in
their
shoes

Other Simon Pulse nonfiction books you might enjoy

**DOING IT RIGHT: MAKING SMART, SAFE,
AND SATISFYING CHOICES ABOUT SEX**
Bronwen Pardes

**THE SOCIAL CLIMBER'S GUIDE
TO HIGH SCHOOL**
Robyn Schneider

**CHILL: STRESS-REDUCING TECHNIQUES FOR
A MORE BALANCED, PEACEFUL YOU**
Deborah Reber

**WHAT IF?: ANSWERS TO QUESTIONS ABOUT
WHAT IT MEANS TO BE GAY AND LESBIAN**
Eric Marcus

From Simon Pulse/Beyond Words

**DOABLE: THE GIRLS' GUIDE TO
ACCOMPLISHING JUST ABOUT ANYTHING**
Deborah Reber

in their shoes

shoes

Extraordinary Women Describe
Their Amazing Careers

DEBORAH REBER

Simon Pulse New York London Toronto Sydney New Delhi

To Derin, my workmate,
playmate, and partner for life

SIMON PULSE
An imprint of Simon & Schuster Children's Publishing Division
1230 Avenue of the Americas, New York, New York 10020
This Simon Pulse edition January 2015
Text copyright © 2007, 2015 by Deborah Reber
Cover illustration copyright © 2015 by Karina Granda
For information about special discounts for bulk purchases, please contact
Simon & Schuster Special Sales at 1-866-506-1949 or business@simonandschuster.com.
The Simon & Schuster Speakers Bureau can bring authors to your live event.
For more information or to book an event contact the Simon & Schuster Speakers Bureau
at 1-866-248-3049 or visit our website at www.simonspeakers.com.
Cover designed by Karina Granda
Interior designed by John Candell
The text of this book was set in Avenir.
Manufactured in the United States of America
10 9 8 7 6 5 4 3 2 1
Library of Congress Control Number 2006928451
ISBN 978-1-4814-2812-5 (hc)
ISBN 978-1-4814-2811-8 (pbk)
ISBN 978-1-4814-4046-2 (eBook)

Photo credits:
Photo of Missy Park copyright © by www.traceyprever.com
Photo of Jess Weiner courtesy of the author
Photo of Nancy Knowlton copyright © by Christian Ziegler
Photo of Chiyo Ishikawa copyright © by Kevin P. Casey
Photo of Severn Cullis-Suzuki copyright © by Jeff Topham
Photo of June Ambrose copyright © by Keith Major
Photo of Melissa Block copyright © by Meghan Gallery
Photo of Lauren Faust copyright © by Deborah Reber
Photo of Amanda Koster copyright © by Rob McKaughan
Photo of Kay Lakey copyright © by Deborah Reber
Photo of Maura Tierney copyright © by Isabel Snyder
Photo of Roxanne Coady copyright © by Tricia Bohan

ACKNOWLEDGMENTS

writing this book didn't actually feel like work at all. I mean, bringing together an incredible group of women to inspire and inform teens? How lucky am I? For their help, guidance, and support in writing *In Their Shoes*, I am filled with gratitude to:

My husband, Derin (aka my rock): Thank you for believing in this idea and encouraging me to make it happen from the very beginning. You are my constant source of support, insight, and love, and your faith in me makes me feel like I can do anything!

My son, Asher: The gifts you give me every day help me grow in ways I never knew possible.

My mom and dad, Dale and MaryLou: You have always believed in my ability to do and be anything. Thank you!

My sister, Michele: Thank you for reading countless outlines, notes, and drafts and giving me invaluable feedback at every stage of this book. Your positive reinforcement is a huge force in my life.

My in-laws, Barbara and David Basden: Thank you for your encouragement and interest in my writing ventures.

My "support team" of Alice Wilder, AnneMarie Kane, Ed Adams, and Renée Adams: I know I can come to you at any time with anything and you're there to share your honest insight, valued opinions, and most of all, your belief in me. I couldn't do what I do without you!

My dog, Baxter: For keeping me company by lying under my desk day after day.

My intern, Anna Minard: Thank you for sharing your great research skills with me, but even better, sharing your enthusiasm for this project and being an excellent sounding board at every step of the way.

Bridget Perry: Thank you for "getting" what I was trying to do and helping me brainstorm the ideas that shaped this into the book it is!

My friends who allowed me to babble on endlessly about my process: Tip Blish, Alison Bower, Mardi Douglass, Peter Koorey, Stephanie Lucash, Darcey Pickard, and Marty Silano.

Ed Adams, Renée Adams, Crai Bower, Britta Couris, Lee Davis, Loch Phillipps, Dave Rosencranz, Lee Skaife, Lisa Viscardi, Chad Willett, Gia Duke, and Sasha Nosecchi, as well as Avon, CARE, the Massachusetts State Police Crime Lab, Scripps Oceanography Institute, and Seattle WriterGrrls: thank you for introducing me to some of the incredible women inside this book.

My agent, Susan Schulman: Your belief in me and my vision for bringing important media to teen girls is truly valued and appreciated.

Jen Bergstrom: Thank you for bringing this seed of an idea to life and realizing its potential.

Michelle Nagler: You know how I feel about working with you. You are a dream editor! Thank you for trusting in me to do what I do best, and for sharing your incredible creative and business skills with me.

Patrick Price: Thank you for being such a fantastic pro to work with on the updated edition.

Cara Bedick: Your perspective and enthusiasm throughout this project has been invaluable. Thank you for taking a special interest!

The extraordinary women in *In Their Shoes*: This book

would be nothing without your stories, inspiration, and advice to bring it to life. Thank you for opening up and letting us inside your work and personal lives. Each one of you is making a powerful mark on the career women of tomorrow!

Russell Gordon, Ann Zeak, Mike Rosamilia, Lisa Fyfe, Joel Avirom, Jason Snyder, and Meghan Day Healey, the incredible designers who brought the content of this book to life: You took a lot of material and packaged it beautifully to make it readable and accessible. Thank you for doing such an amazing job!

My power team at Simon & Schuster, who put their all into making this book a success: Bethany Buck, Paul Crichton, Katherine Devendorf, Jaime Feldman, Lucille Rettino, and Orly Sigal.

And last but not least, to all the teen girls who gave me feedback and provided questions to ask each woman in the book: Thank you for sharing your dreams, goals, and point of view. This book is for you!

CONTENTS

INTRODUCTION

when I was a teen, there were three things my parents heard from me on any given day. The first was "I don't know" as an automatic response to any question regarding why I had done something stupid. The second was the lyrics to some pop song, sung at the top of my lungs while playing the air guitar. And the third? "I figured out what I want to be when I grow up."

This last one always raised eyebrows and drew laughter from my family. After making my announcement at the dinner table (for example, "I'm going to be an animal conservationist and save the giant panda from extinction"), my parents would ask to have it in writing. Apparently they wanted to get it on the record, so the next time I flip-flopped, they could wave it in front of my face, as if to say, "Uh-huh, Deb. *Sure* you're going to join the Peace Corps."

Maybe they had a point. I did change my mind about careers a lot. There was the time I wanted to be a teacher. Then a veterinarian. A rescue worker. Come to think of it, the animal conservationist phase did last a couple of years. Oh yeah, and let's not forget my personal favorite, a "farmer's wife." (I'm not joking. My only defense is too many years of watching *Little House on the Prairie* as a kid!)

Then everything changed. I saw *Broadcast News*, this movie where Holly Hunter plays a high-stakes network news producer. Her character, Jane, was smart. She was sassy. She was even neurotic. *She was me!* From that matinee on, I wanted to be

Jane in the worst way. I wanted her job, her cool Georgetown apartment, her simple bob hairdo, and her invites to press dinners at the White House.

So I went to college and studied journalism and television production, and even put together a few of my own "news pieces" for classes along the way. (I specifically recall producing a hard-hitting segment about the different steps involved in feeding my dog, Ari. Clearly I was well on my way to big-shot newsmaker.)

I researched everything I could about the news industry and interned at the local NBC affiliate in my small college town. It was all falling into place. I'd be Debbie Reber, VINP (Very Important News Producer). I'd waltz through the revolving door at Rockefeller Plaza wearing Prada, my hair in an up-do that looked sensible, smart, and sexily disheveled all at the same time, and hurry off to meet a pressing deadline.

I landed an internship at NBC News the summer before my senior year, where I sat less than a hundred feet away from then nightly news anchor Tom Brokaw. Al, Matt, and Katie Couric at the *Today* show were right down the hall. There I was. Just like I'd imagined. Except it was anything but.

In my internship I saw the real side of news. The window-less work spaces, the layers of foundation worn by on-air personalities, the rigid divide between godlike anchors and lowly production assistants. The drama. The backstabbing. The politics.

Once I graduated, I quickly learned that the kind of job I wanted was nearly impossible to score. I mean, I knew there'd be competition, but I had no clue that I'd be up against recent grads with Ivy League degrees, family connections, and no student loans to worry about while they earned next to nothing fetching coffee for the teleprompter guy. I also learned that most news professionals got their start in smaller television markets like Dayton or Little Rock and worked their way up. Of course I assumed my brilliance and savvy would enable me to go straight to playing with the big boys and girls.

So I gave it a whirl. I used my internship connections to con Tom Brokaw's assistant into letting me interview him under the guise of "postgraduate work" and got meetings with the executive producers of several prime-time news shows who promised to put my résumé "at the top of the pile," but I just couldn't land a job.

Over time, I let go of the dream of becoming "Jane" and began navigating my way through different jobs and careers. Over the past twenty years I've done everything from producing a campaign for children's rights for UNICEF to developing original animation for Cartoon Network. Going from the *Nightly News* to *The Powerpuff Girls*? It wasn't exactly what I'd had in mind. But how was I supposed to know? How was I supposed to understand what my career of choice was all about when I was using a Hollywood movie as a training manual?

And now, here I am. In my (ahem) forties and already on my third career—a writer. This one is sticking, though, because I finally figured out what I want to do when I grow up . . . and I'm doing it. Even though it took me a while, I wouldn't be sitting here today if I hadn't gone through all those different jobs. Still, maybe my journey would have been more direct if I'd had straightforward information about what to expect when I got into the real work world.

As you are likely all too aware, the job market for recent grads entering the workforce, whether armed with a college degree or a high school diploma, is becoming increasingly tight. Because there are fewer jobs available and more competition for the ones that do exist, having an edge is key to forging the career path of your dreams. And I believe that edge comes from the most valuable commodity out there: *information*. That's where this book comes in. Because this book is chock-full of it.

I've reached out to women across the country who are not only great at their jobs but love them to boot, and I've asked each one of them to share what it's really like to be in their shoes. You'll learn not only about the realities of different careers, but even better, what successful women behind these careers actually look like, from *Scandal* and *Grey's Anatomy* creator Shonda Rhimes to surgical veterinarian Anke Langenbach.

I approached the interviews for *In Their Shoes* by asking myself what you—on the verge of making your own career choices—would want to know. So I asked the women to describe the moment they realized what they wanted to do with their lives, what a typical day looks like, what the highs and lows of their job are, how they juggle it all, and what career advice they have for young women like you.

I learned more than I could have imagined. I learned that for most women, there is no such thing as a "typical day." I learned that while almost all the women I interviewed work long hours and consider their job extremely stressful, they wouldn't trade it for anything in the world. I've learned that when it comes to following your career dreams, you can't make a "bad choice"—everything we do along the way somehow fits in with where we end up. Lastly, I've learned that *you really can have it all.*

I absolutely loved meeting the women in this book. In fact, I have to admit that after each and every interview, I had a moment of pause where I thought about making another career shift. (*Is it too late for me to be a forensic scientist? Hmmm . . . what's the cutoff age for joining the Coast Guard?*)

Read on for "a day in the life" of some pretty impressive women, and then ask yourself, *Which one feels most like me?*

To jumpstart your career exploration and dive deeper into the exercises you'll find inside this book, download your free copy of the *In Their Shoes* workbook at www.debbiereber.com.

CAREER SPEAK

there are all kinds of words and abbreviations that are used when talking about college degrees, positions within a company, and other job stuff. Here are some of the more common words and abbreviations you'll find throughout *In Their Shoes*:

AA Associate of Arts, a two-year college degree

AS Associate of Science, a two-year college degree

BA Bachelor of Arts, a four-year college degree

BFA Bachelor of Fine Arts, a four-year college degree

BS Bachelor of Science, a four-year college degree

BUSINESS CASUAL A work wardrobe that's somewhere between jeans and T-shirts and suits—slacks and a top, a skirt and a sweater, etc.

BUSINESS DRESS A work wardrobe that is dressy and professional, like business suits

CEO Chief Executive Officer, a title in business (usually the number one at a company)

CFO Chief Financial Officer, a title in business (usually the number one finance person at a company)

CIO A title in business that stands for Chief Information

Officer (usually the number one information technology development person at a company)

COO Chief Operating Officer, a title in business (usually the number one or number two at a company)

CTO A title in business that stands for Chief Technology Officer (usually the number one technical development person at a company)

DOCTORATE Another way of referring to the graduate school degrees EdD, PhD, or MD

EDD Doctor of Education, a graduate school degree

EVP Executive Vice President, title in business

EXPENSE ACCOUNT The reimbursement of work-related expenses by a company—anything from taxi fare to a lavish entertainment account

GRADUATE SCHOOL Education that takes place after undergraduate school, usually to earn an advanced degree such as an MA or a PhD

HR An acronym for Human Resources, which often refers to the department of a business that oversees all aspects of employees' well-being, including hiring, training, benefits packages, and compensation

MA Master of Arts, a graduate school degree

MBA Master of Business Administration, a graduate school degree

MD Doctor of Medicine, a graduate school degree

MFA Master of Fine Arts, a graduate school degree

OFFICE POLITICS The term used for difficult work situations or relationships within the workplace

PER DIEM A daily monetary allotment provided for people when they're traveling for work, to cover expenses while out of the office

PHD Doctor of Philosophy, a graduate school degree

RECRUITER A person whose job it is to help businesses and organizations attract, screen, and select qualified candidates for available positions

STEM An acronym for science, technology, engineering, and mathematics, referring to fields of study, careers, or educational paths

SVP Senior Vice President, a title in business

UNDERGRADUATE Another way of referring to two- or four-year college degrees

VP Vice President, a title in business

in their shoes

SHONDA RHIMES

TV Show Creator

The Facts

Shonda Rhimes,
*Creator & Executive
Producer,* Grey's
Anatomy *and* Scandal

WHAT? Television show creators dream up TV show ideas—from sitcoms to dramas to reality shows—and convince a network to buy, produce, and broadcast their show.

WHERE? Most TV show creators work out of L.A. or New York City, since these are television industry hot spots, although they can write and develop their ideas anywhere.

HOW? TV show creators need to be amazing writers and have supersmart ideas that fit in with the current television climate. On top of that, they need an agent to set up meetings with television executives so they can pitch their idea. If the execs love the pitch, then the real fun begins in production.

$$$: Ranges dramatically depending on the show and the network . . .

DRESS CODE? Creative and cool . . . or whatever you like

STRESS FACTOR: On a scale of 1 to 10, an 8

she's one of the hottest show creators in Hollywood, and I was thrilled to finagle an interview with Shonda Rhimes, the woman behind *Grey's Anatomy* and *Scandal*, for this book. I spoke with Shonda about how she got her start, what it's like to create a hit TV show, and how she gets it all done. Here's our conversation:

ME: What did you want to do when you were a teenage girl?

SHONDA: I actually thought that I would be a novelist. I read a lot and I also watched a lot of television and old movies. But I really somehow thought that I would be a novelist. I thought that real writing was sitting in a garret somewhere, cold, starving, and pounding out the "great American novel." I loved literature and I majored in English lit in college, but really, when it came down to it, I'm more of a pop culture girl. That's what excites me and the stuff that I sit down to write.

"Most of my time is spent hunched over a computer trying to come up with more ideas for the show, which if you're at all a writer, you find to be extremely fun and liberating."

ME: So how did you decide that you'd rather be writing screenplays instead of novels?

SHONDA: When I got out of school, I was working as an assistant at an ad agency. In my spare time I sat down to put pen to paper, and what came out felt much more like a screenplay than a novel. It was mostly dialogue, and that was the stuff that was really exciting to me, so I went to USC film school.

ME: And look at you now . . . you not only created *Grey's Anatomy* and *Scandal*, but you're also an executive producer of both series. Using *Grey's Anatomy* as an example, can you tell us what you do as a creator and executive producer?

SHONDA: Well, I came up with the idea for the television series, and thus created the series. I wrote the script, I helped pick the director, and we shot the pilot, which is the first episode of a show. When your show is chosen by a network to become one of their shows, you become an executive producer, which means that I oversee the writing on all the scripts, the hiring of all the cast members, and all the editing and postproduction. In an interesting way, it's like running a small country. . . . *Grey's Anatomy* is a small country and I have to run it.

ME: That's a good analogy. It sounds like an amazing job. Is it?

SHONDA: There are parts that are glamorous. I spend a certain amount of time doing interviews and walking down the red carpet and having hair and makeup done for those events. And you know, you do get to hang out with actors and be part of that really great creative process. But the reality of the situation is that most of my time is spent hunched over a computer trying to come up with more ideas for the show, which if you're at all a writer, you find to be extremely fun and liberating.

ME: Was *Grey's Anatomy* the first television show you created?

SHONDA: It was the second television show I pitched and sold, and it's the first television show that was picked up and made.

ME: Wow, that's amazing. I'm sure you know that teens are really into it.

YOU ASKED . . .

"What do you tell yourself that helps you be successful?"
                                                            —ALEX, AGE 14

SHONDA ANSWERED . . .

"My father always said to me, 'The only limit to your life is your own imagination. The only thing that's going to stop you from doing whatever it is you want to do is your ability to envision doing it.' When I was a teenager and he'd say that, I always felt like, 'Oh, come on.' But now it makes so much sense to me. If I come up with the idea, I'm pretty sure I can make it happen."

SHONDA: Yes . . . and it's really exciting because for me, a little bit of what I love about *Grey's Anatomy* is that it's "high school in a hospital."

ME: Yeah, totally . . . that's why I'm hooked! So, what are the hours like? What's a typical day like for you?

SHONDA: I try to get in between eight o'clock and eight thirty a.m., because it's so quiet around here. I do a little writing, answer e-mails, and do phone calls. Everybody else sort of bustles in at about nine and the days are spent doing whatever's necessary at the time. You know, I'll spend a couple hours writing, I'll spend a couple of hours in editing, and I spend a lot of time sitting in a room with the rest of the writing staff coming up with more ideas. Sometimes we'll sit down with the cast and read the script out loud, and that gives me more ideas, and we'll have more notes to go back and keep writing. Now that the show's more popular, it feels like I spend an hour a day doing interviews. I grab lunch if I remember, I try to get home between seven and eight every night, which is not always possible, but I try really hard. And then I spend time with my family, write for a while longer after my family has gone to bed, and then go to bed and get up the next day and it starts all over again.

ME: That's a packed day. Do you have a life on the weekends?

SHONDA: On the days that I take off, absolutely . . . no question. I definitely always take off Sundays. That's my constant. I do not work Sundays mostly because I want at least one full day that I can spend with my family, giving them my full time, my full attention. Sometimes I'll work a little bit in the morning on Saturdays, sometimes I'll work a little in the afternoon. But sometimes I don't do any work at all.

ME: So tell me, is working in Hollywood as cutthroat as some movies and shows portray it?

WHY WAIT?

- Read articles about television show creators and find out how they did it.
- Come up with your own characters and write, write, write about them.
- Follow the trends in TV and watch the highest-rated shows so you can see what makes a hit.

SHONDA: On my shows, we're not very cutthroat. I mean, I think we're fairly relaxed. I think the fact that everybody here really loves their jobs and we're really focused on what we do keeps us from being cutthroat, because there's a lot of work to be done and we don't have time to worry about other people on other shows.

ME: Do you feel like a pioneer in television?

SHONDA: I don't feel like a pioneer. It was a surprising statistic when it was quoted to me that I was probably the first black woman to have her own show on one of the big four networks. But I don't feel like a pioneer so much as I feel like I'm busy still learning and I'm having a really good time while doing it. I'm trying to keep my head down and do a good job.

ME: After reading your blog, it came through loud and clear that you love your job.

SHONDA: I spend my days with the doctors of Seattle Grace Hospital, and that is not a bad thing by any stretch of the imagination. You know, whether they're in my head or I'm going to the stage to talk to the actors, it's a very pleasant way to pass the time. And when you have a job like that, that's the thing you're meant to do because it doesn't feel like work.

ME: What's the most difficult part of your job?

SHONDA: The pace. The pace in television is lightning fast.

Which means that every eight days we need a new script to shoot, every eight days I need to have a new script edited, and every eight days I need to have something ready to go on the air. So the pace is really, really exhausting and you have to keep up. I think it was David Mamet who said that writing a movie is like running a marathon, and writing in television is running a marathon until you die.

ME: That's a great quote.

SHONDA: Yeah. And that's what it feels like. It's a constant never-ending pace. That's the hardest part. That and not getting to spend as much time at home as I like.

ME: What's it been like watching your shows not only survive on the schedule, but become breakout hits?

SHONDA: It's been pretty shocking. It feels really surprising to me that the stuff I come up with in my head at home while wearing my pajamas is stuff that people want to watch. The stuff that the ten writers and I sit around and brainstorm is stuff that people are really interested in. It's always amazing when you feel like people out there can look at something you've created and say, "I see myself in that." They look at one of the characters and they think, *That person's a little like me.* That's an amazing feeling.

ME: Are there any misconceptions out there about being a TV show creator? Anything we'd be surprised to know about?

THEN TO NOW

1991: Graduated from Dartmouth College with a BA in English literature	**1994:** Received MFA from USC School of Cinema-Television	**1995:** Worked as research director for Tollin-Robbins/Mundy Lane Productions	**1999:** Wrote HBO original movie, *Introducing Dorothy Dandridge*

SHONDA: Many people think creating shows is a thing that men do, but more and more women are creating shows. Any time you let someone tell you it's a closed door and you believe them, you're setting yourself up for defeat.

ME: Do you have any advice for girls looking to do what you do?

SHONDA: Go to college. Honestly. And not just go to college, but the best thing you can do to strengthen your writing is to read as much as possible . . . to have a huge knowledge base of literature in all of its forms. I spent my entire childhood living in books, and I feel like that was the one thing that really helped me.

ME: Is there anything else you want to add?

SHONDA: The women around you can be the people who uplift you. The other girls you meet, the other women you meet who are your peers, can be the people who support you and help push you forward as opposed to being your competition. That to me is the most important thing. Some of the great people who helped me in this town have been other women.

2002: Wrote screenplay for *Crossroads*, starring Britney Spears

2004: *Grey's Anatomy* premiered on ABC.

2007: *Private Practice* premiered on ABC

2012: *Scandal* premiered on ABC

In the Field

FIVE MORE CAREERS WORKING ON A TV SERIES

PRODUCTION ASSISTANT (entry-level position) Production assistants, or PAs, support the work of a producer, director, or other production executive. They do their fair share of fetching coffee and running errands, but they also have an opportunity to prove their commitment while learning on the job.

TV SCRIPT WRITER TV script writers work together to develop a series arc and story episode ideas, and then work solo or paired with another writer to write individual episodes. They must have a solid understanding of the show's sensibility, as well as the characters in the series, in order to write scripts that will work on the air.

CASTING DIRECTOR Casting directors work with talent agents to identify potential actors to play the roles in a show, screening a ton of reels and reviewing headshots. After holding auditions, casting directors make their recommendations about who they think should be cast for each role.

LOCATION MANAGER Location managers handle logistics that arise when shooting at a specific location. For example, if a scene from a TV show needs to be filmed at a baseball stadium, the location manager will work with the stadium personnel to work out any logistical details so the TV show can shoot as needed.

PROP MASTER Many TV series hire prop masters to figure out what props are needed for each episode and then buy, find, or build them. Prop masters have to be creative and resourceful in figuring out ways to get the necessary props, especially when they're working under tight budgetary constraints or the item isn't readily available.

YOU NEED TO KNOW ABOUT

Scenarios USA is a nonprofit organization that gives young people ages twelve to twenty-two the chance to write scripts for short films addressing important social issues like peer pressure, HIV/AIDS, self-esteem, and body image. Winners of the "What's the REAL DEAL?" writing contest work with professional filmmakers to turn their scripts into short films. Find out more at www.scenariosusa.org.

For more on writing in Hollywood, check out the screenwriter profile on page 267 and the movie studio executive profile on page 65.

JOANNE B. SGUEGLIA

Forensic Scientist

Joanne B. Sgueglia,
Forensic Scientist

The Facts

WHAT? Forensic scientists study samples and evidence collected at a crime scene to provide proof for police and attorneys as they solve their case and take it to trial.

WHERE? Forensic scientists usually work anywhere within the local, state, or federal law enforcement arena to support the work of detectives, police, and district attorneys. Others might work in independent crime labs, biotech firms, hospitals, or universities.

HOW? To get in the door, forensic scientists need a bachelor's degree in a natural science, like chemistry or biology, although many get graduate degrees in their area of specialization, such as chemistry, botany, or entomology.

$$$: An average salary of $50,000 to $90,000, depending on level of experience, work environment, and geographic location

DRESS CODE? Business casual to casual

STRESS FACTOR: On a scale of 1 to 10, an 8

the popularity of shows like *CSI: Crime Scene Investigation*, *Bones*, *NCIS*, and *Criminal Minds* has spawned a surge in wannabe forensic scientists, but how realistically do those shows portray the career? I turned to forensics expert Joanne Sgueglia to find out. Though today she is a senior manager at biotech firm Life Technologies, when I interviewed Joanne, she described the non-Hollywood version of a career in forensics based on her work at the Massachusetts State Police Crime Lab.

ME: From the outside, your job at the crime lab sounds so cool, and you've been doing it for many years, so you must like it. Was it what you expected when you first got started?

JOANNE: To get in and be trained to do DNA profiling was very much utilizing the skills that I gained in college, but I think the part that was more of a surprise was testifying in court. When you're taking chemistry and biology in college, you don't anticipate that. A lot of very good scientists don't necessarily make very good witnesses, so it takes a certain personality type to be a forensic scientist. So that was the surprise with a twist—it was a different set of skills that I learned on the job. I was testifying after only six months on the job. In those days you were sort of just thrown to the wolves.

"The biggest fallacy on CSI *is the amount of time it takes to do things, along with the fact that one character on the show does what is actually the job of about twelve different people."*

ME: Can you tell us what you do at the crime lab?

JOANNE: I oversee four main units. There's the crime scene response unit, which is the unit that goes out into crime scenes and recognizes, collects, preserves, and transports evidence to the crime lab. I oversee a criminalistics unit, which is the unit that triages* all of the items that come

---

* **THE LINGO:** In forensic science, the term **triage** is another word for classifying or sorting evidence

in from a crime scene and do things like biological fluid identification, identify a particular garment, a rape kit . . . things like that. Then we have our DNA unit, which is my field of expertise, whereby we do DNA profiling on those items that are amenable for DNA testing. And then we have the CODIS or Combined DNA Index System Unit, which is a database of DNA profiles from crime scene samples that gets searched against convicted offender profiles so we can get what we call "cold hits." Within the DNA unit, I make sure that all interpretations of DNA are done correctly and complete a whole host of duties that are overseen by the FBI.

ME: So then how do you actually spend your day?

JOANNE: Earlier in my career, the day would be spent getting items of evidence and bringing them into the laboratory, cutting stains off items, going through different methodologies in our laboratory to get DNA off the fabric, extract DNA, find out if we had enough DNA to continue with the test, and then do some sort of detection method to see if the DNA from the crime scene sample matched the DNA from a particular victim or suspect. That type of day would be working in the lab and looking at the final data to see if little bar codes match up or not. I've come a long way from that. That would be what the staff is doing now. I might spend my day looking into funding for new laboratory instruments, things like that. One of the frustrations and challenges in DNA testing is it's so progressive that as you're using the technology, there's new technology on the way, so you are constantly in a state of transition.

ME: I've read a lot about how DNA testing has gotten so much better in the last twenty years, and that jurors expect a ton of DNA tests for cases now.

JOANNE: A lot of people in the legal field are calling that the "*CSI* effect." Those types of shows have raised a new awareness

YOU ASKED . . .

"What was your inspiration to do this job?"

—ELENA, AGE 14

JOANNE ANSWERED . . .

"I was a biology major in college and a lot of my professors wanted me to go pre-med, but I found that whole environment very competitive, and I wanted to do something that could incorporate street knowledge along with formal education. So I went into a career guidance office and found out about forensics. I always loved shows like Quincy *and* Columbo, *but I didn't realize that the career existed in the same way. I thought it would be fascinating to integrate my love of science with wanting to be part of crime fighting."*

of DNA testing, and now jurors have more questions and more knowledge. They want DNA on everything, and it's actually overburdened the system both for the attorneys and for the scientists, because you have to test more stains on more items that may not necessarily need to be tested, but the jurors are expecting it. Today you have investigators wanting more and more samples tested for comprehensiveness, because it looks better to the jury to say that you tried it.

ME: What are your hours like?

JOANNE: At this level, I work pretty set hours, eight thirty a.m. through five o'clock p.m., Monday through Friday. At different times in my career, though, I've worked really long hours. I was part of the team that identified human remains from the crash of TWA Flight 800 that occurred on Long Island in 1995. We worked for about a year and a half on that project. So if you're working on a disaster or if you're on a rush case, you'll work extra hours.

ME: What kinds of things happen for you to have a good day?

JOANNE: A good day could be if you have a rush case and you get some information so you can solve the case and help the victims' families. That's a good day. When you finally have some sort

> ## THE BREAKDOWN
>
> **IN MEETINGS:** 0–2 hours per day for entry level, 5+ for senior level
>
> **SITTING:** Most of the day
>
> **PUBLIC SPEAKING:** Occasionally
>
> **READING:** Depends on level
>
> **WORKING SOLO:** At least half the day

of DNA match to something in a case that has been unsolved, that can be very rewarding. Or if you have an old unsolved case, called a "cold case," and you get a DNA hit and can finally have an answer, that's a really good day.

ME: Would you say that's one of the best parts of your job?

JOANNE: It's difficult to say. It's complicated, because we do the analysis and we may get a result, but we can't make that result be the answer to a case. So sometimes it's frustrating, especially if it's a highly publicized case. Let's say we get a good DNA profile from a crime scene sample but we can't find the perpetrator. That's out of our hands. But when a rape victim tells you how they feel like they can breathe again because the rapist was caught following a DNA match you made, that's gratifying.

THEN TO NOW

1982: Graduated from State University of New York, Purchase, NY, with BA in Biology

1988–1991: Worked at Lifecodes Corporation as a senior forensic scientist

1991–1999: Worked as forensic scientist II at Suffolk County Crime Lab

1993: Completed training at the FBI National Academy/ University of Virginia

ME: When do things get tense?

JOANNE: Things are very stressful in a forensic crime laboratory. There's constant pressure to get more done with less. It's also a very stringent field as far as quality assurance goes, so bad days might be when you have audits, inspections, or one of your employees fails a proficiency test.

ME: If readers want to become forensic scientists because they think it will be like the show *CSI*, do they have a realistic idea of what they're in for?

JOANNE: The biggest fallacy on *CSI* is the amount of time it takes to do things, along with the fact that one character on the show does what is actually the job of about twelve different people. Forensic science is a field of specialists. For example, our crime lab has a forensic biology department and a forensic chemistry department. There's someone to do the work on the databases; there are different people to go out to do crime scenes; there's a drug unit, which deals with controlled substances; you have bomb arson and fire debris; you have toxicology to see if any date rape drugs are involved; you have a trace department that does hair and fibers and paint and things like that. There is a specialty

> **WHY WAIT?**
>
> - Take biology, chemistry, and physics classes in high school.
>
> - Request an informational interview from a forensic scientist at a crime lab.

1997: Awarded the American Academy of Forensic Sciences Regional Award

1999: Became technical manager of forensic biology at the Massachusetts State Police Crime Lab

2003: Certified by the American Board of Criminalistics

2011: Took job as senior manager, professional services, Life Technologies for any type of substance you're going to analyze. On *CSI*, only a few people do all of that, plus they also go out and do the detective's job. That is very unrealistic.

ME: So one person's job alone might be just collecting trace evidence.

JOANNE: Yes. In trace, for example, they do hair work, fiber work, and paint. So let's say a car hit a bicyclist and paint from the car got onto the bicycle in the accident. Trace will take the paint that came off the car and do some testing. They can look at all the different colors and layers in the paint and try and identify what type of vehicle hit the victim.

ME: How many cases might your DNA group be working on at once?

JOANNE: Each DNA analyst handles approximately forty cases a year. They get their own batch of assignments, about five cases or so at a time. The crime lab itself takes in hundreds of cases a year, and we're backlogged by over a thousand.

WHAT IT TAKES

- Attention to detail
- A compulsiveness to be organized
- A perceptive personality
- Being comfortable speaking (and testifying) in public

ME: Is there anything else you'd like to add?

JOANNE: The one thing I would say is that as much as forensic science can be exciting, every day's not an exciting day. You have to be the type of person who likes putting puzzles together, and in this job, you might be dealing with different puzzles every day.

> ## INTERESTED IN DNA FORENSICS?
> ## HERE'S JOANNE'S ADVICE
>
> - *Take coursework in molecular biology, genetics, biochemistry, and forensic statistics.*
> - *Be sure that you're emotionally able to handle the graphic nature of a crime scene.*
> - *There's nothing sacred when you're in a lab. . . . We have to talk about things that may make some people uncomfortable, so you can't be shy.*

In the Field

FIVE MORE CAREERS IN FORENSIC SCIENCE

FORENSIC PATHOLOGIST Pathologists specialize in examining blood work and determining the cause of an illness or death. Shows like *NCIS, Rizzoli and Isles,* and *CSI* feature forensic pathologists—you usually see them working in a dark room, wearing gloves, and performing autopsies.

FORENSIC ENTOMOLOGIST Because there are insects that literally feast on dead bodies, bugs can be helpful in providing clues as to time of death. Through examining the life stage of insects like blowflies on a dead body, forensic entomologists can pinpoint the exact time of death, a clue that can be very important in murder investigations.

FORENSIC PSYCHOLOGIST Forensic psychologists are experts in the criminal justice system. Some work closely with lawyers, helping them figure out what a criminal's state of mind was during a crime, or testifying in court about the psychology behind a crime. Others might consult with lawyers on jury selection.

BALLISTICS EXPERT The work of ballistics experts usually focuses on ballistic evidence at crime scenes, which is anything relating to guns. Ballistics experts might look for bullets or slugs, help identify what kind of gun was used, and testify about the ballistic evidence in trials.

FINGERPRINT CLASSIFIER   Making a fingerprint match can be a tedious process, and while technology has facilitated it, the actual matching is still a very exact science. Fingerprint classifiers examine fingerprints from crime scenes and use their skills to find a positive match in the hopes of identifying the perpetrator.

YOU NEED TO KNOW ABOUT

The American Academy of Forensic Sciences (AAFS), which you can find online at www.aafs.org, has information on everything concerning forensics and even hosts the Young Forensic Scientists Forum, where you can learn more about schools with forensic science programs and learn how to break into the field.

For more science careers, check out the marine biologist profile on page 101.

LEAH FARESH KARP

Real Estate Agent

The Facts

Leah Faresh Karp, Real Estate Agent

WHAT?   Real estate agents buy or sell real estate—anything from houses or lots of land to office buildings. Real estate agents handle every aspect of a deal, including negotiating offers, coordinating a ton of paperwork, meeting with inspectors, and making sure everything goes smoothly.

WHERE?   Everywhere

HOW?   There are no college requirements for real estate agents, but a high school diploma is required, as well as being at least eighteen years old, taking forty to two hundred hours of training, and passing a written test to get a real estate license.

$$$:   Real estate agents get a percentage of the price a home or apartment sells for, so one who brokers a deal for a celeb could potentially make a million dollars in one shot. Agents working in more typical markets have an average annual salary of $30,000 to $50,000.

DRESS CODE?   Depends on the market

STRESS FACTOR: On a scale of 1 to 10, between a 7 and an 8

from the outside, being a real estate agent seems like a pretty great gig. They get to drive around in deluxe cars, help people find the home of their dreams, sign a few pieces of paper, and sit back and collect their big fee. A closer look shows that it's not as easy as it looks. In fact, a real estate transaction is kind of like a complicated ballet, and the agent is the choreographer.

To get inside the life of a real estate agent, I met with Leah Faresh Karp, an agent in the San Francisco Bay area's hot Marin County market, where a simple three-bedroom home can easily go for more than a million bucks. Leah has been working in the biz for more than twenty years, and she's figured out the secrets of success in her competitive field. I asked Leah what was at the heart of real estate, and she gave me a one-word answer: *marketing.*

"I love matching buyers and sellers together—that's probably why I set my friends up all the time too."

"For me, marketing means always trying to create and tweak new ideas for either showing a property or advertising it differently. I'm always trying to highlight unique aspects of a property and figure out what needs to be said in order to draw the buyers to it. The great thing is that by attracting buyers to my website or by advertising the listing, I'm also marketing myself, which helps me find new buyers to work with,"

YOU ASKED . . .

"How has your career changed your life?"

—CARRIE, AGE 15

LEAH ANSWERED . . .

"I've been doing it from such a young age that I learned about the importance of not just working to get a paycheck, but that it's what you do with the money you earn that determines how you succeed financially. If all I did was work because I wanted to get a paycheck, I would never get ahead. So now I work, get that paycheck, and turn around and invest it in what I do. . . . That's given me a vehicle to be financially successful."

Leah explains. "So I do the creative marketing work, and then I have someone who I employ full-time who does my online marketing."

Because real estate agents work with two different kinds of people—those who have property they want to sell and those who are in the market to buy—and they're sometimes working on a bunch of deals all at once, they are often swamped. In busy markets, they can literally work around the clock.

"The agents that I meet who are at the top of their game work a lot of hours. They probably couldn't even tell you how many hours they work because it's sort of, like, *all the time*," says Leah. "You really can sell real estate twenty-four hours a day."

Leah used to be one of those agents, but having a child changed everything.

"Becoming a mom forced me to face one of the biggest challenges of the job, which is finding balance in your life and being okay with saying, 'These are the hours that I can meet you,' and if it doesn't work and I can't

> ## THE BREAKDOWN
>
> IN MEETINGS: 2–3 hours a day
>
> ON THE PHONE: 4–5 hours a day
>
> ONLINE: 1–2 hours a day
>
> STAYING UP-TO-DATE ON INVENTORY/HOUSE SEARCHING: 1 hour a day
>
> DRIVING IN CAR: Half the day

get someone else in my team to cover for me, accepting the fact that maybe this isn't a client I can work with. Before I had a baby, it was never an issue. I would find a way to make anything happen. Now it's all about making choices and working only with the clients who fit my lifestyle."

That's not to say that Leah is slacking off these days. Hardly. In fact, she still pulls in at least thirty hours of work a week (she worked fifty plus before she had a child), balancing the million different pieces that make up her job. Here's what Leah's day looks like:

6:00–7:00 A.M. *I like to get up before anyone else is awake at my house, because that's when I'm able to fit my exercise in and spend a few minutes actually thinking out my day. I make a list of "to do's" and think about what the day is going to look like and what I need to accomplish. The exercise and quiet time is my favorite time.*

8:30 A.M. *I head off to work, and the first thing I always do is return e-mails and phone calls that are a priority. I try to do the things I like to do the least first, because that's when I'm the most alert and ready. I spend a lot of time prospecting—finding new buyers, finding new sellers, and working on the marketing. The smaller portion of my day is looking at homes or showing real estate.*

12:30 P.M. *I usually don't take lunch—I eat at my desk or in the car. And I always bring my lunch with me, because I don't want to take the time during the day to sit down or go out to lunch, unless I'm meeting a client or having a staff meeting with people who work for me.*

1:00–5:00 P.M. *The afternoon is spent focusing on people who are currently in the process of buying a house, whether it means meeting inspectors, reviewing documents or negotiating and working on contracts, dealing with mortgage brokers and title companies, or returning phone calls. I need to keep all of the pieces moving forward.*

THEN TO NOW

1986–1990: Sales associate, Nordstrom	1990–1994: Took classes at American River College, Sacramento, CA	1990–1992: Bank teller, Wells Fargo Bank	1992–1994: Office manager, State Farm Insurance

You're probably getting the sense that real estate agents

have to be skilled at many things, and you're right. Leah says she always has to think one step ahead, not only when it comes to what's happening with her deals and marketing, but in how she works with people, as well.

"I have to be personable, so that clients feel comfortable talking with me and feel that I understand what their needs are. Part of that is what I consider to be the basics of my job—it's getting dressed and looking presentable, having a clean car with a full tank of gas and just being prepared to go to work. I make sure my cell phone is charged, and I always keep bottled water

WHY WAIT?

- Scour the real estate listings in your weekend paper and visit properties to learn about how they were marketed.

- Get experience working in retail or sales to strengthen your communication and business skills.

and snacks in my trunk to make sure my clients are comfortable and happy," says Leah. "You have to wear a lot of different hats for this one job if you're going to do it successfully."

CHALLENGES

Leah says the biggest challenge of her job is keeping her pipeline full. That means that while she's working with Client A, who is just starting to look at properties, she's also got to make sure she has Client B in the middle of escrow (the financial

1994:
Started working as real estate assistant for father's business

1996:
Became business partner for father's business

1998:
Went out on her own

process regarding the transfer of funds in a sale), and Client C just about ready to finish a deal. Because real estate agents get paid only when all the loose ends of a sale are wrapped up, without this steady stream of clients in different stages of the process, it could be months between paychecks.

WHAT IT TAKES

- Being a "people person"
- Having a good memory
- Being honest, trustworthy, and professional
- Attention to detail

To make matters more challenging, there are a lot of aspects of the job that are out of the agent's control, and that can be frustrating and stressful. There are multiple people in the process, all of whom have to do their jobs right in order for a deal to go through—and of course, the buyer and seller need to cooperate too.

REWARDS

So if real estate is so challenging, why are so many people drawn to the field? Leah summed it up again in one word: *matchmaking*.

"I love matching buyers and sellers together—that's probably why I set my friends up all the time too. When I understand my client's needs and I know what they're looking for and I find the house, I can walk in and say, 'Oh my God, this is the one.' Watching my clients recognize that this is exactly

PAYING YOUR DUES

Don't expect to get your real estate license and dive right into selling multimillion-dollar homes. Beginning real estate agents typically start with less desirable properties and work as associate agents under a more experienced agent to gain experience.

what they were looking for . . . it's just so great. When they have their housewarming party and they call and tell you that they're so happy in the house and the kids love the neighbors' kids—when they really love where they live—that is probably the most rewarding moment."

LEAH'S CAREER ADVICE

- *Make a commitment to what you're going to do and do it for a set period of time before you walk away.*

- *Be passionate about your work—if you don't have a passion for it, you're not going to have what it takes to get through the negative aspects of a job.*

In the Field

FIVE MORE CAREERS IN REAL ESTATE

MORTGAGE BROKER   Unless the person buying a home or office building can pay in cash, they'll be working with a mortgage broker. Mortgage brokers help buyers find a loan to buy the property and handle all the necessary paperwork between the lender and the borrower.

REAL ESTATE APPRAISER   For just about every real estate transaction, appraisers need to get involved. Appraisers check out the house or property that is being bought or sold and determine how much it is worth in the current market.

PROPERTY MANAGER   Every apartment building or rented business space has a property manager who handles everything from making sure rent is paid on time to dealing with plumbing and heating problems. Many property managers say they love their jobs because they never know what to expect from one day to the next.

DEVELOPER   Some people make small (or large) fortunes as real estate developers. Developers are the people who look for opportunities to build new properties—townhouses, shopping malls, apartment buildings, high-rises—oversee their planning and construction, and then hope to make a profit by selling the building or renting it out.

INSURANCE SALES AGENT   Before any bank will lend someone money to buy a home or a commercial space, they need to see proof of insurance, and that's where insurance sales agents come in. These agents sell policies to the person buying the space so if the property is damaged by a fire, flood, or other disaster, the lender's investment is safe.

MISSY PARK

Entrepreneur

The Facts

WHAT? An entrepreneur is someone who starts his or her own business—basically creating something out of nothing. Entrepreneurs must have innovative ideas and find creative ways to get their business up and running.

WHERE? Absolutely anywhere!

HOW? Depending on the kind of business they want to create, some entrepreneurs might start small and fund their venture by themselves, while others might write a detailed business plan and apply for a business loan.

Missy Park, Founder & CEO, Title Nine

$$$: $0 to millions . . . it all depends on how good the idea is, how committed the entrepreneur is to it, and how successful the idea is on the market.

DRESS CODE? Whatever you want!

STRESS FACTOR: On a scale of 1 to 10, between 5 and 10 (Missy says it changes on a daily basis)

there's something impressive about people who take an idea that they're passionate about and bring it to life, with no one telling them how to do it, writing them a paycheck, or giving them health insurance . . . no one guaranteeing them that their idea will be successful. Today entrepreneurship is on the rise, especially among women. Apparently a positive side effect of a fledgling economy is the inspiration to create and innovate. But how do entrepreneurs know what to do? Where do they get their confidence?

There are thousands of women entrepreneurs in the United States, but I chose to interview Missy Park, founder of Title Nine, a hub for women's sportswear and athletic apparel that started as a tiny catalog business in 1989 out of Missy's garage and is now a national name in women's sportswear. In 2013 alone they mailed out more than twenty-five million catalogs and opened their twenty-third store. Missy had a strong vision when she started her company, and I couldn't wait to sit down and find out how she did it. Here's our conversation:

"I'm pretty good at failing, and for me that seems to be the best way to learn."

ME: What were your career dreams when you were younger?

MISSY: My mother and father both said that it was important that I know how to "think." My dad's big thing was, it really doesn't matter what your major is, but you need to learn to write, you need to learn to think critically, and you need to understand how statistics work, because they're important no matter what you do. But I don't believe that you need to know what you want to do at the age of eighteen. I majored in history, mostly because Yale is known for its history department.

ME: I read that you and your college friends talked about trying to create the women's version of Nike when you first got out of school. Is that true?

MISSY: I think that anyone who has played team sports at the

collegiate and even the high school level spends the rest of
their life trying to re-create the unanimity of purpose that you
have when you're part of a team. Women's basketball had been
a varsity sport at Yale for about five years when I got there, and
it was very clear that we were second-class citizens. And there
was a very tight group of us who had an idea about how to
change that in the marketplace once we had graduated.

ME: So how did you get Title Nine up and running?

MISSY: I coached for a couple of years after college and then
moved out to the West Coast because my brother lived here
and it was free room and board. I got a job working for the
North Face when it was quite small, and Fisher Mountain
Bikes, companies whose founders were very much still there
and there was a real passion for the product. My father had his
own business when I was growing up, so I think the idea of that
was very familiar to me . . . it seemed like a good life. I think it
was in my genes to start my own thing, and at a certain point I

YOU ASKED . . .

*"What do you like most about remembering the old days and
your journey to where you are now?"*

—MARYBETH, AGE 12

MISSY ANSWERED . . .

*"You know how we don't always notice when someone we're
around all the time changes because it happens so gradually?
That's almost the way it is with our company. Sometimes I'll look
back on our old catalogs and think, Wow, we've really come
a long way. I mean, we started in my house and the inventory
was in the garage, and now I walk over to our warehouse
and it's twenty-five thousand square feet. It's like, Wow, we've
accomplished a lot. So I certainly have a sense of pride and
progress."*

WHY WAIT?

- You know those little kids selling lemonade on the sidewalk? They're entrepreneurs! It's never too early to try starting your own business.

- Read about famous entrepreneurs like Oprah, Arianna Huffington (*Huffington Post*), and Sara Blakely (Spanx) to find out how they got started.

- Take on leadership roles in activities and clubs to get experience in management.

was like, "Wow, I want to have my own business." I had a total of maybe two and a half years of industry experience. And then I decided to do it and proceeded to learn the business by trial and error. I'm pretty good at failing, and for me that seems to be the best way to learn.

ME: Do you think that not being afraid to fail is an important quality for someone who wants to be an entrepreneur?

MISSY: I do, actually. A buddy of mine once said, "You know, I've seen all kinds of entrepreneurs—some of them are really extroverted, some are really introverted, some are supersmart and some aren't that smart at all, some are really good with people, some aren't. The only thing I can say that they all have in common is that none of them really care about what other people think." Yeah, it's hard to fail and I don't like it, but I'm never thinking, *Oh, I've failed, and what do other people think?* I'm like, *Damn, I wish I hadn't screwed that up,* you know?

ME: Without having someone show you the ropes of starting a company, how did you know that you could make Title Nine work?

MISSY: I didn't. For the first three or four years, I'd resolve that we were going to quit at least once every six months. You know that saying, "Courage is not the absence of fear, but the mastery of it"? The absence of fear is really stupidity. You show me somebody that's never been afraid and I'll show you someone that's either superstupid or living in a box. There were times when I was really nervous and I had a ton of doubts, and that still continues now. But I think that mastering your fear can fuel you to focus on the right things. I think that a lot of girls hate making mistakes, and it just kills me. They're so worried about making mistakes, it's like, "Wow, if you don't make mistakes, how are you going to learn?"

ME: What does your day-to-day work actually involve?

MISSY: I have a lot of interest in the creative side of the business, so I spend a lot of time on that—like looking at products, deciding what's going to go in our product assortment, reviewing how we interact with our customers online, in our stores, and on the phone—that's probably 40 percent of my time. Then I spend 25 percent of my time figuring out what's next. . . . Some people would call that "new business development." I think that's a pretty fancy name for what I do, which is trying to develop other opportunities for us and learning new businesses. I spend the other 35 percent of my time working on employee development stuff—thinking about what the next opportunities are for the people who work here.

ME: Wow . . . it sounds like you wear many different hats.

MISSY: Yes, which is good for me . . . I have a very short attention span.

ME: So, what do you do when things get tense at work?

MISSY: Well, often I'm the one who is causing the tension. . . . I feel like that's my role. I actually think it's a good thing. I need to be able to do it in a way so that we all still love one another at the end of the day, but it's how we get better. One of the things that we talk a lot about is this idea that when we hire people here, you need to feel comfortable both being challenged and challenging others rather than just sort of doing what you're told, because we're growing and things are always changing. You need to be able to think on your feet and say, "Well, this doesn't work anymore."

ME: If you're having a great day, what is it that makes it great?

MISSY: It used to be that a great day at work for me was having the phones ring like crazy, trying to process credit cards, packing up orders while talking on the phone, chasing after the UPS truck, throwing orders at the truck, and then running back and cleaning everything up. That was really fun for me. Now I think a great day for me is when I'm working with a small group of people, all of whom are sort of at the top of their game, and together we come up with a product or an idea that none of us could have come up with on our own. I find that incredibly gratifying.

ME: That's such an interesting perspective, because when I think of an entrepreneur, I think of this sole person running a company. Is it possible to have a balance between work life and personal life when you run your own company?

MISSY: I think work/life balance is probably a lot like finding the job you love—it's an ongoing process. When I was first starting the business, I slept here. I worked all the time, I traveled on the weekends to play rugby or to do photo shoots, and I was really happy doing that. I mean, there might be

THEN TO NOW

1984: Graduated from Yale with BA in history	1984–1988: Worked various jobs in retail	1989: Started Title Nine at the age of 26	1990: Title Nine hired first employee (now she's the CFO)

people who say that wasn't a good work/life balance, but for me it worked great. Then my business became more mature, I grew up, and now I have two kids. When our first child was born, my partner and I were both working in fairly high-level jobs that required a fair amount of travel, and that was a time where we didn't have it right. And it was like, "Okay, now there's a kid in this equation that we really want to spend time with." But about four years ago, Dana left her job and is at home full-time, and we have very clear roles now. And I focus entirely on the business and I have the freedom to do that. Having said that, people always ask me, "Oh, it must be hard juggling a family and a baby and work," and I'm like, "No, it's not hard at all. Family always wins." I've made some compromises. . . . I think I'd rather have more than two kids, but I would have had to start a lot sooner and I wasn't ready then. I don't see work and life as two separate things. I like both a lot, so I don't need to wall them off.

ME: What's it like being able to do what you want with your company?

WHAT IT TAKES

- A great idea (or several)
- Confidence (and, as Missy says, a healthy dose of fear)
- A willingness to fail and assume a financial risk
- The ability to think outside the box
- Being extremely self-motivated

1994: First year Title Nine made a profit

1997: Opened first Title Nine store in Berkeley, CA

2003: Held first Title 9K in Boulder

2013: Opened twenty-third retail store

MISSY: Well, I don't see it quite like that anymore. Now, I am just one of many stakeholders in Title Nine. While technically I do own all the stock, there are many, many folks who are heavily invested in Title Nine. It's my job to make sure that we balance all of those competing interests to get the best, and most sustainable, outcome for Title Nine. We are in it for the long haul and sometimes that means that, in the short run, I don't always get my way . . . and that's a really good thing.

MISSY'S ADVICE

Take more risks. That's it. . . . Just take more risks.

In the Field

FIVE MORE CAREERS WHERE YOU CAN BE YOUR OWN BOSS

SMALL BUSINESS OWNER More than 8.6 million women own small businesses in the United States. While it can be risky, being your own boss is great if you've got the passion. Small business owners may handle product development, marketing, advertising, accounting . . . even pounding the pavement in search of new business.

INDEPENDENT CONTRACTOR OR CONSULTANT This is one career that's difficult to embark on until you've had solid work experience. Independent contractors can be found in any field—the thing they all have in common is an expertise that someone needs. For example, a marketing executive might leave her firm to consult for companies who don't have their own marketing department.

FREELANCE WRITER Freelance writers usually work from home, and they might write anything from magazine articles to marketing materials. Like most self-employed people, free-lance writers are always looking for their next job, even as they're working on a dozen projects at once.

DOG WALKER   In big cities, you can spot dog walkers a mile away because they look like a moving ball of fur. Dog walkers might have up to twenty clients, whose dogs they typically walk while the pet owners are at work. They charge up to thirty dollars a day per dog—this can be a pretty good gig!

STAY-AT-HOME PARENT   This might not seem like a "career" in the traditional sense, but stay-at-home parents have more than a full-time job. Never off duty, they work around the clock—feeding, dressing, entertaining, and educating their children, as well as possibly cooking, cleaning, and doing laundry. The pay's not great (as in . . . there is none!) but the benefits can be.

YOU NEED TO KNOW ABOUT

Junior Achievement, or JA (www.ja.org), is a national organization for children and teens with high school programs that help students foster skills that will be useful in the business world. A number of their programs, like JA Company, JA Titan, and GLOBE, are geared toward educating future business owners and entrepreneurs.

KAMALA HARRIS

District Attorney

Kamala Harris, former District Attorney, San Francisco; current Attorney General of California

The Facts

WHAT? If you've seen legal dramas like *Law & Order: SVU*, then you've seen Hollywood's take on the role of a district attorney. Elected or appointed into their position, district attorneys, or DAs, are the chief legal officer in their jurisdiction, and they prosecute crimes that occur in their counties or cities on behalf of the people.

WHERE? Most cities and counties have a district attorney, as well as a number of assistant district attorneys (ADAs).

HOW? District attorneys need a bachelor's degree and a law degree. They must also pass the bar exam in their state.

$$$: An average of $40,000 to $50,000 a year for attorneys starting out in the district attorney's office, and an earning potential of more than $100,000 a year, depending on the city they work in.

DRESS CODE? Business dress, especially in court

STRESS FACTOR: On a scale of 1 to 10, an 8

kamala harris made national news in 2005 when she was featured alongside Oprah and eighteen other incredible women in a *Newsweek* special report called "How Women Lead: 20 of America's Most Powerful Women on Their Lives—and the Lessons They've Learned."

Kamala was the first woman to ever be elected district attorney for San Francisco, and the first African-American woman to hold the office in the entire state of California. Elected to the position in 2003, Kamala spent the next seven years trying murder cases in San Francisco, creating a new specialist team to deal with gun violence, calling for legislative changes to better protect women and children, and overseeing a whole team of attorneys before being appointed attorney general of California by President Obama in 2011. While she was still a DA, I was lucky enough to get some time on Kamala's packed calendar to find out more about her career.

ME: What were your career dreams when you were younger?

YOU ASKED . . .

"How did you manage to keep a positive attitude and allow the benefits of your dream to outweigh your fear and doubts?"

—BROOKE, AGE 16

KAMALA ANSWERED . . .

"I think that all of us, no matter who we are or what we aspire to do, can sometimes feel overwhelmed with fear and doubt. My mother was a great influence and motivator in my life. She is a very smart woman who is fierce in her honesty and her opinions about what is fair, just, and right. My mother raised my sister and me with a standard that it was never acceptable to do anything other than your best. She never had any doubts about what I could accomplish and always inspired me to overcome any obstacle. In fact, one of the most important pieces of advice she gave me was, 'You may be the first to do many things, but make sure you are not the last.'"

KAMALA: I have always been drawn to issues of justice, public service, and equal rights. Both my parents were involved in the civil rights movement, and some of my earliest childhood memories are of the marching, the passion, the debate, and the emotion about this concept called "justice." My earliest role models and examples of public service were those who were more concerned with work that benefited others, rather than work that made money. My heroes were the architects of the civil rights movement, individuals who were agents for change. Conversations that I heard while growing up were always about the responsibilities of government and the fair distribution of public resources so that those in need are protected and supported. Early on, it was very evident to me that if you were going to have some impact in making sure that justice occurred, becoming a lawyer was a good place to start.

WHY WAIT?

- Public speaking is an important part of the job for most lawyers, so join the debate team at school and brush up on your skills.

- Find out about public hearings in your community. If you feel passionate about the debate, you can even argue your side of the issue in the hearing, no matter your age.

- Some law firms offer internships for high school students, where they can perform administrative tasks like filing and answering phones.

ME: What kind of tasks might you do on any given day?

KAMALA: First of all, it would be erroneous to call this wonderful work "work" in the traditional sense. It is not a nine-to-five job, and no day is like another. It is not only about what I can do in the office during business hours. It's also about what I can do out in the community, whether it is speaking at community events or before fellow lawyers at bar association events. It is continually talking about the need for a criminal justice system

that sees and thinks about all the people it is supposed to protect, including immigrants, children, seniors, and others who
may not feel empowered. It's the work of brainstorming and
thinking about the most creative and efficient ways to solve
some of these problems.

ME: What's the first thing you do when you get to work in the
morning?

KAMALA: I meet with my executive assistant to identify the
most urgent and time-sensitive matters of the day so we can
address them first thing in the morning.

ME: What is the last thing you do before you go home?

KAMALA: Before heading out to any of the one to two community events that are usually scheduled each evening, I debrief
with my chief assistant district attorney and executive assistant
about the day's events. We also look ahead and prepare ourselves for the next day.

ME: Your job appears so cool from the outside, especially for
fans of legal dramas on TV. What's the reality?

KAMALA: The reality is that a prosecutor's job is not glamorous
in the least. Shows such as *Law & Order* do not really depict
how closely prosecutors work with victims and witnesses of
crime, as well as their families. Our interaction with these victims, with their raw pain and struggle and grief, always drives

PAYING YOUR DUES

Attorneys fresh out of law school usually start out as junior
associates, or if they're at the top of their class, as law clerks
for a judge. In these positions they'll do a lot of research for
the attorneys or judges they work for, putting in long hours and
using their salary to start chipping away at law school debt.

WHAT IT TAKES

- Attention to detail and a love of research
- A strong sense of justice and integrity
- Being a great communicator, both written and verbal
- Long, hard hours

home the seriousness and grittiness of the work that we do. So in that regard, TV shows are sanitized versions. And there is no neat conclusion to the day like there is at the end of an episode. After the conclusion of one case, we can't afford to rest on our laurels and watch the credits roll. We have to prepare ourselves for the other twenty cases on our desks. But there are "Matlock moments," such as when we really connect with a jury at trial, or when we make the perfect argument. Knowing that we have done the work necessary to hold a perpetrator accountable for causing harm or injury to another can be immensely gratifying.

ME: What's the best part of your job?

KAMALA: The best part is achieving my goal of creating a world-class district attorney's office. We are focused on the work of keeping San Francisco and its residents safe, and doing that work in a way that is smart. I'm proud that we have significantly increased the conviction rate at trial for felonies. There was a significant backlog of cases in this office, and we have reduced it by more than 60 percent. We have created a priority around the prosecution of gun cases. For the first

THEN TO NOW

Graduated from Howard University	1990: Graduated from Hastings College of Law	1990–1998: Deputy district attorney in Alameda County	2001–2003: Head of the San Francisco City Attorney's Division on Families and Children

time in the history of this office, we created a child assault unit, an environmental unit that prosecutes environmental offenses, and a public integrity unit to go after corruption. We have been reaching out to traditionally underserved communities and taking our show on the road to different neighborhoods instead of waiting for them to come to us.

ME: And the most challenging aspect?

KAMALA: Frankly, how much there remains to be repaired and fixed.

KAMALA'S CAREER ADVICE

The advice I would give to young women, whether they aspire to a law career or otherwise, is to own your power. Know your value and your potential. Don't be afraid of it, don't be intimidated by it, and certainly don't deny it.

In the Field

FIVE MORE CAREERS IN THE LAW

JUDGE Judges are the authority in the courtroom, and they conduct trials and ensure that trials are fair. In trials where there's a jury, a judge explains to the jury how to come to a decision and sentences people who are found guilty. In trials

---

2003: Elected as the first woman DA in San Francisco, and the first African-American woman DA in California history

2009: Kamala's book, *Smart on Crime*, is published

2011: Appointed attorney general of California by President Obama with no jury, they decide the verdict. Most judges are elected into their positions after practicing law for a number of years.

PARALEGAL Also known as legal assistants, paralegals do much of the same work as lawyers, including tons of researching, writing legal briefs, and helping to prepare arguments for trials. Unlike lawyers, paralegals typically don't have law degrees, so they can't give legal advice or present cases in court.

MEDIATOR Mediation can save legal fees and provide parties with a quicker and potentially "nicer" way to resolve disputes by helping two parties at odds with each other resolve the issue by employing an unbiased middle person. Some mediators are on staff at courthouses, while others work for organizations that offer mediation services.

CORPORATE ATTORNEY While most legal TV shows involve dramatic trials, many attorneys never see the inside of a courtroom as part of their job. Corporate attorneys handle legal business for companies. They are required for just about every business transaction, and they must have an intimate knowledge of the business laws on both the state and local levels.

COURT REPORTER Court reporters transcribe every trial as it happens to ensure that there is an accurate legal record of the procedure. Most court reporters use keyboards called stenotype machines, which let them type every word as fast as it's said—good court reporters can type two hundred words per minute.

For more careers in law enforcement, check out the sheriff profile on page 335.

lunch break

SETTING GOALS

Have big plans for your future? Setting goals can be an incredibly powerful tool to keep you plugging ahead. Here are some ideas to keep in mind when setting goals. See which ones work for you!

TRY WRITING A MISSION STATEMENT

A mission statement is basically a sentence or two explaining what the ultimate goal of an organization (or person) is. For example, the mission statement for Step Up Women's Network is "to ignite women and girls to fulfill their potential."

You don't need to know exactly what you want to be to write a mission statement, and you can also constantly revise it. For example, my mission statement for the past ten-plus years has been to "work on creative projects that inspire and empower girls and women." When you have a mission statement that's clear, it's so much easier to make smart choices.

So how about you? Want to give it a try? Here are a few lines to write your own mission statement. Write down something very broad and focus on the things that make you feel excited and inspired:

_____

_____

_____

There's something about putting our dreams and goals down on paper that makes it more likely that we'll accomplish them. Even if no one else ever sees your goals, the act of thinking about what you want to achieve and writing it down forces you to think about the smaller steps that go into reaching the bigger dreams. Try breaking the big goals down into smaller tasks. It makes them feel attainable . . . because they are!

Here's an example: Say you want to be a successful screenwriter. You might map out your goal like this:

MAIN GOAL:

- To be a successful screenwriter by the time I'm twenty-five

MINI TASKS:

- Read William Goldman's book *Adventures in the Screen Trade* this year.

- Watch all the movies that are nominated for best screenplay each year.

- Read one screenplay each month.

- Write in my journal for five minutes every night.

- Look into taking a screenwriting class.

WHY DON'T YOU GIVE IT A SHOT?

MAIN GOAL(S):

_____

_____

_____

MINI TASKS:

_____

_____

_____

_____

_____

_____

KEEP YOUR GOALS VISIBLE

Writing down goals works the best when we put them somewhere we can see them, preferably every day—on your bedroom wall, tacked above your desk, or tucked inside your journal. Goals are almost like "to do" lists . . . and there's nothing more rewarding than checking off a goal once you've accomplished it.

BE FLEXIBLE

Goals change . . . and that's totally fine and completely normal. It doesn't mean that you failed—it just means that you're open to all different kinds of possibilities for your future. There's no better way to be fulfilled in your career and your life than by recognizing when things really connect for you. If you follow your passion, you can't make a wrong turn, because you'll always be happy doing what you're doing, and it will lead you to other amazing opportunities.

If you want to get super serious about accomplishing all your goals, big and small, check out my book _Doable: The Girls' Guide to Accomplishing Just About Anything._

JESS WEINER

Social Messaging Strategist

Jess Weiner, Founder and CEO, Talk to Jess

The Facts

WHAT? When Jess Weiner couldn't find a career title that encompassed everything that she did, she made one up. The result? *Social messaging strategist*, which Jess describes as influencing the social messaging sent to women and girls by working with corporations, engaging experts and thought-leaders, and creating dynamic content that challenges and expands current stereotypes.

WHERE? Actionists do their thing anywhere, anytime.

HOW? Don't expect a course called How to Be a Social Messaging Strategist to pop up in colleges anytime soon. Instead focus on studying things that feed your interests and inspire you, get clear on your message, and believe in your ability to be a change agent.

$$$: The sky's the limit.

DRESS CODE? Pajamas to dress pants—depends on where that day's adventures take you

STRESS FACTOR: On a scale of 1 to 10, a 9

when I first heard about what Jess Weiner was doing with her life, I thought, How cool is that? Here's a woman who created a career by following her passion and working on projects that connected with her purpose. Like any trailblazer, Jess is a risk taker with a clear vision, and following her gut has certainly paid off. In addition to being the founder and CEO of her own consulting firm, Talk to Jess, she's also a successful author—writing books like her recent bestseller, *Life Doesn't Begin Five Pounds from Now*—writes a column for *Seventeen* magazine, is the global ambassador for the Dove Self-Esteem Fund, and even makes appearances on TV.

I've known Jess for many years, so it's been inspiring to watch her entrepreneurial career evolve from what she used to describe as being an "actionist" to where she is today. Jess filled me in on her fascinating career journey in our conversation. . . .

ME: One of the things I love about your story is that you've always designed your career to match your vision. Can you tell us a bit about your earlier work as an actionist?

"I didn't have anyone showing me how to do exactly what I wanted to do."

JESS: From the time I was a little girl, I loved to perform, loved to create, loved to make up stories. So I decided I wanted to be an actor and performer. Then when I was in my teens, I struggled with eating disorders, and as I dealt with figuring out who I wanted to be in the world, I was afraid of going further into acting because I thought people were going to tell me all the time to lose weight or straighten my hair or change my nose or look different. When I was eighteen, I came to the conclusion that I didn't want to put myself out there in a way that would damage my self-esteem any further.

ME: That was pretty insightful at eighteen years old.

JESS: I just knew I didn't want to make a career out of having people comment on what I looked like. At the same time, as part of my recovery from my eating disorder, I was sitting in groups with women and talking about body image and our addictions, plus I still was in love with storytelling. So I started writing stories about the girls in my treatment program and performing them as one-woman shows on campus. That's kind of where it all began, and over the years, I refined it into being an Actionist. I didn't have anyone showing me how to do exactly what I wanted to do.

ME: I love that, the whole idea that there are many different ways to go about reaching the same destination.

JESS: Yeah, me too. But when I was in college, it was challenging to be a twenty-one-year-old senior trying to figure out how to make money at it. All my friends were going out to get their "jobs," and there I was with no idea how to make a living at what I was doing. I just knew that I loved it so much, I was going to have to break the rules and make something up.

ME: So how did you get started?

JESS: I took a grant-writing class at a community college because I thought that maybe I wanted to start my own business. My

YOU ASKED . . .

"If you could do it all over again, would you?"
                                              —CRYSTAL, AGE 12

JESS ANSWERED . . .

"Absolutely. I would even take all of the bad stuff that happened to me as a teenager and all of the things that wrapped themselves around into making this a career for me. All the hard work, frustration, pain, and discouragement gets wiped away when you do what you love and you see that you've affected someone else. That kind of happiness is irreplaceable."

final exam was to write a grant and submit it, so I did that. My grant application was accepted and I got five thousand dollars from the Eli Lilly Foundation, and at the age of twenty-one I started a social issues theater company in Indianapolis without a clue as to what I was actually going to do. So I wrote plays and

THE BREAKDOWN

IN MEETINGS: 10 to 20 meetings a week

ON THE PHONE: Constantly

ONLINE: Constantly

SITTING: Not very often!

PUBLIC SPEAKING: All the time!

WORKING SOLO: A lot

WRITING, DAYDREAMING, AND IMAGINING: A lot

got actors together to perform for anybody who would have us—high schools, middle schools, colleges. We'd put on these plays and get people to talk about things. And my career just slowly started taking off after that.

ME: Let's shift to the present. My gut is that you don't have an "average day," but could you tell me what a typical day might look like if, say, we were peeking through your window?

JESS'S (UN)USUAL DAY ———————————————

I usually get up between six thirty and seven in the morning. Then I meditate or go for a walk, usually for about a half hour, just so I can start to clear my head. Then I come back and I write in my journal. I write in my journal every day, even when I don't feel like it, because it's the one place I can get out all the crazy thoughts in my head. My whole morning routine takes about an hour, and it starts my workday.

    Next I check in on what's happening in pop culture, because I need to stay up to date on trends and what's going on in the media. So I check first thing in the morning because

I'm looking at East Coast feeds. After I check into pop culture, I answer some e-mails.

After that, I typically go to meetings with clients if they're in Los Angeles, or I do Skype meetings with my clients if they're on the other side of the country. And so I probably have, like, two to four hours of meetings every day. Later in the afternoon, I come back and I do some writing, because I'm the editor in chief of the Dove Global website, so I write columns for them.

Now I'm married, and so I actually really like family time. Believe it or not, most nights I turn off my computer at six thirty p.m.

JESS: As you can see, I have a really unstructured day. The trick for me and my job is to not overwork. The tendency is for me to push myself because there's no one over my shoulder telling me I only have fifteen minutes here and fifteen minutes there. The challenge is to strike a balance, because my life is my work, and my message is my life.

ME: Can you tell us about the transition from your work as an actionist to a social messaging strategist?

JESS: In 2007, when I became the global ambassador for the Dove Self-Esteem Fund, I got a firsthand look at how a company and brand as large as Dove could have such a positive

THEN TO NOW

1995: BA in theater arts, Pennsylvania State University	1995: Created the ACT Out Ensemble in Indianapolis	2000: Founded Parallax Entertainment, Beverly Hills, CA	2003: First book, *A Very Hungry Girl*, is published

impact around the world for girls and women. I became very interested in figuring out how I could help influence the messaging, and deliver the messaging and shape it for moms and girls to hear in a way that they could use. And so that started my interest in social messaging, and then I became a strategist about four years ago.

WHY WAIT?

- Discover where your passion lies.
- Volunteer with organizations whose causes feel close to your heart.
- Offer to be an intern for a person you admire.

ME: So, what exactly do you do in your job?

JESS: My company works with media—networks, studios, producers—as well as brands and businesses, who all want to reach women and girls. We work with them to come up with the most creative and nonstereotypical campaigns, to challenge the inner working of those companies to look at girls and women differently. So sometimes the work I do is completely internal and, you know, people won't know about it on the outside, but I'll be doing my work and workshops on the inside. And also it's about helping these brands find the right partners—great influencers and ambassadors that can help them spread their message.

ME: That's so cool. Once again you're blazing your own trail!

2003: Appeared on *Oprah*

2005: Second book, *Life Doesn't Begin 5 Pounds from Now*, is published

2007: Became global ambassador for the Dove Campaign for Real Beauty

2008: Became a contributing editor to *Seventeen* magazine

2011: Changed the name of her business to Talk to Jess

JESS: I think what I realize now is that my whole life I've been an entrepreneur and a social entrepreneur at that, an entrepreneur really focused on changing or shaping a social issue. I never called myself that. And when I look back at my history as an entrepreneur, it means that I change and grow with my career. I hope that the girls reading this book give themselves enough space to let their career evolve and not to really get stuck in what their business or career is from year to year. We change as people, and it's obvious that our work would change too, but sometimes it wasn't that obvious for me. Looking back, it's been a natural growth, but I don't think I was prepared to think about growing like that, actually.

ME: Did you have any fears around making those big changes?

JESS: Oh yeah, tremendous fear, and a lot of it is for two reasons. One is that personal fear of, like, well, wait a minute, I set this goal, but am I allowed to change it? And the other is that I had a public career—I wrote books, I spoke publicly about my own personal issues, I was very transparent about my life and my work. And then over the last couple of years, I've had to go quiet about that because I now work in such a sensitive way with clients that I can't talk about it publicly. And that made me worry that people would forget me. You know, will I be less relevant? Are people confused by what I do? And I struggle with all of that.

ME: I know that so many girls are inspired by what you do. What advice would you share for girls who want to follow in your footsteps as a change maker?

WHAT IT TAKES

- Being self-motivated and a self-starter
- Passion, passion, passion!
- Confidence in yourself and your message
- Being a good communicator

JESS: Unfortunately, in my opinion it's not enough just to sign a change.org petition. Girls need to understand how businesses run so we can really change them at the core level. It's important that they articulate that they don't like a campaign, that's still really important. But I think they expect the campaign to change because they don't like it, and that's where I want to educate them. If girls are interested in that, I think one of the ways to do it is to work in those fields with this idea of change in mind and find out where you can apply that. I think there are a lot of ways that we can apply the desire to change the media by actually working within the media.

JESS'S CAREER ADVICE

- *Make it up—all of the great career niches out there have been created by someone!*

- *Surround yourself with friends and family who say yes to your dreams and validate your vision.*

- *If you see somebody doing what you want to do, don't be afraid to grill them. Offer to take them to lunch. E-mail them! Ask them to be interviewed. Find out what their lives have really been like.*

In the Field

FIVE MORE CAREERS WHERE YOU CAN INSPIRE THE WORLD

MOTIVATIONAL SPEAKER   To be a good motivational speaker you need: (1) a strong message that inspires other people, (2) a healthy dose of charisma, and (3) a love of being in front of an audience. Motivational speakers might work for themselves or for an organization that wants to promote a cause or message.

LIFE COACH   This is a fairly new career, but its future looks pretty hot. Most life coaches work for themselves, and they're hired by people who want to get their life on track—everything from creating a plan for landing their dream job to helping them keep their life in balance. See the life coach profile on page 423.

YOUTH PROGRAM DIRECTOR   Have you ever joined a youth organization like the Girl Scouts, or maybe a religious youth group? Every one of these organizations has directors who figure out what programs their organization's members might be interested in, like writing workshops or group volunteer activities, and then make them happen.

ACTIVIST   Activists are passionate about a cause or idea, and their work is all about creating change. Activists are the people behind all the big "movements," like the civil rights movement or the women's lib movement, and they usually work for organizations that are trying to change government policy.

VOLUNTEER COORDINATOR   Most of us have volunteer experience, and it's a good thing, too—the work of volunteers is what helps keep even multinational organizations running. Volunteer coordinators help find new volunteers, train them, and make sure their work has a positive impact.

YOU NEED TO KNOW ABOUT

Idealist.org (www.idealist.org) is the online hub for people from more than 165 countries who want to take action and change their world. You'll find links to thousands of nonprofits, opportunities to volunteer, career resources, and a section with info on how to get involved in the causes you care about.

JULIE GEORGE

Child Therapist

The Facts

Julie George, Behavior & Education Consultant

WHAT? Behavior and education consultants are child therapists who typically work with children on the autism spectrum to help them strengthen their communication, academic, social, and functional skills.

WHERE? These specialized therapists might work for universities, schools, therapy conglomerates, or be self-employed consultants like Julie.

HOW? You'll need at least a master's in education, psychology, or counseling, and to become a Board Certified Behavior Analyst (BCBA).

$$$: An average annual salary of $67,000

DRESS CODE? Casual to business casual

STRESS FACTOR: On a scale of 1 to 10, a 6.5

as the percentage of children with autism—a developmental disorder that affects the brain's development of social and communication skills—continues to climb, people like Julie George are going to become more and more crucial. Take a look at Julie's time line and you'll see that she's had a fascinating career journey that includes working in a group home, being a special ed teacher, running an autism program in a middle school, being a behavior and educational consultant at a university autism center, and finally running her own private practice, where she is today.

When I sat down to talk with Julie, her love for working with this population of children was palpable. Here are the highlights from our conversation.

"I don't get a lot of reinforcement back from kids. I've had to find those other reasons as to why I'm doing it and what I love about it. I love the challenge of the work. That's what keeps me there. It's challenging. It always makes me think. It always makes me have to go and read articles and come up with new stuff, and I love that. I love constantly coming up with new ideas."

ME: First things first. In the simplest of terms, how would you describe what you do?

JULIE: I work with kids on the autism spectrum, doing social skills coaching, executive functioning skills, and working with them on emotion regulation. I'm using applied behavior analysis (ABA), which is a type of therapy we use with kids on the spectrum, but it's kind of a mix between behavioral stuff and cognitive stuff. I like to think of myself as a coach—giving them advice, having them try out some new things, and asking them to come back and let me know how it went.

ME: Can you give us an example of what that actually looks like in practice?

JULIE: I have a kid right now who's having a really hard time. She's just started middle school and has resistance around making friends, so we've set up some goals for her. Each week she has to do something different, like sit in the cafeteria, and then pick a table to sit at. Finally I said, "I would like you to find some girls to sit with," and so she did. It was really cute because she was like, "I asked this girl to sit with me, and she said yes, and now I sit with her and her friends every day." And I said, "How does that make you feel?" And she answered, "It feels good," and then she said, "Who am I kidding . . . it feels awesome!"

ME: Love that story! Did you always know you wanted to work with special needs kids?

JULIE: Actually, coming into the world of autism was total happenstance. I originally thought about being a science teacher. But when I met with my counselor at university, she recommended I do their dual certificate in general education and special education, because you end up being more marketable. At the time I wasn't really open to it. . . . I didn't want to work with that population. Then when I transferred schools, my best friend's sister encouraged me to do their special ed program. Again, I didn't want to do it, but I decided to try working with young girls with special needs at a group home just

YOU ASKED . . .

"Will I be able to have a social life while I pursue my career?"
—SAVANNAH, AGE 15

JULIE ANSWERED . . .

"Yes! I feel it is really important to have a social life while pursuing your career. It is vital to maintain a community of family and friends that you can reach out to when you need support or when you just need to have fun. While your social life may not look exactly like all your friends', you should always make sure to carve out time to connect with others. It's vital for your mental health!"

THE BREAKDOWN

IN MEETINGS: 1 hour

ON THE PHONE: 1 hour

SURFING THE WEB: 2 hours

E-MAILING: 2 hours

SITTING: 3 hours

PUBLIC SPEAKING: 30 minutes

READING: 1 hour

WORKING SOLO: 3 hours

CONDUCTING SCHOOL
  CONSULTATIONS: varies

to see. I showed up on the first day and the girls had severe mental retardation and autism and I was like, "I cannot do this." But my dad's a real stickler about not quitting things unless you have something else, and he told me I wasn't quitting the job until I had another one. And while I was searching for my other job, I ended up falling in love with it. So from there, I decided to go into the special ed program, and that's kind of how it narrowed down.

ME: It sounds like you almost "fell" into this career.

JULIE: Yes . . . if someone had told me when I was eighteen I would be doing the work I am doing, I would have laughed at them. There would've been no way I could have even wrapped my head around this kind of work, but I also recognize that I have a gift and a talent for working with these kids that I wouldn't have discovered if I hadn't been paying attention to doors opening.

ME: Let's shift to today. I know you have your own private practice. What is your work schedule like?

JULIE: Because I work with kids who are in school all day, I tend to work in the afternoons and evenings. So I only work with kids Monday through Thursday—Friday is an office paperwork day. When I see kids, I generally start anywhere between one and three in the afternoon and go until about seven or eight at night. I've got some nice chunks in there do my own thing too, and I can do e-mails from home. One day a week, I spend doing school consultations. But ideally, I try not to see more than four clients a day.

ME: Why do you limit the number of clients you see each day?

JULIE: When you're a therapist, you're the parents' lifeline in a lot of ways. So when parents are feeling anxious, there are a lot of phone calls. Inevitably part of my session is always talking with the parents, and it pulls more energetically because I feel like they need more from me on an emotional level. I'm super-sensitive to other people's energies and emotions, so I need my own time to make sure I can clear the energy, the emotion, and the stress.

ME: How do you do that?

JULIE: One of the things I got into last year was Self-Care Friday. Every Friday I dedicated an hour to doing something just for myself. It could be a bubble bath. It could be taking a walk. It could be getting drinks with friends—whatever was going to fill me up. I think doing this work, and teaching kids a coping routine, and teaching them self-talk, and breathing, and doing strategies, along with doing this Self-Care Friday, has really helped me to understand the practice of self-care and what that can do for you.

ME: I imagine there might be challenges working with autistic kids. What's difficult about your job?

JULIE: These kids can have some really outrageous behavior. So having to work through that is hard. Like last week one girl I work

WHY WAIT?

- If there is an inclusion classroom in your school, volunteer to get experience working with children on the autism spectrum.
- Read books that feature autistic characters, like *Marcelo in the Real World* and *The Curious Incident of the Dog in the Night-Time*.

WHAT IT TAKES

- A love of working with children
- Oodles of patience
- A willingness to do personal growth work
- Creativity and problem-solving skills
- Good communication skills

with had a really bad session and she got up and dumped my bottle of water all over me. And for me, that's the teaching moment. It's like, "Okay. I'm not going to scream. I'm going to tell you how I'm feeling. And I'm going to go take a break because I'm feeling overwhelmed right now. And I'm feeling scared. My heart's racing, and that was really unexpected." Getting them to a place where they can overcome some of those behavior challenges is, by far, the most taxing.

ME: That sounds really hard. Yet I can tell from the way you talk about your work that you see this as a perfect fit for you.

JULIE: I've picked a population of kids to work with that aren't super "thank-you kids." They're not coming to therapy going, "Wow, you're awesome! Thank you so much for working with me and getting me to change!" Instead they're like, "Oh my gosh, how long am I going to have to see you?" I don't get a lot of reinforcement back from kids. I've had to find those other reasons as to why I'm doing it and what I love about it. I love the challenge of the work. That's what keeps me there. It's challenging. It always makes me think. It always makes me

THEN TO NOW

| 1994: Started college at Northern Arizona University, Flagstaff | 1998: Transferred to Arizona State University | 1999: Began working with HOPE group as ABA therapist | 2001: Graduated with BA in education, with emphasis in special education | 2001: Special education teacher, Gilbert Elementary School, Gilbert, AZ | 2006: Graduated with MA in elementary education, reading emphasis |

have to go and read articles and come up with new stuff, and I love that. I love constantly coming up with new ideas.

ME: Do you have any stories you can share with us of a successful outcome?

JULIE: Just the other day a girl I work with came in and said, "I think I'm ready to make friends. I think I'm ready to let them in." And I was like, "Let who in?" She said, "The social world." And I said, "Oh, okay, that's good. Tell me more about that." And she said, "I just realized that I'm the only one holding myself back." And I just wanted to start bawling, because she was right. Watching these kids come out of their bubbles and their autism worlds, and pick up what's going on around them and find joy in that, is by far the highlight.

ME: Therapist as a career is often portrayed in TV shows and movies. Do you think Hollywood gets it right?

JULIE: Not necessarily. I think they're getting closer to it on the show *Parenthood*. They had an ABA therapist on there for the character Max, who has Asperger's. But in general, no, because it always comes across as you just sit and talk, or you just sit and play games. For me, I always go in with a goal in mind and the steps of how we're going to get there. All the kids have goals they're tracking themselves, so they actually fill their goal sheets out every week to see how they're doing. I think it's pivotal for kids at these ages to see how far they've

2006: Special education teacher, Tyee Middle School, Bellevue, WA

2010: Began classes in applied behavior analysis at University of Washington

2010: Behavior and education consultant, University of Washington Autism Center

2012: Passed Board Certification for Behavior Analyst

2013: Launched private practice

come and not just hear it from us, but for them to actually witness their progress and see it change over time. So it's more than just sitting on the couch and sharing your feelings and emotions.

ME: One last question. How would you define being successful at your job?

JULIE: For me, it's about being successful on two different levels. I'm always wanting to be really practical in the advice and the strategies I give, and so when kids are doing well and families are happy, I feel like that's successful. And then when I start to see growth in kids and the parents' anxiety levels ease and they start to relax more, that's also being successful. I was actually just called into a school district to do an evaluation for a kid, and the dad said to me at the end of the session, "You came in without knowing our kid and took this bird's-eye view and you captured our son perfectly. You know exactly what his behavior is and exactly what to do for it." It's moments like that I think, Okay, I'm on the right track. I'm doing the right thing.

JULIE'S CAREER ADVICE

When you're going down a career path, keep going with it, and check in with yourself, and make sure it's filling you and it's filling you on the level that you want it to. Check in with yourself and be like, "Is this what I want to do?" I think there's also a little bit of letting the path unfold too. It's important to pay attention to those signs and those doors when they're opening or figure out the meaning when doors are closing.

*FIVE MORE CAREERS IN THERAPY AND
SOCIAL WORK*

FAMILY SOCIAL WORKER   Also known as family services social workers, these people specialize in family dynamics and provide support for issues ranging from parenting problems and difficult relationships to children with special needs. Family social workers usually work for government agencies or family services agencies.

FOSTER CARE CASEWORKER   The foster care system finds temporary homes for more than a half-million kids in the United States who have been abused, neglected, or abandoned, and caseworkers act as advocates for these kids—matching them with foster parents, recommending programs, and helping to determine when and if a foster child should be reunited with his or her parents.

SUBSTANCE ABUSE COUNSELOR   Substance abuse counselors work with people who have drinking or drug problems, and help them address their abuse and come up with strategies for recovering from their addiction. Substance abuse counselors might work at rehab centers, for hotlines, or in hospitals.

SOCIAL POLICYMAKER   These social workers help shape government laws and policies that affect populations who might not have a lot of support, such as the homeless, child abuse victims, and drug abusers. Social policymakers work with the government to develop ideas, programs, and policies to create positive change.

CLINICAL SOCIAL WORKERS   Clinical social workers specialize in counseling people or providing what's known as "psychotherapy," or therapy that deals with mental and emotional disorders. Some work in mental hospitals or in psychiatric wards at hospitals, while others might start their own private practice to see clients independently.

YOU NEED TO KNOW ABOUT

If you're interested in being a child therapist working with autistic children, Autism Speaks is a great online hub of information. Dive into research, explore intervention tool kits, and read their active blog to learn more about the reality of life with autism and the latest conversations around this childhood epidemic. Find out more at www.autismspeaks.org.

ALLI SHEARMUR

Movie Studio Executive

The Facts

WHAT? Movie studio executives wield much power when it comes to what movies get made, who stars in and directs them, and how they get produced.

WHERE? Most movie studio execs work on the big movie studio lots like Universal, Paramount, and Sony, which are primarily located in Los Angeles, although a number of movie studio execs work out of New York City.

Alli Shearmur, Movie Studio Executive

HOW? These jobs are supercompetitive—a background in film, being in the right place at the right time, and a willingness to pay lots of dues are all key.

$$$: Between $100,000 and $1 million a year or more, plus bonuses, depending on level

DRESS CODE? Business to business casual, with creative flair

STRESS FACTOR: On a scale of 1 to 10, an 8 for stress (and "a 10 for enjoyment!" says Alli)

alli shearmur has been a part of the movie studio power structure in Hollywood for a number of years. As an executive at Walt Disney Pictures, Universal Pictures, Paramount Studios, and Lionsgate, she has overseen the day-to-day development of big studio features such as *The Hunger Games*, *Erin Brockovich*, *The Bourne Identity*, the *American Pie* trilogy, and *Charlotte's Web*.

I caught up with Alli in Los Angeles and swung by her office on a studio lot full of old Hollywood charm and bustling with activity. While I waited outside her door, I caught up with her assistant, who was doing ten other tasks at the same time, bolstering the stereotype that the movie industry is extremely fast paced. Once inside her office, Alli and I got comfortable on plush couches, and she shared with me the ins and outs of the job of a movie studio executive.

ME: What were your career dreams when you were younger?

ALLI: The first memory I have of even thinking about what I wanted to be was when I was in first grade. My teacher asked us, "What do you want to be when you grow up?" And I remember drawing a picture of the answer, not writing it out. I literally drew a princess with a crown and wand. That changed, because by the time I got to junior high, I had already become deeply obsessed and fallen in love with the movies, and I knew with all my heart that I wanted to work in the movie business.

"The reality is, this job is like being in a class where you have tons of reading and way more homework than anybody else."

I didn't know that a job as a studio executive even existed until seventh or eighth grade, when I read a magazine article about a prominent studio executive. And I remember thinking that maybe someday, that could be me. From then on, anytime I had any exposure to film or a conversation about film, I knew that it was a world I wanted to work in.

ME: It's amazing that you had such a clear vision of what you wanted at such a young age.

ALLI: It's a really strange thing, I admit. But it was really luck that I stumbled upon that article back when I was a teenager and got to read about the movie executives of the day and track their careers. It was also really lucky that there were so many amazing women in Hollywood paving the way at studios like Sony, Universal, and Paramount. It truly inspired me to believe that this career was a possibility.

ME: I have to say, in writing this book I haven't met many women who are doing exactly what they dreamed they would be doing when they were so young. What does it feel like?

ALLI: It is the luckiest thing in the world. I remember one of my best friends in high school went to California and she came back with a plaque for me that said, "I'd rather be in California." At my sweet sixteen party, I'm literally photographed with a director's clapboard. That's how much I loved it. I would stay inside and watch *Roman Holiday*, *Philadelphia Story*, every version of *Phantom of the Opera*, while my siblings were playing outside.

ME: So is it still exciting to you?

YOU ASKED . . .

"Did you have any struggles along the way?"

—TIFFANY, AGE 19

ALLI ANSWERED . . .

"I'd say the biggest struggle I had was self-doubt. But I stayed connected to my passion and my dream and stuck it out long enough to find people who mentored me and showed me the way."

THE BREAKDOWN

IN MEETINGS: Half the day

ON THE PHONE: Half the day

ONLINE: At least 4 hours while on phone, at least 1 hour at home

READING: At least 1½ hours a day, plus 3–4 hours each weekend

ALLI: Yes! I have not lost the love and excitement for being around screenwriters, directors, and actors. I never will, ever. But what I have learned is what unbelievably hard work making a movie is, and how much hard work all people working in all the facets of the movie industry do. It's hard work, it's long hours, and it's not always glamorous.

ME: So what does the hard work really entail? What does being a movie studio executive mean?

ALLI: As a movie studio executive, you are the godparent of a film from the moment it's an idea until it's completed. First you buy an idea that someone has verbally pitched to you, or you've read a screenplay, a book, or an article and you've decided, "Hmm, that's a good idea for a movie." So you hire a writer and, just like an editor does at a publishing house, you work with that writer to develop the best written version of that story for the screen that is emotional and unpredictable, and funny if it's a comedy, moving if it's a drama, or terrifying if it's a horror film.

You're also responsible for figuring out how much the movie would cost to make. Then you go out and you find a director. When you have the director, you actually "cast" the movie. Then you bring this entire package to your bosses and tell them that this is a movie you believe in your heart and soul will be entertaining and profitable.

Then when they say yes, your job is not over. Because then your job is to be the godparent of that project through every phase of production. In prep, when the crew is hired, in production while the film's being shot, and in postproduction while the editor is putting the film together, the composer is scoring music, and the effects people are adding effects. And at the same time, it's making all the people involved in all of those decisions feel good about their role. Depending on what level you are in your career, you may be doing this for more than one movie at a time. When you become a VP, you're responsible for one or two of these a year. As SVP or EVP, you're responsible for maybe three or four. And as a president of production, you might be responsible for a slate of between sixteen to eighteen of these a year, as well as managing all of the people in the staff who are part of the creative group, production, legal, business, and music, and who help make these movies possible.

ME: Wow! It seems like having a great assistant is critical for a movie studio executive.

ALLI: Yes, it is. And assistants to movie studio executives work extremely hard and put in long hours, but it can be a great opportunity for the right person to discover if the path of a movie studio executive is for him or her.

ME: I e-mailed your assistant at eight a.m. on a Sunday to confirm our meeting, and I got a reply back from him within minutes. I couldn't believe he was working on a Sunday morning!

ALLI: Well, I started out working as an assistant when I first got into this business. And it's a great learning experience, because you're not just answering the phone and handling schedules—you're really a part of the process, and it is just such a great glimpse into the career.

ME: So are the TV shows and movies that portray the job of a movie studio exec as being hip and glamorous unrealistic?

ALLI: The reality is, this job is like being in a class where you

WHY WAIT?
- Watch tons of current and classic movies of all genres.
- Read the books behind some of your favorite movies to see how they've been adapted for the big screen.

have tons of reading and way more homework than anybody else. Imagine doing a term paper on every script that you're reading. That's just one part of the job. Watching dailies, which is the film that's shot on a daily basis, is also required. And watching dailies is a privilege and needs to be done with complete concentration, so phone calls and e-mails have to wait until the screenings are done. On top of that, there are a lot of people who call you because they have questions that need answers, and most of the time, the answers can't wait a day or two. On top of that, you have to read several papers a day—the *New York Times*, the *Los Angeles Times*, the *Hollywood Reporter*, *Variety*, the *Wall Street Journal*. And it's not unusual to read an entire novel or six-hundred-page manuscript in one night. So imagine you're in a class where you have more reading and more written homework than any of your friends—that's what being in my job is like.

ME: With such an incredible amount of work to do, how do you get it all done and still stay sane?

ALLI: You prioritize and focus only on those scripts that need

THEN TO NOW

Graduated from University of Pennsylvania	Received law degree from University of Southern California Law Center	Director of comedy development, Columbia Pictures Television	1994–1997: VP of production, Walt Disney Pictures

attention by the end of the weekend. You create your own due dates and deadlines. You hire very smart people and you rely on them, let them do their jobs, and trust them.

ME: How about being a woman in your career—is it particularly difficult, especially because you're a mom, too?

ALLI: I don't really feel like there have been any limitations as far as being a woman in the business. I actually feel like I've had the good fortune of working among great women who make it seem very doable, and not one of them seemed to have their personal life impaired because of their job. It just happens to be that like many working women, we can't be home during the day for our children. I also work around my daughter's schedule. She's up at six thirty, so I set the alarm clock for five in the morning. That way I get an hour and a half of work in every day before she even wakes up. What I won't do is be around her and be on my BlackBerry or on a phone call or be reading a script. She is the center of my attention when we're both home.

ME: Tell me what kinds of things make a studio executive's day.

ALLI: A great day can be when an actor you're dying to do a movie with says yes, or a script comes in better than you ever imagined, or maybe a director you dreamed of directing a movie says yes. Or sometimes you'll just be sitting in a creative meeting with a writer, director, actor, or producer, and it's just

| 1998–2004: EVP of production, Universal Pictures | 2004: EVP of production, Paramount Studios | 2005: Promoted to co-president of production, Paramount Studios | 2008: Named president of production, Lionsgate | 2012: Started Alli Shearmur Productions |

PAYING YOUR DUES

You'll need to spend one to three years being an assistant to a movie executive, where you'll earn little money, work long hours, and do a lot of phone and scheduling work. The great part is, you'll be on the inside, and after paying your dues, you'll have a greater chance of moving up to the next level.

an absolutely fulfilling conversation that you know is going to end with the movie being better. Any one of those things can make a great day.

ME: And what are the biggest challenges, besides having more work than you have time to do?

ALLI: There are two main challenges. There tends to be a lot of change in the entertainment business, and you have to be a personality that can remain fluid and not become shaken by a business that is in constant transition. Another interesting challenge is that it's a very social business, so your work doesn't end when you leave for the day and go home to do your homework. There are no regular hours. And there are very few boundaries. There's nothing regular, routine, or predictable about it.

ME: Is there a particular project that you're most proud of?

ALLI: I'm proud of all of them, but two of the films about which I have the greatest pride are *The Bourne Identity* and *The Bourne Supremacy*. That franchise is something that I nurtured from the beginning. The director of the first film brought the book to me and together we developed the screenplay, and together we dreamed that Matt Damon would play Jason Bourne. I par-

WHAT IT TAKES

- Being persistent and willing to pay your dues
- A blend of creative and business sensibility
- Able to handle change and instability

ticipated in many decisions relating to that movie, and the idea that the films were considered by some to be redefining the spy genre felt incredibly exciting for someone who loves film as much I do. When I watched the final cut of *The Bourne Supremacy*, I was moved when I saw that the filmmakers had named the hotel where Jason gets his memory back the Brecker Hotel, which is my maiden name. That meant a lot to me.

ALLI'S WORDS OF WISDOM

I never skipped one step. I was a secretary, I was a junior executive, I was a midlevel executive, I was the slightly higher midlevel executive. I never skipped any grades as far as moving along on this career path, but by the time I was promoted to senior executive, which I was never 100 percent sure would happen, my experience gave me a tremendous sense of what to do and what not to do. I learned a lot by watching, and it's a perfectly fine way to progress, to not have your career miss a step and to not become overly impatient along the way. You need to have a sense of faith that if you stick it out there is a chance that it really can happen for you.

In the Field

FIVE MORE CAREERS WORKING IN THE MOVIES

DIRECTOR OF PHOTOGRAPHY Every shot of every movie has been carefully planned out by directors of photography (DPs or cinematographers), who need to understand lighting, cameras, and different types of film stock. Those at the top of their game can leave as much of an impression on a film as the director or the actors.

SCRIPT SUPERVISOR Script supervisors take detailed notes about what happens every day of a film shoot, including dialogue changes, what scenes were shot, and how many "takes" the director filmed for each shot. They also help prompt actors who forget their lines while rehearsing or filming.

FILM EDITOR After a movie has been filmed, the music scored, and the sound effects created, it is handed off to an editor, who works with the director to put the pieces together, scene by scene, note by note, frame by frame. Editors dictate the pacing of a film—the tiniest tweak to a scene or shot can change the way an entire film feels.

CASTING DIRECTOR Before an actor can be cast in a new movie, they must first impress a casting director. Casting directors work with talent agents to identify potential actors to play the roles in a film, screening a ton of reels and reviewing hundreds, if not thousands, of headshots. After holding auditions, casting directors will make their recommendations about who they think should be cast for each role.

GAFFER In the production of a film, the gaffer is another word for "chief lighting technician." Gaffers not only plan what lights are needed for each scene, but they also work with the crew to get the lights set up and make any necessary changes on the set as shooting progresses.

YOU NEED TO KNOW ABOUT

The Internet Movie Database (www.imdb.com) is the go-to source for any and all info relating to movies. Here you'll find a searchable database of every movie ever made, inside scoop and trivia on the movies and their stars, and articles on moviemaking.

For more on writing in Hollywood, check out the TV show creator profile on page 1 and the screenwriter profile on page 267.

DENISE GERSHBEIN

Design Creative Director

The Facts

Denise Gershbein,
Executive Creative
Director, frog design

WHAT? Creative directors work in a variety of environments in arts and entertainment and play a key role in developing and shepherding creative ventures, from products and advertising to motion graphics and publishing.

WHERE? Creative directors can work for small boutique design firms or large corporate agencies and just about everywhere in between, in cities across the country.

HOW? You'll want to start out with a bachelor's degree in a creative field and get some solid work experience in areas like copywriting, designing, graphic design, branding, or art direction. After you've put in the time, you can parlay your experience, passion, drive, and business savvy into this coveted role.

$$$: An average annual salary of $110,000

DRESS CODE? Creative and cool . . . or whatever you like

STRESS FACTOR: On a scale of 1 to 10, a 7 (says Denise, you create your own stress . . . or lack of it)

denise gershbein is the executive creative director for frog, a global innovation firm that combines research, strategy, technology, and design to create products and services. In our interview, Denise shared her journey from graphic designer to creative executive and brought us inside her busy work world at frog's San Francisco studio.

ME: How would you describe exactly what it is that you do?

DENISE: I design products and services—everything from mobile phones to health-care devices to online services (like Netflix). And I design everything from the mobile phone itself, to the apps that run on it, to the visual design of everything you see on the screen. Said even more simply: I study how people learn, think, and interact, then I design and make things that help them do that.

ME: When you were in college, did you see "creative director" in your future?

DENISE: I thought my career would be about designing the visual aspect of things: posters, packaging, reports, corporate identities. I was also interested in psychology, philosophy, education, and writing. I didn't know what that meant or how I'd tie it together, but I knew that I not only cared about how things looked, but also how and why people use and understand things. So while I was designing printed annual reports, I was wondering, how can I communicate this idea in a better way? What is the person reading this report thinking? What's the most important message? Within a few years I knew I wanted to go to grad school to continue to explore this crossover between design, education, philosophy, and psychology. I found a great program that combined product design and computer science, where I

"The best part of my job is what I call 'awake moments,' which is when I help someone see something or do something in a new way."

YOU ASKED . . .

"Did you have doubts about your career after you started it?"
—MEGAN, AGE 13

DENISE ANSWERED . . .

"Everyone has doubts, no matter who you are or how successful you are! I've always looked at my doubts, though, as a sign that there was some interest, some passion, some hidden curiosity in me that needed paying attention to . . . a clue to the next exciting thing, not a warning of something I've 'done wrong.' I look at my career as an ever-emerging idea. There is always some new current to follow, some new branch to explore. And at any time, I can explore any new branch I choose. So there is no reason to think in terms of 'second thoughts.'"

learned about design research and how to make things. So it was an evolution of what I had been doing in graphic design but in a whole new direction.

ME: So would you say a graduate degree is necessary to be a creative director?

DENISE: Not directly, no. Many people do have graduate degrees, though. In my field, a graduate degree signals you are super passionate not only about your field and the skills required, but also that you have a very strong personal point of view you want to explore in-depth.

ME: So let's switch gears to your actual workday. What's the first thing you do when you get into work?

DENISE: This question gives me an "ugh" feeling, and I'm hesitant to answer it, because this is something I think I could be doing better! Honestly, the first thing I do is fight fires. I look around—at people, at my e-mails, at messages—and I see if there is anything happening that is a huge priority and needing my immediate attention. I try to put the attention there first. I think I could do this differently, though. What I'd like to do first is quietly sit with a cup of tea and review my to-do list for the day (I'm a big list person, as it helps me take the pressure off my brain and put it onto paper for safekeeping), and then have a block of time, an hour or two, when I could be focusing on conceptual work, like reviewing teamwork, writing an article, or creating concepts for a new product idea or process. I find I do my best creative thinking first thing in the morning, and that, unfortunately, is exactly the time of day when I find myself focusing on work "emergencies." To clarify, there really are no such things as "emergencies" in this field— I have to remind myself of that daily. It's just a kind of stress we put on ourselves to deliver the best work.

ME: I've heard that hours at design firms can be brutal. Is that the case for you?

DENISE: My in-studio hours are usually right about forty hours.

THEN TO NOW

1991: Graduated from Savannah College of Art and Design with BFA in graphic design	1992: Graphic designer for Abrams Design Group	1994: Began working as a freelance graphic designer	1995: Graphic designer for Heiney & Craig	2001: Graduated from Stanford University with an MFA in product design

That's thanks to my son—I get him to school in the morning, and I'm home in time for dinner (unless I'm on a business trip). But I'm also on e-mail in the morning while I'm getting ready, and checking in after my son goes to sleep, so that can easily add another ten to twenty hours to the week.

> **WHAT IT TAKES**
> - A sense of curiosity and wonder about the world and people
> - A desire to see your ideas made in the real world
> - An optimistic point of view

ME: So, are you ever truly "off duty"?

DENISE: Well, I'm a creative person, and my work is creative, so in that sense, I'm always working. I'm always thinking about design, technology, culture, society, and what I'd like to create, change, and see happen. I'm always thinking about possibilities, ideas, connections. So that's one way I'm never "off." Because of that, I tend to communicate with coworkers and clients whenever ideas strike. Also, in my role, I have to be reachable by my clients, my team, and my own managers for critical issues. We are a global company, which means lots of time zones to manage, so it's not unusual to do calls or e-mail at strange hours.

ME: With such an intense schedule, is it possible to have a personal life too?

2002: Became an interactive designer at Advisory Software

2005: Began working at frog design as a design analyst

2007: Promoted to principal designer, frog design

2008: Promoted to associate creative director, frog design

2010: Promoted to creative director, frog design

2013: Promoted to executive creative director, frog design

ON ANY GIVEN DAY, DENISE MIGHT BE ──────

- *Meeting with teams to review designs*
- *Meeting with team leads and directors to give feedback on the direction of a project concept, the client relationship, or thoughts on how to mentor and direct team members*
- *Meeting with the studio general manager to discuss the studio: recruiting, culture, client relationships. We talk about things that are currently going on, and plan what we want to do to make things even better.*
- *Attending client pitches—sometimes far away, sometimes nearby, sometimes in our own studio.*
- *Giving presentations to our people in the studio on design, or process, or just inspiring things that I want to share*
- *Time sheets! Expenses! Yuck.*
- *Reading and researching (the web, people I follow on Twitter) about interesting things that are happening in my own field, but also things that are totally unrelated, as sometimes the best ideas come from surprising connections between disparate ideas*

DENISE: I'm able to balance work and personal pretty well. . . . What's throwing me off these days is being a single mom. Right now I'm doing well balancing time for my son, time for myself, and time for work . . . but not time for relationships, both personal and romantic. That's a struggle. I always put my son and myself before work, and thankfully, I work at a place where it's possible to do that. I've come to terms with the fact that there are only so many hours in the day, and my own energy and stamina are a finite resource. So I pay attention to what's most important and accept that I can't do everything every day. Actually, now that I say that, I realize that's my secret. It's really important, and it's taken me years to learn that and be okay with it.

ME: What would you say are the best parts of your job?

DENISE: The best part of my job is what I call "awake moments," which is when I help someone see something or do something in a new way. It might be a client, a designer, or a person who uses the products I design. Also really, really cool are the times we travel to crazy places to do crazy things. Like the time we were working on a food project, and we spent the day in a fancy restaurant making a gourmet meal just by playing around with ingredients. Or the day we ran a workshop at NASA. On those days, I say to myself, "I get paid to do this? This is crazy!"

ME: That does sound pretty awesome! On the flip side, what are some of the challenges?

DENISE: The stress of managing one hundred things at any given moment, which doesn't come so much from being a designer, but from being a manager and director. Being at a director level takes me further away from the actual hands-on design work, but it's design at another level: It's about designing teams, programs, process, relationships. That's really stressful and complex, but also very exciting.

ME: Are there any myths out there about your job and field that you'd like to clear up?

DENISE: I think people think that design is about sitting at an art table all day, surrounded by pens and paintbrushes and paper, making pictures. First off, much of the design craft has become very digital—design on computers, for computers, and other screens. Secondly, a big part of design work is going out and looking at and being in the world, not just sitting down and drawing things.

ME: One last question: What does being successful at your job mean to you?

DENISE: If I have made things and put them into the world, or created a process that people use, or facilitated a group of people toward action . . . and those things have made at least one person have an "awake moment" where they were able to see themselves or be more than they imagined they could be, then I think I've done what I was put here to do.

DENISE'S CAREER ADVICE

Don't aim for a career or a position. Life changes, you change, and there are curves and bumps along the way. Rather, follow what you love to do. Be willing to explore, to experiment, to piece together the bits that you learn about yourself along the way, so that you create a path for yourself rather than just blindly following some prescriptive path someone else has dictated.

In the Field

FIVE MORE CAREERS IN CREATIVE DESIGN

GRAPHIC DESIGNER Graphic designers typically work for magazines, newspapers, and other publishers. Their tools of the trade are usually computers, and their talents lie in using colors, fonts, photos, and more to come up with creative ways to communicate visual messages.

WEB DESIGNER Just about every business, big and small, has a website, many of which were created by a professional web designer. Beyond the actual coding and visual design of a site, this hot job often includes figuring out interface design, search engine optimization (SEO), and user experience (UX) design.

TECHNICAL DESIGNER Technical designers, or TDs, often work for companies that deliver products or services, and their job is to interact with both the designers and the manufacturers to ensure that the quality of the end result meets the company's expectations and needs.

CREATIVE SERVICES MANAGER Some large companies and brands have in-house creative services departments to meet internal creative needs. These managers harness creative services—from graphics and video to copywriting, art, and photography—to create materials needed for presentations, trade shows, meetings, and more.

DIGITAL DESIGNER This career title encompasses any design jobs working in digital visual media. This might mean 3-D modeling for an animation studio or developing digital platforms for mobile phones. The best visual designers have a strong design sense coupled with an understanding of user experience (UX).

YOU NEED TO KNOW ABOUT

The American Institute of Graphic Arts (AIGA) is the professional association for designers, which brings together practitioners, enthusiasts, and patrons to amplify the voice of design. On their website you can learn more about design careers, read inspirational stories about designers, watch free webinars, and more. Visit the AIGA online at www.aiga.org.

NANCY PEARL

Librarian

The Facts

Nancy Pearl, Librarian

WHAT? Librarians take care of the books and documents in a library, as well as deal with the public to help them interact with the library materials.

WHERE? Librarians work in public libraries, schools and universities, museums, nonprofit organizations, and historical institutions.

HOW? Most professional librarians have at least a bachelor's degree, if not a master's, in library science.

$$$: An average of $58,000 per year, but could be more or less, depending on the type of library—public or private—and where it's located

DRESS CODE? Casual to business casual

STRESS FACTOR: On a scale of 1 to 10, a 3

if ever there was a librarian who's achieved "celebrity status," it's Nancy Pearl. Nancy, who was the executive director of the Washington Center for the Book at the Seattle Public Library until her retirement in 2004, is a serious book expert and frequent guest on TV programs like the *Today* show and NPR's *Morning Edition*, where she talks about her recommended reads. She is also the author of more than ten books herself, including *Book Lust* and *Book Crush*. But perhaps Nancy's most interesting (and bizarre) claim to fame is that she has her very own action figure. Yes, you heard right: *action figure*. The librarian action figure, which can be found in kitschy boutiques around the country, is a little statuette of Nancy with a finger to her lips, as if to say "shush."

Nancy and I got together in a little coffee shop on a rainy day in Seattle, and the fact that several people approached us while we were talking, saying, "Aren't you Nancy Pearl?" and then introduced themselves like giddy fans, reconfirmed that she is indeed a celebrity librarian extraordinaire. Here are some highlights from our conversation:

"A librarian is not solely a person who retrieves information—the public library really is the heart and soul of a community."

ME: You knew you wanted to be a librarian from the time you were ten years old. What is it about being a librarian that appealed to you?

NANCY: I come from a family of do-gooders, people who really believed that you could change the world and make it a better place. And for me, the way that I understood even at ten that you could make the world a better place was by being a librarian, especially a children's librarian, and opening up the world of books and reading to kids who might be in unfortunate home situations or in other difficult places in their lives. Books have that unique ability in that you can both lose yourself and find yourself in the pages of the same book.

ME: So now, reflecting back, did you achieve your goal?

NANCY: Yes, I do think that librarians make the world a better place. A librarian is not solely a person who retrieves information—the public library really is the heart and soul of a community. I think that through recommending good books to read or through programming that they do, librarians make a library a living, breathing place.

ME: So what kinds of things do librarians in a public library actually do?

NANCY: I think one of the most exciting things is putting people together with good books. A lot of people come to the librarian and say, "I just finished this book, I loved it, can you find me another one exactly like it?" And the trick is to figure out what it is that they meant by "exactly like it" and find that book. Another important task is helping people find information for life skills, whether it's the address of the gas

YOU ASKED . . .

"What, if any, are your regrets?" —MOLLY, AGE 16

NANCY ANSWERED . . .

"I think my general regret is that I let fear of the unknown stop me from doing things that I really wish I could have done. When my husband and I were first married, people of our generation were picking up and moving to a place in the world where they wanted to live without having a job there, and just sort of saying, 'Okay, we'll just go there and get a job.' We would never have done that. . . . It was too scary. That sort of fear of just taking a leap is something that I really regret. I also believe at the same time that all of those wonderful things that have happened to me in the last decade or so happened as a result of everything else I had to go through. But generally, I think that fear is an awful sort of hang-up—it's a distraction in your life."

company or where to register to vote, that kind of thing. So all of that is accepted within the librarian's job description.

But I think that what a librarian ought to be doing a lot of is bringing the community into the library for book discussion groups, poetry readings, and author visits, and showing the public that the library isn't just a collection of dead books or books that

WHY WAIT?

- Volunteer at the library in the teen section or get a job at a bookstore.
- Read books in all different genres.
- Keep a reading journal where you write your thoughts down about your favorite books and the impact they had on your life.

only come alive when you read them. It's a place that breathes. My personal mission has always been to both deepen and broaden a user's experience with works of literature. So if somebody only reads fiction, for example, I will always look at the library in a more holistic way to try to get them out of that fiction section and show them that there are great books in other parts of the library.

ME: I *love* reading, but it also puts me to sleep, so it takes me a while to get through a book. How do you get all your reading in?

NANCY: It depends on the books that I'm reading. I think that books say to you, "Okay, this is how fast you should read me," so it's really hard to say how much time I spend reading. I've arranged my life at this old age of mine so that I don't do much else but read and write about the books that I'm reading. I think that reading is a choice that you make, and so you choose to read a novel instead of the newspaper or instead of a magazine or you choose to read a novel instead of play a game. My downfall is FreeCell on the computer, so I choose to read rather than playing a FreeCell game or something like that.

WHAT IT TAKES

- A love of books and research
- Good people and organizational skills
- Being comfortable working with computers

ME: What do you think are the most challenging things about being a librarian at a public library?

NANCY: Dealing with the public. . . . You're really a public servant. It's the public who pays your salary, and you owe them your best thinking and your courtesy, and sometimes that's very hard, as it is for anybody who's dealing with the public. There are actually a lot of similarities between retail and being a librarian. And so people tend to think of librarians as being sort of solitary readers who just sit at their desk or catalog books. And sure, there is that part of the library, but when you're working in a public library, you're on the desk a lot, you have to have good interpersonal skills and you have to be a people person. The people who use the library to find good books or information for making themselves a better person, that's the best part of society. And so you get to meet such interesting people.

ME: Are there any other stereotypes about librarians that you want to bust?

NANCY: I think one of the misconceptions is probably that librarians are stuffy and boring and don't read. And of course, there are some that are like that, but most aren't. Take teen

THEN TO NOW

Received MA in library science from University of Michigan

1998: Was named Fiction Reviewer of the Year by *Library Journal*

1998: Developed breakthrough public reading program, "If All of Seattle Read the Same Book"

NANCY'S FAVORITE AUTHORS FOR TEENS

- Sarah Dessen
- Deb Caletti, especially *Honey, Baby, Sweetheart*
- Pete Hautman, especially *Godless*
- M. T. Anderson, especially *Thirsty* and *Feed*

librarians—they generally go into that field because they're really interested in teen books. They're people who have read those books and stand up for the rights of the teen in the library, and I think that's really important. When you have a teen librarian who is identified as such, that's somebody you can really trust, who knows what books are really good and who knows what you're going through.

ME: Do you make a distinction between your work and your personal life?

NANCY: Robert Frost has a poem in which he talks about when love and work are one, and I think that should be the goal. I've been fortunate enough that there's never been a separation between what I do in my work and what I would choose to do if I weren't in this job. I guess that's one result of knowing at age ten what I wanted to do. I've always just loved to read and escape into the pages of a book.

2003: Book Lust was published

2004–2005: Recipient of the Women's National Book Association Award

2004: Retired as executive director of the Washington Center for the Book at the Seattle Public Library

2009: *More Book Lust* is published

NANCY'S CAREER ADVICE

Take your work seriously, but don't take yourself seriously.

In the Field

FIVE MORE CAREERS IN LIBRARY SCIENCE

CONTENT MANAGER   Content managers create and manage the content of a website or online portal, keeping it up-to-date and providing information. Many content managers have some knowledge of HTML or other web languages so they can program the content themselves.

DATABASE ADMINISTRATOR   Just about every company tracks data electronically, such as customer and inventory information. Keeping all of this data organized, secure, and accessible to the right people is the job of database administrators. These people set up, design, and maintain the databases, backing up information as needed.

INFORMATION BROKER   An information broker is someone who does research, like market research or patent searches. Some information brokers specialize in researching a particular kind of information, and all of them use the Internet and special online information databases to do their work.

INDEXER   If you flip to the back of a nonfiction book, you might find an index listing references to names, terms, and concepts within the book and their corresponding page numbers. Indexers create these indexes to help researchers and others easily find what they're looking for.

TAXONOMIST   Originally taxonomy was a field of biology, and the job of taxonomists was to identify and figure out what family or "class" different organisms belonged to. Today it has a broader definition, and taxonomists classify different types of information and nonliving objects.

YOU NEED TO KNOW ABOUT

The American Library Association (ALA) at www.ala.org is the primary organization for anyone working in the library sciences. Their website hosts information about conferences and other events, online learning opportunities, career opportunities, ALA publications, and more. If becoming a librarian is your thing, dive into this site for a full-immersion experience.

For more on working with books, check out the independent bookstore owner profile on page 441.

lunch break

NETWORKING
(IT'S NOT A DIRTY WORD!)

The term "networking" gets a bad rap, but it's really just another word for connecting, as in nurturing professional relationships with people. And the truth is, it's an invaluable tool when it comes to exploring career paths and future job opportunities. Not sure how to network? Don't worry—here are a few of my trade secrets:

- Keep track of people you meet who might be good connections for you down the road. Put their names in a notebook and write down what they do, when and how you met them, and any other personal information or anecdotes they shared with you.

- Ask everyone you meet for a business card, and write notes on the back about the person.

- When you see people doing jobs that you want to learn more about, try to set up informational interviews with them. Informational interviews give you a chance to ask people every little detail about what they do, while giving you the opportunity to show people who you are. See the Lunch Break on Page 137 for more info.

- Don't let people forget you! If I meet someone I want to stay in touch with, I make it my job to stay on their radar so they'll remember me if I call to ask for a meeting or favor. A great way to stay fresh in people's minds is to send e-mail updates with big news (like a new job or a school graduation) or even send annual holiday cards. But don't overdo it—limit your contact to two times a year so you're seen as a go-getter and not a nuisance.

- Keep expanding your pool of connections by asking everyone in your network for the names of other people you could meet and speak with.

- Be memorable! When you meet people you want to add to your network, remember their names, shake their hands, and be superprofessional in your communication with them.

MAUREEN SHIRREFF

Advertising Executive

*Maureen Shirreff,
North American
Creative Director for
Dove, Ogilvy & Mather*

The Facts

WHAT? Advertising executives work for ad agencies, whose business is developing campaigns for products ranging from Diet Coke to iPhones. Creative execs like Maureen manage the way a campaign looks and feels, from concept through production, while account execs manage the relationship between the client and the agency.

WHERE? While both big firms and small boutique ad agencies are scattered throughout the country, the major players are based primarily in New York, Chicago, and Los Angeles.

HOW? People in advertising have a BA in anything from English and philosophy to business and marketing.

$$$: An average of $75,000 to $150,000 for an executive, plus bonuses

DRESS CODE? Typical days are business casual, while meetings with clients might call for something dressier.

STRESS FACTOR: On a scale of 1 to 10, can reach an 8

one of the most revolutionary ad campaigns in recent years is the Campaign for Real Beauty from Dove, a global company specializing in personal care and cleansing products. The campaign consists of print ads, thought-provoking viral videos, and educational materials, all with the goal of creating "a world where beauty is a source of confidence and not anxiety." Behind the scenes I found Maureen Shirreff, North American creative director for the Dove brand, working out of her office at global ad agency Ogilvy & Mather in Chicago.

"I was kind of heavy when I was younger, so I always had body issues. When I started working on the Campaign for Real Beauty, I realized that in some weird way, it was helping me tackle some of that stuff. And here I am getting paid for it. . . . How great is that?" Maureen says.

Maureen didn't always know she wanted to work in advertising. She found her passion by knowing her strengths and keeping her eyes open for a career that would allow her to express them all.

"Until I was in my early twenties I had not a clue what I should be doing."

"Until I was in my early twenties I had not a clue what I should be doing. I knew I was creative, I loved to draw, I loved

---

YOU ASKED . . .

"What is it that picks you up when things go wrong or you seem to be stuck?"

—ERI, AGE 13

MAUREEN ANSWERED . . .

"Music. It's a wonderful thing that I need to have around me when I get stuck on a creative problem. I have an amazing sound system in my car, so I usually drive around and listen to Earth, Wind & Fire, Stevie Wonder, gospel music. . . . It just does something to me. If your spirit can get lifted up a bit, it's amazing how you tend to look at obstacles differently."

to do theater, I loved fashion, I loved architecture. I loved all these things, but I didn't know what job that would be a good fit with. My parents were really great about supporting me by saying, 'You're going to find it and it's going to find you.' That really came true for me," she explains.

Maureen's been in advertising for more than thirty years, so clearly she went down the right path. I asked her to break down for me exactly what she does as a creative director, and here's what she had to say:

"I'm responsible for the creative side of all of the advertising for the Dove brand—that includes television, print, and cause-related efforts. All of the messaging that the consumer hears about Dove usually comes through me. I supervise anywhere from fifteen to twenty creative people working on the advertising for different Dove products, and we do things like come up with creative ideas and work with the account folks to get our ideas approved, supervise the production for the ideas that we sell, work with photographers to shoot the print ads, go on production shoots for the TV ads, and work with editorial houses to finish commercials.

THE BREAKDOWN

IN MEETINGS: 1–2 hours a day

ON THE PHONE: 1–2 hours a day

ONLINE: 1–2 hours a day

SITTING: Much of the day

PUBLIC SPEAKING: 1–2 hours a week

READING: 1 hour a day

THEN TO NOW

| 1975: Graduated from Northwestern University with a BS in speech | 1975: Worked as a typist at O. O. Mallegy Co., Chicago, IL | 1977: Worked as bank teller at Water Tower Trust | 1978: Got first "creative job" as the art director for John Lucas & Co. | 1980–1983: Held various entry creative positions at Foote, Cone & Belding agency |

WHY WAIT?

- Get involved in school activities like the debate team, where you need to think of a "persuasive" way to convey information.
- Start paying attention to commercials and ads in magazines, on the sides of buses, and on billboards. Could you come up with a better campaign?
- Rent *Picture Perfect, What Women Want,* and *Thank You for Not Smoking* for a Hollywood (read: nonreality) glimpse of agency work.

"If you see a commercial for Dove right now, I would have done that, from the inception of the idea all the way through the production process. The only thing I don't do is actually deliver the commercial to the networks and push the button that gets it on the air, but pretty much everything in between, I'm involved in," she explains.

Because Maureen's business is an international one, she does a lot of traveling all over the world. She's out of town at least one week a month, which might not sound like a lot, but the time away generally makes her in-office days more full. For every trip she goes on, Maureen has to plan for it, get from point A to point B, have her meetings, travel home, and then fill in her creative team on everything that happened on her trip.

She says, "There are parts of the travel that I really like, because when I'm away I can mentally focus on the bigger picture. I do miss my family a lot, although my children are now

1983–1987: Storyboard illustrator and junior art director at BBDO agency

1987: Rejected by airline company to be a flight attendant

1987–1993: Was a freelance art director

1993: Hired as creative director at Ogilvy & Mather

2000: Promoted to North American creative director of Dove at Ogilvy & Mather

PAYING YOUR DUES

Most people working in advertising start out in an entry-level assistant position. Expect to spend one to two years doing a lot of photocopying, finding scrap art, preparing presentations, and other support tasks while earning as little as $20,000 a year.

in college and living independently. When they were young, it ripped my heart out. But what I love about it is that when you go into another office, you're there to get a job done and so you're really productive. You're also building relationships, which is the cornerstone of a global brand like Dove. I've got to have really strong relationships with Ogilvy folks in different offices and with clients in different parts of the world."

I asked Maureen to tell us what the reality of working in advertising is versus what we might expect based on the Hollywood version shown in shows like the period drama *Mad Men*.

"I think advertising is sometimes portrayed as this kind of villainous backstabbing environment where you're up for hours on end and you're fraught with despair because you can't come up with creative ideas. It's portrayed in a very tense, dramatic way, and yes, it has that, but there is so much joy there too. I don't think that gets a fair shake. Yes, there are a lot of ups and downs. You might come up with an idea and your creative director hates it or the client hates it. But when you are able to get something sold in and protect it so that it actually gets on the air and does what it's supposed to do, and you begin to sell product and people notice it, that's a pretty big high."

WHAT IT TAKES

- Creativity
- Thriving in a fast-paced environment
- Being open to constructive criticism
- The ability to think on your feet and handle pressure

> **MAUREEN'S CAREER ADVICE**
>
> - *Don't beat yourself up if you don't know exactly what you want to do. Start by getting in touch with who you are as a human being and give life a chance to reveal itself to you.*
> - *Network whenever you can.*
> - *If you're interested in advertising, don't worry about being 100 percent sure what you want to do when you're first starting out. Take any job you can find at an agency, and you'll eventually discover where you belong.*
> - *Trust your instincts!*

In the Field

FIVE MORE CAREERS IN ADVERTISING

TRAFFIC MANAGER   (entry-level job) Because there are so many stages of an ad campaign, traffic managers track schedules and budgets and control the flow of "traffic," making sure that production stays on track and deadlines are met. The traffic department is where many people start out, since it's a great way to learn what goes into creating an ad campaign.

MEDIA PLANNER   Advertisers pay big bucks for their commercials to be shown during a hit TV show or have a two-page spread in a magazine, and media planners are the ones who make it all happen by figuring out where to purchase advertising space for the products they represent.

ACCOUNT EXECUTIVE   Account execs have to be good at dealing with clients, crunching numbers, and communicating with creative departments. Most account execs juggle only a few clients, and their main job is to manage the relationship between the agency and the clients.

COPYWRITER   Copywriting is often perceived to be one of the more glamorous jobs in advertising, because copywriters come up with the "tag lines" that become popular, like Nike's "Just Do It." They also write all the content of an ad, so they have to know how to write creatively and effectively about products using very few words.

RESEARCH DIRECTOR   In advertising, research directors analyze data regarding how efficient or effective an ad campaign is, conducting focus-group tests to find out how the consumer responds to different advertising strategies or trying to determine whether or not people are buying the advertised product.

YOU NEED TO KNOW ABOUT

The Advertising Educational Foundation's website (www.aef.com) offers videos to download, case studies about different advertising campaigns, a list of must-read books, and career advice from the pros.

DR. NANCY KNOWLTON

Marine Biologist

The Facts

Dr. Nancy Knowlton, Sant Chair for Marine Science at the Smithsonian's National Museum of Natural History

WHAT?   Marine biologists study the plants, animals, and organisms that live in the ocean.

WHERE?   Most marine biologists work at marine research centers and often lecture at a university biology department. Not surprisingly, they tend to work in coastal areas, where they have easy access to the ocean.

HOW?   Marine biologists at the level of Dr. Knowlton or those teaching in a university need a doctorate, which involves a four-year degree in biology, a related master's degree, and a PhD in a specific area of marine biology. Marine biologists with a master's degree can teach at the high school level or at an aquarium.

$$$:   An average salary of $45,000 to $65,000, but can earn more than $200,000 depending on experience and position

DRESS CODE?   Casual to business casual (and sometimes a wet suit!)

STRESS FACTOR: On a scale of 1 to 10, an 8 (but Nancy says the stress is mostly self-imposed)

one of the top marine biologists in the world is Dr. Nancy Knowlton, the go-to person for the ocean at the Smithsonian's National Museum of Natural History in Washington, D.C. Nancy has a beautiful office on the mall, a long rectangle of green that stretches from Congress to the Washington Monument and beyond. From here, Nancy both directs a team of scientists researching coral reefs and leads the Ocean Portal (http://ocean.si.edu), the Smithsonian's online source of ocean information and inspiration for students, teachers, and ocean lovers around the world.

Nancy didn't always know she wanted to be a marine biologist, but she's always been a "science junkie."

"My first science love was really astronomy. My parents had gotten me a nice telescope when I was little, and I used to spend a lot of time looking at the planets. Then in tenth grade I took a biology course with a really wonderful teacher, and that's what turned me in the direction of biology rather than astronomy or other sciences," she explains.

A SPECIAL DIVE

Last October I went on a cruise to the southern Line Islands, which are a series of very isolated islands in the middle of the Pacific Ocean between Hawaii and Tahiti. These islands are so remote that they don't suffer from the effects of fishing and pollution, which makes going to them like traveling backward in time, before people had such a huge influence on the planet. We were trying to figure out how these protected reefs function, and the job of my team was to study the small organisms that live in the cracks and crevices of the reef. Every day we would get up and go on a dive and collect pieces of dead coral to bring back to the boat.

In the afternoon we'd break the coral up into tiny little pieces, putting all the animals and plants that we found in little cups. Over the course of the day, we would find hundreds and hundreds of tiny animals. First we would photograph them and then we'd freeze them or put them in alcohol to study them when we got back, some for genetics and some for more traditional studies. During that trip, we followed the same routine every day for nearly four weeks. It was actually exhausting, because the diving is hard and you have to lug equipment and buckets and buckets of heavy seawater and samples up to the main deck of the ship. And the days were long—we'd be working from about eight in the morning to ten or eleven at night or later, and then we'd sleep for eight hours (if we were lucky) and get up to do it all over again. It's very physical work, but it's fun, too, because you see all these amazing organisms, and the physical activity is nice. Plus, you're in this beautiful place where we'd see dolphins and manta rays, sharks and turtles, and all sorts of things in the water. It's spectacular, breathtakingly beautiful.

Since marine biologists can specialize in many different areas, I asked Nancy to describe what her work is all about.

YOU ASKED . . .

"How the heck did you go through college without having your brain explode?" —ROSIE, AGE 19

NANCY ANSWERED . . .

"That's funny—I never felt like my brain was near exploding. I guess for me, college was hard, but it wasn't out-of-control hard. I know there were times that I stayed up all night to study for exams and write papers. I think the thing you have to do when you feel like your brain is on the verge of exploding is say, 'Okay, I'm going to do this this morning and I'm going to do this this afternoon' and break it into bite-size pieces. If you take it one piece at a time, it really helps with the exploding brain syndrome."

"I study coral reefs, so at least once a year, and hopefully more often, I go out in the field—my list of dive sites over the years includes Jamaica, Brazil, West Africa, and small islands across the Pacific and Indian Oceans. Each year I return to Panama to study coral spawning. Coral reefs undergo what's called 'mass spawning,' where all of the different colonies release their eggs and sperm into the water simultaneously once a year. This is a 'mega event' and it's very interesting biologically, so I go and study that because, although coral reefs are famous in the public eye, we actually know relatively little about the organisms that live there," she explained.

"One of the projects I'm working on now is to figure out how many species there are in coral reefs. The published estimates range from less than one to nearly ten million species, so there's a huge range, and they're horrible estimates, because they are so uncertain. We really don't have a clue what's out there, and moreover, we don't have a real sense of what we're losing as reefs become more and more degraded.

THE BREAKDOWN

IN MEETINGS: 2 hours a day

ON THE PHONE: 30 minutes a day

ONLINE: 1–2 hours a day

SITTING: Most of the day

PUBLIC SPEAKING: 1–2 hours per week at most

READING: 1 hour a day

WORKING SOLO: Much of the time

THEN TO NOW

1971: Graduated from Harvard University with BA

1978: Received PhD in marine biology from UC Berkeley

1979–1983: Was an assistant professor of biology, Yale University

1996: Became professor at the Scripps Institution of Oceanography, University of California at San Diego

So one of the projects I'm working on now is trying to figure out what we're losing so we know how to focus our conservation efforts."

When Nancy gets back from her research expeditions, the lab work begins, although at Nancy's level, it's mostly her team of scientists who analyze the samples she has collected in the field.

"I define the nature of the project, organize it, raise the money, and do a certain amount of the fieldwork. Then I organize the work, and at the end I play a big role in writing the papers that come out of the research," she explains. Nancy also fills her very busy days with guiding the Ocean Portal website, raising funds, developing new programs, and reviewing the work of other scientists. She also does a lot of writing for academic journals and lectures both to scientists and the general public.

With all that work, one can imagine that it would be challenging to find enough time in the day to get it all done. Nancy says that the more successful she's become, the more she is asked to do things, juggling many different tasks to keep them all afloat and supervised. And while she says the travel is still exciting—in the past year alone Nancy traveled to Taiwan, Panama, Indonesia, the Philippines, and France—it's also draining.

Still, the payoff is obviously worth it. Nancy's passion for her work came through loud and clear in our conversation. I

2001: Founded the Scripps Center for Marine Biodiversity and Conservation

2001: Joined the Advisory Board of the National Geographic Conservation Trust

2007: Named Sant Chair for Marine Science, National Museum of Natural History (Smithsonian)

WHY WAIT?

- Rent a snorkel, mask, and fins the next time you're at an ocean or lake.
- Take biology and AP science courses in high school.
- Visit a nearby aquarium—many offer volunteer opportunities or special programs just for students.

asked her to tell me what keeps her going . . . what she really loves about her work.

"The core of what makes science fun is finding out something that you didn't know before. For a while I was working with a guy named Rob Rowan on the diversity of the little single-celled algae inside coral that are responsible for the productivity of reefs. In earlier work Rob had figured out that there were a lot of different species, and we were working on a project to understand what controlled all this diversity, and why you found some types in one place and different types in another.

"We had done a lot of work in Panama, and there was a major 'bleaching' event, which occurs when the water gets too hot and the whole symbiosis between these algae and the coral breaks down, so we went back out to the field where we had worked before to figure out what was going on. It was amazing because we could look at the reefs and realize that the bleaching was differentially affecting the different types of algae—after five minutes swimming on the reef we knew exactly what was happening. It was extraordinary. It was

PAYING YOUR DUES

After years of school, most marine biologists spend their first three to four years working in a postdoctoral position doing research under a more senior scientist.

almost like having a whole jigsaw puzzle in a box, shaking it up, and then throwing it on the ground and having it land assembled. It was a classic 'eureka' moment.

"It's also great when you've worked hard on a project and you send it out for review and it comes back and it's been funded. Or if

you give a lecture and people are really receptive and enthusiastic; that always feels good. Just knowing you're making a contribution is a great feeling."

She loves the rave reviews that her popular book *Citizens of the Sea* has received and fondly recalls the exhibit of a giant crocheted coral reef that she brought to the museum, a community craft project that linked science, conservation, art, and math. And recently she was recognized for all her contributions by being elected to both the American Academy of Arts and Sciences and the National Academy of Sciences. "It was quite a week!" she says.

She added, "I'm also very proud of the Center for Marine Biodiversity and Conservation that I created, because it's transformed the Scripps Institution of Oceanography and made conservation a major part of the activities there. We raised many millions of dollars and trained a large number of students, and I feel like we made a huge difference in terms of creating the next generation of scientists. Many are now here in Washington, helping to create policies that are informed by good science. I'm very proud of that." Nancy stays connected by going back to the center each year with her husband to attend a seminar they sponsor that brings leaders in the field to the campus.

"I don't consider myself in the ranks of Einstein or Charles Darwin, but in a more modest way, I've made a major contribution to marine biology, and I've made a major contribution to the institutions I've worked at. It's funny, some people are really driven by the recognition they get by being on the morning news or something like that, but I have to say what really drives me is the sense of doing something that will make a difference a hundred years from now."

NANCY'S ADVICE

- *Always make sure you enjoy what you're doing. You spend an awful lot of your life working, and if you love what you do, it doesn't really feel like work.*

- *Focus on the goal you're heading for, especially if what you're doing at the moment feels frustrating.*

- *For a career in science, it's important to do well in school. Take your studies seriously and get into the best college or university that you can.*

In the Field

FIVE MORE CAREERS AS A BIOLOGIST

BOTANIST Botanists study plants, and depending on their area of expertise, they might focus on plant identification or how certain plants interact with animals and other living organisms in their environment. Botanists can work in botanical gardens, universities, private companies, or government agencies.

ZOOLOGIST Also known as wildlife biologists, zoologists study all aspects of animals, from their behavior and biological structure to how they interact with their environment. Many work in zoos and oversee the care of the animals there, while others might study animals in their natural habitats.

BIOCHEMIST   Biochemists specialize in the chemical composition of living organisms, studying areas like reproduction and metabolism. Most spend their time doing scientific research for large biotech firms or government agencies, and though it's not an absolute requirement, most biochemists have an MD or PhD.

GENETICIST   These scientists study heredity in living organisms. Most geneticists work in laboratories researching different genetic technologies, while others become genetic counselors who discuss genetic risks of hereditary problems, like some birth defects, with soon-to-be parents.

MICROBIOLOGIST   Some organisms are so tiny, they can't be seen by the naked eye. Microbiologists work in laboratories, using high-powered microscopes to study these organisms. They might work in the food and drug industry, within environmental organizations, for government agencies, or for large companies.

YOU NEED TO KNOW ABOUT

The website www.marinebio.org is full of information relating to marine biology, including facts about different marine species, info on marine conservation and why it's so important, and a list of schools offering courses and degrees in marine biology.

CHIYO ISHIKAWA

Museum Curator

Chiyo Ishikawa, Deputy Director of Art, Seattle Art Museum

The Facts

WHAT? Curators plan and organize exhibitions of art and other collections for museums—coming up with new ideas for exhibitions, figuring out how the art will be exhibited, planning how the event will interact with the public, and organizing tours, lectures, and interactive presentations.

WHERE? The majority of curators work for museums or at historical sites.

HOW? Curators typically have a PhD in art history, and many specialize in a certain art style or time period.

$$$: An average of $45,000 to $150,000, depending on the size of the institution and the home city

DRESS CODE? Business casual

STRESS FACTOR: On a scale of 1 to 10, between a 4 and a 9 (depending on what's going on)

there's something intriguing about museums—they're full of so much history, the artwork on display is often worth millions of dollars, the atmosphere itself somehow feels . . . creative. The people behind the exhibits are called curators, and to find out more about what they do, I spoke with Chiyo Ishikawa, deputy art director and chief curator for the Seattle Art Museum. We met in Chiyo's office at the museum, which at the time of writing was being renovated under Chiyo's supervision. We caught up on a cool Friday afternoon.

ME: Can you tell us what you do at the Seattle Art Museum?

CHIYO: I'm the curator of European painting and sculptures in the museum, and that means I research our collection of art, present it through exhibitions, work with our conservation department if anything needs to be cleaned or restored, and present the collection to the public.

I am also an exhibition curator, so that means organizing the exhibitions, either from our permanent collection or from work that comes in from outside the museum. We curators are ambassadors for the art, so when we do exhibitions, we have to raise money, market the exhibition, and train docents. We're kind of the point person for everything that reaches the public about the show.

"Our most rewarding times are when we are down in storage looking at art objects and getting ideas."

When we're planning exhibitions or installations, a lot of my time is spent staring at a computer screen, or on the phone or in meetings, but I will say that our most rewarding times are when we are down in storage looking at art objects and getting ideas. It's a wonderful job. I've been doing it for twenty-four years, and there's always something new you can do, even with a small collection like we have here.

ME: Do curators usually specialize in one area?

CHIYO: Yes. The training for somebody who wants to be a

curator is to get a PhD in art history, and it's also helpful to have museum experience. The way it works in graduate school for art history is you start out generally and then you focus, focus, focus. So by the time you're writing your dissertation, it's about something pretty narrow. But what you ultimately end up doing depends on where you work. If I were at the Metropolitan Museum of Art, I'd focus on one little century or art from one region. But at a small, general museum, it's a lot of fun for me because I go from the dates 1200 to 1800. So yes, there is specialization, but at our museum we think about everything in a larger context.

ME: Are most curators people who grew up wanting to be artists?

CHIYO: It's more people who love art history . . . who love art and who love history. It's an incredibly different thing from being an artist. I think it helps to have done studio art—it really gives you empathy for the objects—but it's more of an engagement with looking at other things.

YOU ASKED . . .

"What is more important: success or significance?"

—CHARLENE, AGE 17

CHIYO ANSWERED . . .

"I work for a nonprofit, so if we're talking about financial success, I'd have to say significance. For me, success is a feeling of satisfaction and love of your colleagues, and enjoyment and excitement about coming to work every day. People go into this profession for love—they have low salaries, they work really hard, they usually work much more than a forty-hour week. We get our satisfaction from people coming to our talks or giving tours in the gallery and having people thank us afterward. I think that museum curators uniformly would answer that significance is more important."

ME: So how did you know this is what you wanted to do?

CHIYO: When I was twelve, my dad was on a sabbatical. We bought a VW bus and drove around Europe off and on for six months. We went to lots of museums and churches, and I totally loved it. I didn't really realize how meaningful that trip was until I was in college, struggling with my desire to be a studio artist, and I discovered I was a lot more comfortable talking about other people's art than I was trying to come up with something on my own.

THE BREAKDOWN

IN MEETINGS: Half the day

ON THE PHONE: 30 minutes a day

ONLINE: 1 hour a day

SITTING: Most of the day

PUBLIC SPEAKING: Occasionally (for special exhibitions and events)

WORKING SOLO: 1 hour a day

ME: What is it about museums that you love?

CHIYO: My dad was the assistant director of the Des Moines Art Center when I was born, and he worked for college art museums while I was growing up, so I was surrounded by art and by artists—they were just part of our world. I had so much fun going to little exhibition openings as a child, and I grew up knowing that art was special. So I think I had an inherent interest in it. Initially I wanted to be a dealer because I wanted to help artists, and then once I started graduate school, I saw how hard it was to write about contemporary art with any distance. I really wanted to have the ability to stand back and make judgments that I could be more confident about, and so I went back to the fifteenth century, and that's what I studied for the rest of graduate school.

ME: Do you ever look around and see what you're actually doing and think, "How cool is this?"

WHY WAIT?

- Take art history classes if your school offers them and get to know the works of the masters.

- Visit local museums and libraries to view art of all kinds and see what you're drawn to; inquire about volunteering or becoming a docent.

- Curate your own exhibit at school.

CHIYO: Yeah, I do feel really lucky. I work in a beautiful place, and that alone makes me feel kind of spoiled. Just being at a place where everybody is visually aware is wonderful, and it can be something as minor as seeing interesting clothes in the hallway that gives me a little lift every day, to looking at wonderful works of art that are coming into the collection. It's never routine here, and I love that. I also love that a big part of my job is seeing things in other cities, and that's certainly a big part of why people become curators—so they can travel. If you're going to work with objects, you really have a responsibility to know everything you can about them, and that often involves seeing where they come from.

ME: I didn't realize that travel was such a big part of your job.

CHIYO: I travel multiple times a year: once or twice to New York, sometimes to L.A., and to Europe at least once a year. When I was working on a Spanish exhibition, I was going to Spain for two weeks at a time, because you need to establish relationships in person and you need to see objects firsthand

THEN TO NOW

1969:
First trip to Europe and exposure to great museums and art

1979:
Graduated from Hampshire College with BA

1982:
Began working on master's and doctorate

1983–1985:
Interned at the Metropolitan Museum of Art in New York

1986–1987:
Volunteer internship at the Museo del Prado, Spain

1989:
Received PhD from Bryn Mawr College

that you want for the exhibitions. . . . It's where you get your inspiration. And every curator here always comes back from a trip with three or four good things—making a new collegial connection, hearing about an exhibition that might be good for us, promoting an exhibition that we might take to some other place. Personal contact is what really keeps you viable.

ME: Are there any tasks that are typical for a curator?

CHIYO: You think of the idea, you think about how you're going to communicate ideas through the art, and then you think, Okay, I've got this plan, I want to talk with educators about it to see if I'm communicating it well, if it makes sense to them, and if not, how can I change it? So those are kind of the ideal curatorial tasks, but there also are practical matters, like when a work of art that is being acquired was damaged in transit and you have to work with conservation to see what happened. There are also tedious things like submitting our budgets for the year. There can be talking to the public, giving lectures.

PAYING YOUR DUES

Many future curators spend one year as an intern while getting their PhD, where they might do things like researching, photocopying, writing, and attending meetings. Others might be a curatorial assistant until graduation, at which time they move into an assistant curator position.

| 1989: Interned at the Museum of Fine Arts, Boston | 1990: Hired at Seattle Art Museum as assistant curator of European paintings | 1994: Promoted to curator of European paintings and sculptures | 2001: Promoted to chief curator of collections, Seattle Art Museum | 2005: Named deputy director of art, Seattle Art Museum |

Or a really fun part of the job is bringing works into the collection. It's a challenging job here at the Seattle Art Museum, because we don't have many acquisition funds and it's hard for us to compete with private collectors. But we work with donors who give things to the collection, and sometimes we identify something that we want and we raise money for it. One of the things I love about working here is that we're all dedicated to the same goal of making the museum better and making more people love art.

ME: Is the portrayal of the world of curators in the movie *The Da Vinci Code* realistic?

WHAT IT TAKES

- An acute visual sense
- A love of research
- An interest in putting things together in interesting ways
- Being open to new ideas

CHIYO: All of the intrigue and sleuthing and people poisoning each other and stuff . . . we're a far more mundane world than that. I do think curating is a fairly romantic field, but it's also very tied to revenue projections and what level the art labels are hung so that they're not over people's heads. There are a lot of practical issues that are a part of it too. For me it's a good balance, because you get to stimulate your imagination as one part of the job and then you ground yourself and keep your head out of the clouds with other aspects. As far as *The Da Vinci Code* is concerned, of course I like it when people become interested in art, but to me, there are so many fascinating and interesting things about Leonardo da Vinci that don't involve murder and strange rituals.

INTERESTED IN BEING A CURATOR? HERE'S CHIYO'S ADVICE

- *Learn to look at art—training your eye is the fundamental skill that will sustain a curatorial career. When looking, always ask why. Why did the artist put that color there? How would the painting change if he hadn't? How does the background contribute to a portrait? Who is the main character in a narrative painting? This questioning attitude will lead to understanding the artist and will help the student or curator explain to others how the painting works.*

- *Learn other languages! Art historians need to read German and at least one other language. When conducting research in other countries, it's very useful to be able to communicate in the native language.*

- *Don't try to fit a mold, but really think about what you want to do and how you're going to get there.*

In the Field

FIVE MORE CAREERS AT A MUSEUM

GUEST RELATIONS MANAGER   Most museums are visited by millions of people every year. Guest relations managers handle everything guest-related, including parking, admissions, maps, information centers, and programs and activities for guests, with a goal of making sure that museum visitors have a positive experience.

CONSERVATION SCIENTIST   If you're a science junkie with a love of art, you might be interested in being a conservation scientist. They use their science background to research art artifacts by examining art to make sure it's authentic or conducting tests on artifacts to help museum conservators better preserve them.

EXHIBIT DESIGNER Just as a set designer in a theater creates worlds for the actors to perform in, an exhibit designer in a museum creates the space for art exhibits. Exhibit designers figure out who will be visiting the museum and how to best create an exhibit to show off the work in a way that will be most comfortable for visitors.

GIFT STORE MANAGER Most museums have gift stores that carry art prints, jewelry, books, and other goods reflective of the museum. Gift store managers interact with visitors from all over the world and are typically responsible for hiring and managing employees and keeping the store stocked.

ARCHIVIST If you think of a museum as being similar to a library, then an archivist is the equivalent of a librarian. Archivists organize and catalog the information or material that is important to a museum, including photos, films, art documents, magazines, and computer disks.

For more art careers, check out the photographer profile on page 296.

LEANNE LUSK

Coast Guard Lieutenant

The Facts

Lt. Leanne Lusk, Coast Guard

WHAT? The Coast Guard is the branch of the U.S. armed forces concerned with maritime law enforcement and safety, which means anything having to do with the coasts, ports, and inland waters of the United States, as well as international waters.

WHERE? The Coast Guard, whose motto is "Wherever America Needs Us," has units located throughout the United States, mostly in coastal cities.

HOW? Coast Guard officers need a bachelor's degree and must attend a seventeen-week-long Officer Candidate School (OCS) or, like Leanne, graduate from the Coast Guard Academy.

$$$: Salary depends on rank. For officers like Leanne, it's anywhere from $40,000 to $200,000, depending on your level and number of years of service.

DRESS CODE? Some type of Coast Guard uniform, depending on rank and the work. Leanne wears dark blue slacks and a light blue shirt, a name tag, and shoulder boards.

STRESS FACTOR: On a scale of 1 to 10, a 5

when i interviewed leanne lusk, she was a lieutenant in the Coast Guard based in San Francisco, and while you might assume that Coast Guard jobs involve working at sea, Leanne works on land in an operational position. In Leanne's unit, the Coast Guard has three primary missions—homeland security, search and rescue, and law enforcement. Leanne's official title is assistant enforcement officer, and while her work encompasses a little bit of all these components every day, no two days are ever the same. Here are some examples of the kinds of things Leanne's job entails.

"I'm not someone that people would look at and think I'm a federal law enforcement officer. . . . I really like breaking out of that mold."

- **Planning for marine events:** Leanne puts together security plans for San Francisco marina events like Fleet Week or Tall Ships.
- **Managing search-and-rescue boats:** Leanne manages seven small boat stations and four patrol boats within northern California, so any issues that come up regarding these boats and stations are her responsibility.
- **Developing training plans for stations:** Leanne comes up with training plans to help other stations run more efficiently.
- **Coming up with security plans:** When presidential candidate John Kerry visited San Francisco, he wanted to go windsurfing in the bay, so Leanne met with the Secret Service and came up with a security plan for while he was in the water.

While a recruit who goes through boot camp graduates as an "enlisted person," Leanne got into one of the highly competitive military academies—the Coast Guard Academy, located in New London, Connecticut—and spent the next four years earning her BS in government and being trained as an officer.

When Leanne graduated, the protocol was that the first assignment for officers had to be on ships, but they changed the rules so that today grads can move straight to a land job like the one Leanne's in now. I asked her to walk us through her early career journey:

"When I first got out of the academy, I went to work on a three-hundred-seventy-eight-foot ship out of Alameda, California. Our missions weren't locally based—we generally covered the Pacific Ocean, so I did several trips up to Alaska, where we did fisheries enforcement and search-and-rescue kind of stuff like you'll see on that *Deadliest Catch* show on the Discovery Channel. We also went down off the

THE BREAKDOWN

IN MEETINGS: 2–3 hours a day

ON THE PHONE: 2 hours a day

ONLINE: 3 hours a day

SITTING: Half the day

STANDING: Half the day

PUBLIC SPEAKING: Not daily, but often

READING: 2 hours

WORKING SOLO: 4 hours

YOU ASKED . . .

"Did you know what you were doing when you were my age?"
—ANNIKA, AGE 16

LEANNE ANSWERED . . .

"No. When I was seventeen I applied to colleges, planning to major in premed or political science. I didn't have any money for college and I was looking for a way to pay for it, so I talked to a recruiter and he told me about the Coast Guard Academy. I didn't think I had a shot in the world of getting in, because my high school GPA was a 3.85 when I graduated high school, and I thought I needed a 4.0. But I applied and got selected as an alternate. So I got into UC Davis and was planning on going there when I got a call saying that I had been selected for the academy. And that was it."

WHY WAIT?

- Visit a Coast Guard base near you and see if you can "get under way" with their crew for a ride-along.
- You can start the application process for the Coast Guard Academy as early as your junior year. It's competitive, so get excellent grades in high school!

coast of Mexico and Panama to do alien migration 'interdiction,' which was dealing with people who were trying to illegally enter the United States by taking a boat to Guatemala or Mexico and then a bus into the United States. We also did counter-drug operations with people who run drugs on speedboats.

"That assignment was for two years, and we would generally get under way for three to four months, come home for a couple months, do maintenance on the ship, and then leave again for another three to four months. While I was onboard, I got qualified to drive the ship and bring a helicopter in for a landing on the deck. I also got qualified as a law enforcement boarding officer, as well as being in charge of all the weapons systems onboard," Leanne explained.

So do you have to be a thrill seeker to be in the Coast Guard? Leanne thinks so. Throughout her career she's done some fairly dangerous jobs, like boarding other boats. As she explained, you never know what you're going to find onboard—there could be dangerous drug runners.

THEN TO NOW

1998: Graduated from the Coast Guard Academy with a BS in government

1998–2000: Worked on the Coast Guard cutter Morgenthau as a deck watch officer, gunnery officer, boarding officer, and landing signals officer

2000–2003: Worked for the International Training Division, teaching courses in twenty-two countries

Now that Leanne is working on land, it's not all high adventure all the time, but it's still pretty action-packed. Here is how Leanne described a day in her life.

LEANNE'S (UN)USUAL DAY

My workday starts at seven a.m., so I leave my house and get here between six forty-five and seven fifteen, depending on traffic. I used to have my own office, but now I share it with four other people. I work just downstairs from the command center, and I have a gorgeous view of the Bay Bridge out my window, so I look out at the water all day.

The first thing I do when I get here is check my e-mails and follow up on any issues that came up the day before. At eight a.m. there is a command briefing that goes over all of the cases that involve the Coast Guard. That usually takes about a half hour.

Then I come back to my office, and basically the rest of my day is spent putting out fires. I always have a list of projects that I'm working on. For example, if I'm putting together a security plan for events like Fleet Week or Tall Ships or something like that, I would be doing

WHAT IT TAKES

- A sense of adventure and public duty
- Being in good physical shape
- Working well with a team

2003: Began working as assistant enforcement officer at Sector San Francisco

2004: Started working toward MBA at University of Phoenix

2011: Promoted to search-and-rescue analyst, Office of Search and Rescue

2013: Received MBA

2013: Became deputy director, Sexual Assault Prevention and Response Military Campaign Office things like attending planning meetings. Like yesterday I had a meeting with the Red Bull airplane guys to plan the security and safety zones for Fleet Week. Or I might have other issues come up that concern our units. There's not a cookie-cutter type of day.

For lunch, we have a cafeteria called a galley. It's $3.50 for lunch, and you can't beat that for an all-you-can-eat meal. But I usually end up bringing my leftovers in from the night before and working through lunch at my desk.

My workday officially ends at three o'clock, but I usually go home somewhere between five or six, and then I have traffic on the way home too. It's a long day, but there's a lot that goes into it and it's really rewarding. And once I'm home, it's not always over—I always make myself available twenty-four hours a day. In my last position, I used to stand a one-week duty that was a twenty-four-hour-a-day duty, where I was available by telephone and I was briefed on any case that happened in northern California for search and rescue, homeland security, law enforcement, and any ships of interest coming into the port. One night I had nine calls between one and five in the morning.

Leanne told me about one of the more high-profile cases that she worked on. In 2005 a woman threw her three babies into the San Francisco Bay. Leanne was out at dinner cele-brating her stepmother's birthday when she got the call. She dropped everything and drove back to work to cover the oper-ational aspect of planning the searches for the children, as well as meeting with the San Francisco Police Department's media people to coordinate press releases.

"It was a long night. . . . I was up until about two thirty a.m., went to bed, and got back up at four thirty to prep my captain and take him to the press conference. I just slept in my office on the couch. I was actively involved in the case, which ultimately became a homicide investigation, from the beginning all the way until noon the next day, when I got relieved so I could go home and finally get some sleep," Leanne says.

Like many women in this book, Leanne says one of her biggest challenges is juggling work and family life, especially since she's a mom of two. She's a self-described go-getter and loves being dedicated to her job, but it takes an effort to make sure she has enough time for her husband and children.

But talk to Leanne about the Coast Guard and it's obvious that the benefits of the job clearly outweigh the downsides. "I love that I can retire when I'm forty-two years old because I'll have twenty years of active duty and I won't have to work another day in my life. . . . My husband, too, because he's also on duty. We'll be able to watch our son's and daughter's school events or whatever they want to do; we'll be there to support them. They won't even be teenagers yet when Mom and Dad will be home all the time," she says.

"I also love that when I come to work, I don't know what that day will be like. It's really exciting, and I love being involved in the action. Particularly in the job I have right now, the stuff that you read in the newspaper or see on TV is the stuff that I'm actively doing."

I asked Leanne what it was like being a woman in the military, since traditionally it's been such a male-dominated career path. Leanne pointed out that out of all the armed services, the Coast Guard has the highest percentage of women. And she loves busting stereotypes about what women can and can't do.

"I'm not someone that people would look at and think I'm a federal law enforcement officer. . . . I really like breaking out of that mold. I know that I can get dropped in a country anywhere in the world and survive. . . . I know how to take care of myself," she says.

Note: Since I first interviewed Leanne, she's risen through the ranks of the Coast Guard and is currently the deputy director of the Coast Guard's Sexual Assault Prevention and Response Military Campaign Office at headquarters in Washington, D.C. She's also on tap for a big promotion to the rank of commander. Go, Leanne!

LEANNE'S ADVICE

- *To be successful in this career path, find an area that you're passionate about—search and rescue, law enforcement, engineering, driving ships and small boats, being involved internationally—and go for it!*

- *Don't think that a decision you make when you're seventeen or eighteen is going to affect the rest of your life. I thought I was going to go to the academy, serve my five years, and then do something else. But I've stayed here and it's been extremely rewarding for me.*

In the Field

FIVE MORE CAREERS IN THE MILITARY

AIRCRAFT LAUNCH AND RECOVERY SPECIALIST   In the opening scene of the classic movie *Top Gun*, aircraft launch and recovery specialists are standing atop a huge aircraft carrier in the middle of the Indian Ocean. These specialists oversee the equipment that helps aircraft take off and land on an aircraft carrier.

MEDICAL CARE TECHNICIAN   In the civilian world, medical care technicians could be compared to nurses' aides. In the military, they generally work in military hospitals, aboard ships, or in mobile field hospitals, administering first aid, taking pulse and temperature, prepping operating rooms, and feeding, bathing, and dressing patients.

EMERGENCY MANAGEMENT SPECIALIST Emergency management specialists train for and plan responses to future disasters, as well as respond to various real-life emergencies, whether it be a terrorist attack or a natural disaster. There are emergency management specialists in all five branches of the military.

SPECIAL FORCES OFFICER Special forces officers have to be ready to do just about anything, anytime, anywhere. Their job is to be trained in many different skills, from parachuting and swimming to survival techniques, and they are in a "constant state of readiness" for the call to report for duty.

INTERPRETER Interpreters in the armed forces interpret for people who speak foreign languages or translate other written languages into English. Unlike civilian interpreters, those in the military might help to interview or interrogate prisoners of war or translate foreign documents or messages that are intercepted.

KRISTEN COLBY

Nurse

Kristen Colby,
Registered Nurse (RN)

The Facts

WHAT? Registered nurses are health-care professionals who do things like perform physical exams, provide health counseling, administer medication, coordinate care, and more for their patients.

WHERE? Nurses work in a variety of settings, including hospitals, nursing homes, community health centers, clinics, and more.

HOW? Most nurses have a bachelor's or associate's degree in nursing, but some can be accredited through a vocational nursing program. Nurses must pass a national licensing exam to become an RN.

$$$: An annual salary of $65,000

DRESS CODE? Nursing scrubs

STRESS FACTOR: On a scale of 1 to 10, a 5

nursing is one of the most stable careers out there, and predictions are that the need for nurses will continue growing over the next few decades. I connected with Kristen Colby, an RN from northern California who has forged a unique career using her nursing degree and medical records background. Rather than work in the same unit day after day, Kristen "floats" to different floors and departments at the hospital, sometimes working as an RN and other times as a nurse case manager.

Here's Kristen's peek inside her atypical nursing life.

ME: I love that you've created your ideal nursing career based on your experience, background, and lifestyle. Can you tell us about the kinds of activities your job might entail on any given day?

KRISTEN: The wonderful thing about my particular job is that there really is no "typical day"! If I'm working as a bedside nurse, I show up, get a report on my patients from the previous shift, do my physical assessments of my patients, attend to their immediate needs (which usually lasts all shift), and do my charting as I can fit it in between patient care. Some days are rushed, and others are more mellow. It all depends on my patient load and how they are doing—tests and procedures ordered, amount of medications they are on, whether I get a new admission or have a postoperative patient, or if I have to discharge a patient.

"I have never regretted my career decision. It is always easy to find a job wherever I go, the pay is excellent, and you have a feeling of satisfaction at the end of your workday—what more could you ask for?"

ME: It sounds busy already! So what kind of actual hands-on tasks might you be engaging in with these various patients?

KRISTEN: Because I have different types of patients every shift I work, what I do throughout the day varies—I could be inserting catheters and putting nasogastric tubes in, or I could be starting IVs, or simply giving meds, bathing my patient and making their bed, controlling their discomfort with meds and nonpharmaceutical measures, advocating for them with calls to the physicians. It's always different, and I always get a chance to get a cool washcloth or warm blanket to comfort my patient in a time of sickness or injury. Sometimes just being a listening ear helps ease a patient's anxiety. The hospital I work at has excellent nurse-patient ratios, which allows me to do patient education, which I enjoy immensely.

ME: How about when you're doing your nurse case manager work. Does that look different?

KRISTEN: If I work as a nurse case manager, I arrive at work, print up a census of patients so I know my caseload for the day, attend "huddles" where I hear reports from the nurses on their

YOU ASKED . . .

"Did you ever doubt your ability to make it in your career even after you got started in it?" —**JORDAN, AGE 15**

KRISTEN ANSWERED . . .

"No. My nursing program was very 'hands-on' with two eight-hour days of clinical experience per week, so by the time I got out into the 'real world,' I could hardly wait to take care of patients without an instructor following me around. Though I started out caring for many more patients than we do now with California nurse-patient ratio laws—and went home some evenings about to throw up from the intense multitasking required (and the knowledge that I could harm or kill someone if I made a significant error)—I never gave up. I changed my environment and left on a travel assignment, finding out that many hospitals have better nurse-patient ratios (California law requires maximum ratios now, fortunately). Nurses are in high enough demand that if you are unhappy in one place, you can find another job elsewhere."

patients so we can better assist with discharge planning, and assess whether the patients are the appropriate status. It's satisfying to help assure everything is set up for the patient to be discharged home safely with plenty of support. I set the patient up for home oxygen, IV antibiotics, home health services,

THE BREAKDOWN

ON THE PHONE: 30 minutes

SITTING: 30 minutes

STANDING: 8 hours

READING: 30 minutes

TAKING CARE OF PATIENTS: 12 hours!

and work closely with the physicians and bedside nurses in managing the patient's stay and discharge.

ME: It sounds like you have incredibly full days. Do you work long hours?

KRISTEN: As a per diem registered nurse, this varies greatly. Depending on the amount of shifts I'm needed to fill in and how many I choose to take, I can work six hours in a week or I can work forty. For me, it all evens out. I prefer to have the stress of wondering if I will get enough hours each week over the stress of knowing I have to be at the same place at the same time every day. My bedside nursing shifts vary based on the unit, but are always twelve hours long. They usually start at eight a.m. and end at eight thirty p.m. My nurse case management shifts are seven thirty a.m. to four p.m.

ME: I can tell that you love your job. What are the best parts for you?

KRISTEN: I live in a ski resort town, and our hospital, though small, sees a lot of tourists, which makes my job even more exciting, with more variety. And my wage is excellent—as a per diem, I make enough to *not* work full-time. And I can always find work, no problem.

WHY WAIT?

Many hospitals and nursing homes are open to teenage volunteers, who do things like visit with patients, give tours, and more. Spending time in a hospital will give you a better idea if this is the right work environment for you.

ME: That's so great, especially in today's job market. It sounds like you have a lot of freedom to do what you want to do too.

KRISTEN: The flexibility and variety of my job is wonderful, but the *best* part of my job is that when I go home after a shift, I know that I helped people who were in a bad place. I choose to work on holidays like Thanksgiving and Christmas, not only for the time-and-a-half pay, but to care for patients who would rather be home. Getting letters from my patients thanking me for my care or having a patient thank me for my care later on— making a positive difference—that is why I chose nursing.

ME: I can only imagine that being in a position to help someone going through a difficult time must be super rewarding.

KRISTEN: One time I ran into a patient at the supermarket who recognized me and got teary telling me that she was very ill in ICU a year ago and I was so sweet and caring and that, as her nurse, I helped her get through such a tough time. That is the most amazing, satisfying feeling ever—to make a difference every single day of your career.

THEN TO NOW

1999: Graduated from American River College with an AS in nursing

1999: Took job as hospital staff nurse at St. Joseph Hospital, Eureka, CA

2002: Graduated from Humboldt State University with a BA in liberal studies

ME: What an awesome story. . . . Love that! Are there any downsides?

KRISTEN: For me the most challenging aspects are dealing with state and federal regulations, individual facilities' politics, and system failures that prevent nurses from doing their job to their highest potential. And sometimes I'm dealing with situations where the patient is declining and the family dynamics prevent the best decisions being made for the patient. Some of the most frustrating days of my career have been due to those two factors.

WHAT IT TAKES
- Compassion
- Integrity
- Flexibility
- Patience
- Teamwork
- The ability to multitask
- A stomach for dealing with bodily fluids

ME: Since you have chosen an alternative approach to nursing as a career, can you tell us more about what that looks like in terms of work/life balance?

KRISTEN: Absolutely! I choose to be per diem, so when I take time off, I simply do not get paid. But I earn a higher wage and I bank my money, and it all evens out. And with my flexible scheduling, I choose when I work. Many hospitals allow a certain amount of self-scheduling, but you must still adhere to X amount of hours per week. I am responsible for working a minimum of five shifts per four-week schedule—and of course I

2003: Worked as RN registry nurse at Shasta Regional Medical Center

2004: Became staff nurse at Tahoe Forest Hospital, Truckee, CA

2009: Nominated for Nurse of the Year, Tahoe Forest Hospital choose to work more than that, but I tell them when I am available to work. I make myself as flexible as possible so I can pick up last-minute shifts and extra projects as needed. I choose my work days around my life. I *love* this part of my job. After fifteen years of nursing, I am not burned out. Psychologically, this is liberating, and it reflects positively in my attitude with my patients and coworkers.

ME: That's so cool. And I think it's a good reminder that we often have a lot of choice in determining what our career looks and feels like. I just have one last question for you: Do have any advice for teen girls who are hoping to become nurses?

KRISTEN: Research the many, many types of nursing you can do. You don't have to work as a full-time nurse in a hospital if that doesn't appeal to you. You can be a camp nurse, work with Doctors Without Borders internationally, work in a doctor's office or an outpatient surgery center, where you have weekends and nights off—the possibilities are much larger than most people think. You can be a travel nurse (I've done it—my housing, rental car, mileage all paid for), a registry nurse where you work whenever you choose, or a per diem nurse like myself. You can go on to be a nurse case manager or a risk manager nurse, a resident assessment coordinator on a long-term care unit, an education nurse—the possibilities are endless. And each job has its own wonderful rewards. I have *never* regretted my career decision. It is always easy to find a job wherever I go, the pay is excellent, and you have a feeling of satisfaction at the end of your workday—what more could you ask for?

In the Field

FIVE MORE MEDICAL CAREERS

HOME HEALTH AIDE   When people are unable to leave their homes or live independently due to illness or injury, they may receive the regular support of home health aides. These specialists either visit or live with homebound patients and offer personal care, including administering medication, checking vitals, and helping with day-to-day care.

PHARMACY TECHNICIAN While pharmacists are responsible for providing medication to patients either in hospitals or pharmacies, pharmacy technicians work behind the scenes performing administrative tasks like counting tablets, labeling bottles, and more.

MEDICAL SECRETARY   Medical secretaries manage administrative tasks associated with everything from wellness visits to surgeries. They might handle things like dealing with insurance claims and scheduling appointments or transcribing medical records and other correspondence. Certified medical secretaries must have a working understanding of medical procedures and be highly organized.

ULTRASOUND TECHNICIAN   If you've ever had an ultrasound at a hospital, there's a good chance it was performed by an ultrasound technician. These specialists are trained to administer ultrasounds and capture images of internal organs that can then be used by doctors for diagnosis.

MEDICAL INTERPRETER   When hospital patients don't speak English or have limited command of the language, a medical interpreter will be brought in to facilitate communication between the medical staff and the patient. Because they might have to explain complex procedures to their patients, medical interpreters must be familiar with medical terminology and procedures.

YOU NEED TO KNOW ABOUT

The American Nursing Association is the primary organization serving the more than three million nurses in the United States. Their website houses information on all things nursing, from legislative and policy issues to career information for different types of nursing. Find out more at www.nursingworld.org.

lunch break

INFORMATIONAL INTERVIEWS

When i was looking for a job in television news after graduating from college, I discovered this amazing thing called the "informational interview." An informational interview is a meeting where there is no job at stake. It's simply an opportunity to talk with professionals about their work, get tips on how to break into a company or industry, and most important, give people the chance to get to know and like you. A clever cover letter and a lot of persistence could just get you in the door.

As a twenty-two-year-old with very little experience, I managed to meet with the executive producers of ABC News's *20/20*, the newsmagazine *Day One* (no longer on the air), PBS's *MacNeil/Lehrer NewsHour* (now *PBS NewsHour*), the head of broadcasting for UNICEF, and a small television production company called Globalvision. While nothing happened immediately, as a result of those initial informational interviews, I eventually got job offers!

Here are just a few advantages to informational interviews:

- You can do them anytime—even as a high school student.

- Most people are happy to sit down with you (if they can fit it into their schedule) and talk about what it is they do and answer any questions.

- Contacts made through informational interviews can be valuable job contacts down the road.

- By asking for an informational interview, you're showing people that you're motivated and serious about your future.

The best place to start identifying possible interviews is with friends and family. Let people know what you're interested in and see if anyone has a connection to someone doing your hoped-for career. You can also ask your guidance counselor if any alumni have the job you want—sharing an alma mater is a great way to get someone's attention. Lastly, don't be afraid to send a letter to someone you don't know and ask them for a meeting. If you're professional in your communication and the person you're writing to isn't too swamped with work, you've got a good chance of landing a meeting.

Here are some more "do's" and "don'ts" that will prepare you for successful informational interviews:

DON'T	DO
Address your query "To whom it may concern" or "Dear Sir or Madam."	Address your e-mail or letter to an individual, and make sure to spell his or her name correctly!
Ramble on in your query and forget to clearly state why you're writing in the first place.	Be specific about what you're asking for—a half hour of their time for an in-person or on-the-phone informational interview.
Demand that the person reply to your letter.	Suggest that you'll follow up with a phone call in several weeks.

DON'T	DO
Call the person every day and get frustrated that they haven't returned your phone call.	Be patient and check in by phone no more than once a week.
Show up late or unprepared for your informational interview.	Come to the informational interview on time, dressed appropriately, and prepared with great questions (see below for examples).
Take the fact that somebody offered you free career advice for granted.	Send a personal thank-you note (handwritten is the best kind) to the person you met with

SAMPLE INFORMATIONAL INTERVIEW QUESTIONS

1. How did you get into this line of work?

2. What does your job entail?

3. What magazines do you read about your job? Are there any helpful organizations or websites I should know about?

4. What classes should I take in college?

5. Does your company offer internships?

6. What advice do you have for me about breaking into this career?

7. Can I get in touch with you down the road when I'm ready to look for a job?

DR. ALICE WILDER

Educational Psychologist

Dr. Alice Wilder, Head of Research and Development/ Producer, Preschool Television

The Facts

WHAT? Educational psychologists study how learning takes place and find ways to make it more effective. They do anything from coming up with ways to help a learning-disabled student get more out of a class to determining whether or not a new teaching tool impacts students' grades.

WHERE? Many educational psychologists work in schools, but they might also end up in hospitals, counseling centers, or even the world of preschool television.

HOW? Many educational psychologists have doctoral degrees, which means being in grad school for up to seven years, but there are different job opportunities in educational psychology for all levels of degrees.

$$$: An average of $70,000, but depends on level of education

DRESS CODE: Casual to business casual, depending on the day

STRESS FACTOR: On a scale of 1 to 10, a 7

until I worked with her, I had no idea that anybody did what Alice does. I met Alice while working for the hit preschool show *Blue's Clues* at Nickelodeon. One of the reasons the show has such a powerful impact on kids is because Alice took the time to ensure that the content of the show made sense.

While the show was in production, Alice spent a ton of time with preschoolers—acting out scenes from upcoming *Blue's Clues* episodes, playing the same games that the characters on the show might play together, and seeing if the script was as engaging, comprehensible, educational, and interactive as the writers and show creators wanted it to be.

Today she's still having an impact in the world of educational programming for preschoolers, but on a much larger scale. In addition to working on individual shows, she is the educational adviser responsible for developing the Amazon Originals curriculum for kids and is helping implement Amazon's unique educational point of view into the development of new series, all while juggling a host of other consulting gigs like working on shows for CBeebies and Cartoon Network Asia, as well as acting as chief content officer for children's digital publisher Speakaboos. If you're thinking that Alice is more than a little busy, you'd be right. It's a juggling act, and one she lets us peek at through her day-in-the-life-of diary.

"I also love how honest preschoolers are (if they don't like the story I'm reading, they will ask to leave!)."

ALICE'S JOURNAL

7:00 A.M. My alarm is going off. And I'm not a morning person. But I have to get up. I'm going to a preschool this morning to act out a new script for a show I'm working on. I will come to life when I am sitting in front of the kids and getting to talk to them—they always bring me to life and actually transform me. When I get in front of them, I channel my inner child and use my creative energy to act out the characters and problem solve on the spot, keeping in the back of my mind the series' goals, writer's goals, learning theory, child development. . . . It's a fun challenge that changes with each and every script. We were up late getting the materials ready to show the kids, and it is snowing outside. I flip on the TV, hoping for a "snow day." Adults wish for snow days too! But alas, school is on, and I need to get myself to those kids, who are sure to be full of a lot of energy! Today is definitely a "jeans day," since I'll be on the floor playing with preschoolers. If I had meetings later in the day, I would be in business casual.

8:30 A.M. Head out the door. Since I'm not going straight to the office, I can't walk, so I jump on the subway and head downtown with hordes of other New Yorkers. As always, I've got my big blue bag in tow. . . . Inside it are things I never leave

YOU ASKED . . .

"What was the toughest obstacle you had to face in order to be who you are today?" —**SARAH, AGE 16**

ALICE ANSWERED . . .

"Low self-esteem. When I was in college, I registered for a business course, and one of the requirements was a presentation in front of the class. As soon as I heard that, I wanted to drop the class. When I started at Blue's Clues I used to whisper my notes in the creator's ear, not believing in the value of what I had to say. What helped me was going into schools every week and talking with preschoolers . . . the audience themselves. My voice had to be heard because it stood for them, not for me. My voice became respected on the show and in the industry because it had the integrity of representing the kids, and this gave me confidence. And now you can't keep me quiet, especially on matters of kids' voices being heard."

home without: my MacBookAir, iPhone, extra thumb drives, my Internet hotspot, chargers, my notebook full of things to do (because there are just too many things I need to keep in my head), and my makeup so I can freshen up if I make it to the gym later that day.

THE BREAKDOWN

IN MEETINGS: 1–2 hours a day

ON THE PHONE: 1–2 hours a day

ONLINE: 8–10 hours a day

READING: 1 hour a day

SITTING: Most of the day, unless at a preschool or in in-person meetings

WORKING SOLO: In a parallel work–type way, almost always

9:00 A.M. *Research time. I like sitting on the floor and playing. . . . I don't know why. Maybe because I'm short? Maybe because I've always liked to sit on the floor? I gather four or five preschoolers around me, tell them my name, and ask theirs. When we're doing this, I try to notice something unique about each one of them—maybe one has something sparkly on her clothing, maybe another is wearing really cool sneakers—and talk about it with them, the idea being to make the kids feel as comfortable around me as possible. After all, I'm just a stranger coming in to read them a story. The tricky thing about researching with preschoolers is keeping them talking about the same thing I am, especially if they don't like the story.*

Once I start reading the story (which is the episode script in storybook form), I really get into it to make it more interesting for the kids. I act it out and play the part of different characters. If they like the story and are listening, it's easier. If they don't, it's going to be an exhausting forty-five minutes, and I'd better figure out what isn't working in the script. Something I love about researching with preschoolers is how silly they can be. Like today, the script I was researching had a joke in it. We were transforming a wolf from "little" to "big." But instead of spelling "big," we spelled "pig." When the preschoolers thought about changing a wolf into a pig, they lost it . . . all-out belly laughs. They just kept laughing and saying, "Again! Again!" By this time I was laughing so hard, I had tears rolling down my cheeks. It was so cool seeing them having such a good time and knowing it was educational, too (after all, we were teaching preschoolers spelling!). I also love how honest preschoolers are (if they don't like the story I'm reading, they will ask to leave!).

10:00 A.M. While the rest of my research team was working with other groups of kids, I tested the same script with some older kids, this time five- and six-year-olds. They totally got it. They were entranced in the story and screaming out answers as we played along. They made all of the connections. Today I brought the writer of the script with me so we could get a sense of what was working and what wasn't. It's kind of like "cheating," but in a positive way. We're just trying to find out what works before we spend the money and time to make the actual episode.

WHY WAIT?

- Be a teen peer counselor at a youth hotline.
- Volunteer at a hospital or clinic.

1:00 P.M. Back at my home office. I jump on a quick conference call and then switch over to a development meeting for another show I'm helping to get off the ground. I'm on the line with the network

THEN TO NOW

| 1988: Graduated from Skidmore College with a BA in psychology | 1991: Graduated with an MA in educational psychology, Columbia University | 1993: Started working on doctorate, Teachers College, Columbia University | 1995: Hired as the director of research and development/ producer, Nick Jr.'s *Blue's Clues* | 1998: Received EdD in educational psychology, Teachers College, Columbia University |

executives, creator, and writer. My job is to be the four-year-old in the process, to let people know how the series and each episode works for the audience and what the positive educational impact could be in kids' lives. For just about every show I work on, the creators and writers start with a show "bible." I am assigned to read the bible and provide notes from a kid perspective and pull out and define the educational point of view with an eye toward how it fits with our network's über-curriculum. Once we are all on board with the creative, we pick one of the story ideas from the bible for the writer to use to bring the series to life! Once that is written and the bible is revised, we will all get on the phone and talk through notes and ideas or we will each write notes and e-mail them back to the writer for revisions. So much happens electronically that we could be working together on an idea from anywhere in the world. The great part about that is ideas can be shared from anywhere, and it's efficient. The not-so-great part about that is face-to-face time is part of the magic of the creative process.

4:30 P.M.: There is a draft one script, an animatic, a rough-cut animation, stories in progress, and a conference presentation

WHAT IT TAKES

- A passion for education
- A strong interest in research
- Strong analytical and communication skills

2008: Co-creator, head of research and education, PBS Kids' *Super Why*

2010: Co-creator, executive producer, *Cha-Ching: Money Smart Kids*

2011: Chief content officer, Speakaboos

2012: Educational advisor, Amazon Studios Kids' Programming *prep sitting on my desktop. All of these things need to be done right away, so I quickly prioritize and set to work reading or watching and giving notes. I am pretty detail oriented, so each one takes me some time to get through. I'll do as much as I can and then what I don't finish, I'll finish after I go out for a few hours OR make a plan for times I can fit in the notes I won't get to today. My desktop remains cluttered with to-do items and may look like a mess, but it makes organizational sense to me! Plus, these days it's not really possible to be ahead of the work, so I have to become Zen with always feeling the pressure of deadlines. It's an exciting time in educational kids' media, and having this much to do means there is a lot of opportunity to have a constructive and positive impact in the lives of kids, their families, and even in classrooms and libraries!*

6:30 P.M. I meet a friend, grab a bite to eat, and head uptown to Columbia University (my alma mater) to hear my "education hero," Jerome Bruner, speak. Aside from having a cool job, it's nights like this that make living in New York worth all the stress and hassle. His talk tonight was called "Educating a Sense of the Possible." After hearing him talk, I feel like I got a dose of inspiration that will last a year!

10:30 P.M. Ah . . . nighttime. I am happy to be back in my apartment. I always need at least an hour or two of downtime before I go to bed . . . "me" time. But in today's digital world there isn't really such a thing as downtime—e-mails don't stop coming in (and the expectation seems to be that they need to be answered right away), productions send scripts and animatics at all hours, there has to be time to Tweet, check Instagram, Tumblr, and quickly look at Facebook. So I sit on the couch with my laptop on my lap, my iPad not far away, and my iPhone plugged in on the table next to the couch. I just can't seem to get to bed before midnight or one a.m. I want to . . . in fact, I need to. Every day feels as if there is not a moment of downtime. I consciously enjoy the fact that I love what I do every day and also love time for space and connecting with friends. "Work hard. Play hard." But I know that I need to get off to bed; tomorrow is another full day! Before I go to sleep, I figure out what time I have to get up in the morning (it changes every day, and luckily, I thrive on the variety of my work and life) and read a page or two of a book before I collapse in exhaustion. The last thing I do before I turn out the lights is list a few of the things I have to be grateful for and tune in to my ten-minute meditation! Looking forward to tomorrow!

In the Field

FIVE MORE CAREERS IN PSYCHOLOGY

RESEARCH PSYCHOLOGIST   These psychologists often work in universities, splitting their time between teaching and conducting research on things like memory, behavior, learning, and perception. Many research psychologists spend a lot of time writing articles about their research for academic journals and publications as well.

SCHOOL PSYCHOLOGIST   Chances are you've crossed paths with a school psychologist before. School psychologists do things like deal with problem students, come up with ideas to support gifted and talented students, and work with teachers to make their classrooms more kid-friendly.

FAMILY THERAPIST   Family therapists are like marriage counselors, except they examine the whole family dynamic and the role each family member plays in any problems there may be. Family therapists usually have their own practice, and their patients come to their office for therapy sessions.

TRIAL PSYCHOLOGIST   Trial psychologists are hired by prosecutors and defendants to help them strategize how to win their cases by giving them psychological insight into picking a jury, planning opening and closing statements, and figuring out a plan for the trial.

CLINICAL PSYCHOLOGIST   Clinical psychologists work with mentally and emotionally disturbed people, or people going through a difficult time, and give them tools to deal with their problems. Some clinical psychologists work in hospitals or counseling centers, while others might have their own practice.

For more careers working with children, check out the Child therapist profile on page 55 and the teacher profile on page 407.

JAYNE MORGAN

Accountant

The Facts

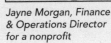

Jayne Morgan, Finance
& Operations Director
for a nonprofit

WHAT? Accounting is the business of tracking the money that goes in and out of any company, organization, or wallet, and while many accountants file taxes and conduct audits, others develop financial plans for businesses and even run organizations.

WHERE? Accountants work in just about every industry and company imagineable. Others might be self-employed.

HOW? Most companies require a four-year college degree in accounting, finance, or business. Becoming a CPA (certified public accountant) means passing a special exam and working a number of hours in accounting. Getting an MBA is a good idea for people with high career aspirations.

$$$: Starting salaries average $53,000, while experienced accountants can earn $80,000 to $200,000 plus for management and executives, depending on the company.

DRESS CODE? Business casual at auditing firms and suits in supercorporate environments.

STRESS FACTOR: On a scale of 1 to 10, a 7

when i interviewed jayne morgan, she was an accountant and the finance and operations director for the nonprofit NESsT in Santiago, Chile, and she busted one myth about accountants right away. Contrary to popular belief, accounting really isn't about "math" per se. In fact, according to Jayne, the most complicated math an accountant will do is addition and subtraction . . . perhaps division on the rarest of occasions. As she explained, accounting is a "system" for tracking financial information. "You don't need to be good at math, but you do need to be good at following systems and procedures, and have the type of mind that likes to work within a rigid framework." She adds with a laugh, "Although I couldn't live without *my* calculator, and I can only use *my* calculator—that is one stereotype about accountants that's actually true."

"I couldn't live without my calculator, and I can only use my calculator—that is one stereotype about accountants that's actually true."

I asked Jayne how and when she knew she wanted to be an accountant, and she gave me her story.

"When I was in high school applying to colleges, I had no idea what I wanted to do. So my dad recommended that I apply to the business schools at all these universities, because no matter what you decide you're interested in, there's a "business" behind it. So if you're interested in medicine, you know, every hospital needs to be run—there's a "business" behind it. If you want to work in the movie industry, there are accountants and finance people behind every movie production. Once I was in business school, I really enjoyed accounting, because of that idea that it gives order to whatever business you're in," Jayne explained.

Jayne began her career like many accountants—working with one of the "Big Five" accounting auditing firms. PricewaterhouseCoopers recruited her out of college to be an auditor in their Chicago office, and in this competitive, entry-level position, she "audited" companies, meaning she

YOU ASKED . . .

"What did you have to give up to get to where you are?"
—NATALIE, AGE 16

JAYNE ANSWERED . . .

"I had to give up a lot of evenings and weekends! To be successful, you cannot expect to work from nine to five, and you have to be ready to do whatever it takes to get the job done. Accountants work with a lot of strict deadlines, which sometimes means working long hours."

reviewed their financial books, making sure that everything added up and checking receipts for equipment against the equipment itself. She spent most of her time either on-site with clients or working in computer programs like Excel, which she used to add invoices and review documents.

"When you do an audit, usually you start with the physical documents like receipts or contracts or loan agreements. The first part of the process was to review those documents, and the second part was to enter the information into specialized accounting programs," Jayne says.

Accountants fresh out of college might spend a couple of years "paying their dues" as an auditor and then take their experience into the corporate world, where they might be hired as an in-house accountant for a company. Unless they're like Jayne. Then they might move to South America to run the financial side of a small nonprofit organization. I asked Jayne to

THE BREAKDOWN

IN MEETINGS: 1 hour a day

ON THE PHONE: Less than half an hour a day

ONLINE: 2 hours a day

SITTING: Nearly the whole day

READING: 1 hour a day

WORKING SOLO: 7 hours a day

WHY WAIT?

- Get a job at a bank—many will hire high school students to work as tellers.

- Get comfortable using Excel—it's one of the biggest tools for accountants. (If you need help getting started, try doing an online tutorial.)

- Manage your own money matters. Create your own spreadsheet in Excel or try using a budget program like Quicken to keep your own "books."

explain what she did for the organization, NESsT (Nonprofit Enterprise and Self-sustainability Team).

"I work in a small international organization, and I'm not just behind my desk all day entering numbers into Excel. I'm using financial analysis and budgets to help support other people's programs. I play a big role in making sure that the organization is running properly, making sure our technology systems are working, helping with funding or hiring decisions, and so on. So it's human resources, technology, everything. . . . I really love my job, love the people," Jayne says.

Because the accounting industry is so regulated by the federal government, and there have been a number of high-profile accounting scandals over the years, one of the challenges of being an accountant is staying up-to-date on changing regulations and the fast pace of the business environment. But when pressed, Jayne admits that while this is a

THEN TO NOW

1997: Studied abroad in Madrid, Spain	**1998:** Interned at Merrill Lynch in Boulder, CO	**1998–2000:** Worked part-time job as forensic accounting assistant at RGL Gallagher in St. Louis, MO	**2000:** Graduated from Washington University in St. Louis with BS in business administration

challenge, she actually enjoys the continuing education too. In fact, she likes pretty much everything about her job.

153

ACCOUNTANT

"There's definitely a certain satisfaction in being able to have everything in order so things can run efficiently, and being able to provide management with the information they need to make decisions about the company. No director of any company or nonprofit could make decisions without the necessary information, and one of the key pieces of information is financial information. So what I really like is being able to have accurate records of the past and use them to forecast into the future to help make decisions," she says.

According to Jayne, the job opportunities and the potential to rise up the ranks are enormous for people with backgrounds in accounting.

"People are really impressed when you put in your time with one of these accounting firms—it looks great on your résumé. Accountants are in very high demand because in order to understand finance, you have to know what's behind the numbers, and that's what accountants know. So if you have a lot of experience in accounting, you can easily make a transition into other business areas."

WHAT IT TAKES
- Strong computer and analytical skills
- Paying attention to detail
- Being procedure-oriented

2001: Passed the CPA exam in Illinois

2000–2001: Associate at Pricewaterhouse Coopers, in Chicago, IL

2001–2002: Senior associate at PricewaterhouseCoopers, Santiago, Chile

2002: Hired as finance and operations director, NESsT, Santiago, Chile

In the Field

FIVE MORE CAREERS YOU CAN HAVE WITH AN ACCOUNTING BACKGROUND

FINANCIAL AUDITOR (can be entry-level career) Financial auditors examine the finances of a company or organization to ensure that everything the company reports about their finances is accurate. Many typically work for the "Big Five" accounting firms such as Deloitte & Touche and PricewaterhouseCoopers.

BUDGET ANALYST Behind the budget of every company, organization, or government office is a budget analyst, who tracks budgets throughout the "fiscal" or financial year and creates new ones each year based on projected income and spending.

FINANCIAL PLANNER As the economy fluctuates and uncertainty reigns, financial planners are becoming increasingly important. They help companies, families, or individuals handle their money, whether it's setting up a retirement fund, paying off college debt, or saving to buy a dream house.

TAX ACCOUNTANT While many tax accountants are busiest during "tax season" preparing tax returns, they support their clients year-round by handling things like audits or the complicated tax implications of a merger between two companies, as well as staying up-to-date on ever-changing tax regulations.

MANAGEMENT ACCOUNTANT Management accountants typically work in large companies and analyze the structure of an organization as it affects the financial bottom line. They are always looking for ways to reorganize a company or reallocate resources so the company can be financially efficient.

YOU NEED TO KNOW ABOUT

Start Here—Go Places (www.startheregoplaces.com), hosted by the American Institute of Certified Public Accountants, is a great website to learn more about accounting, find out what courses to take in high school, and discover job and internship opportunities.

SEVERN CULLIS-SUZUKI

Environmentalist

Severn Cullis-Suzuki, Environmentalist

The Facts

WHAT? While "environmentalist" isn't necessarily an actual job title you'll find at a company, environmentalists are people who aim to protect and improve the environment through their work, which might involve things like education, engineering, and research.

WHERE? Some work for nonprofit organizations or government agencies, while others might work in academic institutions or for environmental firms.

HOW? Environmentalists should take science and biology classes in high school and get an undergraduate or graduate degree in some sort of social or environmental science.

$$$: An average of $40,000–$55,000, but varies widely depending on the organization

DRESS CODE? Casual to business casual

STRESS FACTOR: On a scale of 1 to 10, between a 5 and a 9

while there is no cookie-cutter career description of an "environmentalist," any way you shake it, that's what Severn Cullis-Suzuki is. Her father is world-renowned scientist Dr. David Suzuki, and his passion for nature and the environment clearly rubbed off onto Severn at a very young age. So young, in fact, that Severn spoke at the first-ever International Earth Summit in Rio de Janeiro in 1992. She was only twelve years old.

Since then, she has continued to speak out about the environment, using her voice and her passion to educate others about the plight of the earth and the need for people to improve their relationship with its natural resources. I talked with Severn about her work and what it means to be an environmentalist.

ME: We hear the word "environmentalist" used all the time. What is an environmentalist?

SEVERN: Actually, one of the things that I'm trying to do personally and professionally is to reevaluate what the term "environmentalist" means. I think one of the biggest problems that we have with respect to our environment is how we've really externalized it. How it's this thing that certain people deal with

"One of the challenges . . . is becoming so absorbed in the problems that you forget to enjoy your life. Burnout is a really big problem in activist communities."

YOU ASKED . . .

"What does being successful mean to you?"

—ASUKA, AGE 16

SEVERN ANSWERED . . .

"I would say that being successful is being happy. But I also think that if I can have a small ecological footprint and I can live without causing harm to the environment, to me that would be a pretty big success."

WHY WAIT?

- Start an environmental club at your high school or in your community to raise awareness of issues you're passionate about.

- Read biographies of famous women environmentalists like Rachel Carson or Julia Butterfly Hill for inspiration.

- Start at home! Recycle, take shorter showers, turn off lights when you leave the room, and keep electrical appliances unplugged when you're not using them.

and we call them "environmentalists" or we talk about "environmental problems" or the "environmental movement." In reality, the environment is everything that surrounds us. It's the air that we breathe, it's the food that we eat, it's our health, it's our economic interactions. What I'm trying to do is redefine our relationship to our resources and to one another in a very grand way.

ME: How are you trying to do that?

SEVERN: The first thing is education. Right now I'm in school again and educating myself. I've been active in environmentalism for a long time, and after I finished my undergrad degree, I was public speaking and writing and doing a lot of educational stuff. But I went back to school because I realized I wanted to learn more about different worldviews and different ways of managing our environment. Right now I'm doing a master's in

THEN TO NOW

1992: Spoke at the International Earth Summit in Rio de Janeiro, Brazil, at the age of twelve

1993: Awarded the Global 500 Award by the United Nations Environment Programme (UNEP), Nairobi, Kenya

1997–2001: Commissioner for the UNEP's Earth Charter Commission

2001: Research intern at Pinkaiti Research Station, Brazil

2002: Graduated from Yale with a BS in biology

ethno-ecology and studying with First Nations* here in British Columbia, learning about environmental attractions and the economy. That's the first step. Another step is to translate what I'm learning into my personal life, as well as teaching others what I'm learning about. I don't have a career plan or step-by-step process in my mind, but I do think that people who are interested in environmental studies, environmental engineering, and sustainability will have a lot of career options.

ME: You've done a lot of public speaking about the environment. Do you see yourself continuing to do that in the future?

SEVERN: I think I'll always be doing that. I started when I was quite young, and it's just part of my role as a communicator.

ME: You were only twelve years old when you spoke at the Earth Summit in Rio. How does doing so much at such a young age impact you now?

SEVERN: I'm not sure. The Earth Summit was a pretty big

WHAT IT TAKES

- A willingness to make changes in your own life
- Dedication and commitment to your cause
- A willingness to fight "uphill battles"

---

* **THE LINGO: First Nations** is a term used in Canada to refer to the indigenous people of North America, sometimes called Indians or Native Americans

| 2002: Founded the Skyfish Project, an Internet-based think tank | 2002: Took part in a twenty-one-city speaking tour across Japan | 2003: Hosted documentary *A View from the Summet* for broadcast on Canadian television | 2004: Enrolled at University of Victoria, B.C., for master's degree | 2010: Documentary about Severn, *Severn: The Voice of Our Children*, is theatrically released |

event. I'd say that was probably the biggest speech I've given in my life. So it's kind of funny to have this precedent set right off the bat. But I find it a useful tool when I'm speaking today, because as a story it really captures people's imaginations. It shows the potential for anyone to make a difference, and people love the imagery and the idea of a child going to the Earth Summit and speaking to world leaders. It's almost like it has a life of its own.

ME: Your work and your life really seem to be one and the same. Is there any separation between the two?

SEVERN: It really seems that what my life is about and what my work is about are one and the same. I consider myself lucky in that regard. It's also kind of hard because some of the issues are kind of overwhelming, so it's difficult to not bring that into your personal life all the time.

ME: Can you talk more about that? What are the challenges of your work?

SEVERN: Well, one of the challenges that I'd say is true, not only for environmentalists, but also for activists, is becoming so absorbed in the problems that you forget to enjoy your life. Burnout is a really big problem in activist communities. I was just talking to my parents this weekend, and I was going on about how there is such heavy ecological pressure on our ecosystems right now and it's pretty hard to look up from that, and my mom reminded me that life is pretty good. There are always going to be problems . . . it's part of the human condition, part of being alive on Planet Earth. To forget about the positive is really part of the problem. So we've really got to work on personal sustainability as well.

ME: When do you feel like you're having the biggest impact in your work?

SEVERN: It's really hard to measure when you're dealing with raising awareness or conveying ideas. But at the same time, whenever I reevaluate things and consider whether I'm making a difference, I come back to the realization that planting seeds in people's minds about possibility for change is a really important starting point, especially in the industrialized world, because our actions have incredible impact around the world.

And so starting with conversations and opening up new avenues of thought and realizing the impact of our actions is really important, but it's really hard to measure. Sometimes when I'm giving speeches I think, *Oh man, who am I to be giving a speech on what I think? I mean, this is just what I think.* So when I give talks, that's exactly what I say. I say this is what *I* think, and then I ask the audience to think for themselves, and that's pretty much my main message. Think! Think about your actions.

Afterward young women will often come up to me, and they'll have a bunch of questions or they want to talk about what they're interested in or they'll thank me for being there. And that's why I'm justified in being up there. Because we should be speaking out. So it's pretty rewarding to get that feedback.

ME: I think that being able to speak out and inspire others is a real gift.

SEVERN: Yes, but we *all* have voices.

ME: Last question—have you ever thought about doing anything else?

SEVERN: I plan on doing *everything* else!

In the Field

FIVE MORE CAREERS WORKING TO SAVE THE ENVIRONMENT

ECOLOGIST Ecologists study the relationship between people and other living organisms and the environment in which they live. Many work in academic settings, where they teach and do research, while others might work for government agencies or for-profit companies to ensure new products are environmentally friendly.

ENVIRONMENTAL EDUCATOR If you're passionate about the environment and aren't afraid of speaking out, you might consider being an environmental educator. These educators usually work for government or nonprofit organizations, and they educate the public about environmental issues through lectures, hikes, and tours.

OUTREACH DIRECTOR Environmental outreach directors usually work for nonprofits focused on environmental issues, and they develop campaigns to get public attention, form alliances with like-minded organizations, figure out ways to identify volunteers, and hold community events in support of the organization's cause.

ENVIRONMENTAL FIELD SPECIALIST When a company's work potentially impacts the natural resources of the environment, environmental field specialists go out in the field to collect water and soil samples to research how the operation of the company is affecting the environment and then write up reports based on their findings.

FUEL ECONOMY RESEARCHER As the price of gas continues to skyrocket, fuel economy researchers are becoming more important. They develop ways for people to rely less on traditional fuel, whether by creating alternative power sources such as biodiesel or by developing more efficient modes of transportation.

YOU NEED TO KNOW ABOUT

The National Resources Defense Council (www.nrdc.org) is a nonprofit environmental action organization with more than a million members. On the website you'll find out about important environmental issues throughout the world and get involved as an online activist.

ANKE LANGENBACH

Veterinarian

Anke Langenbach, Veterinary Surgeon

The Facts

WHAT? Veterinarians are medical doctors who specialize in the care of animals, from Fido and Fluffy to livestock and even zoo animals. Vets do everything from tending to injured or sick animals and administering vaccinations to performing surgeries.

WHERE? Many work for small animal hospitals, where they deal primarily with people's pets, while a smaller percentage work in laboratories, zoos, or in their own private practice.

HOW? Veterinarians must attend an accredited four-year veterinarian medical school program following undergrad and pass a number of exams. Most states also require a veterinarian to be licensed to practice.

$$$: An average annual salary of $93,000 a year

DRESS CODE? Lab coat or surgical scrubs

STRESS FACTOR: On a scale of 1 to 10, can range from a 3 to a 10

as a serious animal lover, there's always been a part of me that has dreamed of being a veterinarian. Veterinary surgeon Anke Langenbach said that she hears that a lot. For whatever reason, being a veterinarian seems like such a cool job to many teens, but a lot of people shy away from the career when it comes down to actually making the choice to pursue it. Perhaps it's because vet schools are so competitive? Perhaps it's because people are intimidated by the amount of schooling?

None of those reasons deterred Anke, who knew she wanted to be a veterinarian from a very young age. I recently had a chance to catch up with Anke to talk with her about her work.

ME: When did you know you wanted to be a veterinarian?

ANKE: When I was ten years old.

ME: Was there any one thing that sparked that interest?

ANKE: I always dragged home everything that was broken and needed help—earthworms, the neighbor's cats, frogs. I used to take frog eggs out of a dirty pond by this industrial area behind our house, and I raised them in the yard. My dad could never cut the grass—there were little frogs everywhere. I guess you could say I never thought about doing anything else.

"It feels so good to know that I put a new hip in and now this dog is going to be able to jump in the car or run again."

ME: I think that's great. And now that it's what you're doing, is veterinary work what you expected it would be?

ANKE: No. When I went into veterinary medicine, it was certainly because I had a love for animals and a love for science, but I worked mainly with veterinarians who did this old English-type work, getting called out to the farm to help with a calf or something . . . large animal work. Then, as I went through veterinary school, I realized that's not really what I wanted to do.

ME: So what kind of veterinary medicine did you end up going into?

ANKE: I'm what's called a veterinary surgeon. I went through veterinary school, and after that I did another four years of training to specialize in small animal surgery. So what I do is fix things that your general veterinarian doesn't fix, such as broken bones, torn ligaments, and I perform back surgeries, hip replacements, and things like that. I work only on a referral basis. So people with animals can't just call me and say they need to see me—they have to go to their veterinarian, who would refer them to me.

ME: What kind of animals do you do surgery on?

ANKE: Mainly dogs and cats, but I also work with the local wildlife group and help them with birds and other wildlife animals such as raccoons and squirrels and bats, some owls. Tomorrow I'll do surgery on a little bunny. I do that for free on the side.

ME: Where do you actually work?

ANKE: I work within a big animal hospital in Virginia. It has an emergency clinic with about ten emergency doctors and lots and lots of technicians, a cardiology group, an internal medicine group, and a surgery group. I own the surgery practice,

YOU ASKED . . .

"How did you accomplish all of the work that you've done over the years?"   **—ANASTASIA, AGE 13**

ANKE ANSWERED . . .

"One task at a time, with lots of long hours and lots of coffee."

and I have two other surgeons that work for me.

ME: Well, I'm very impressed!

ANKE: *(laughs)* It's fun. . . . I enjoy what I do.

WHY WAIT?

- Volunteer at a local shelter or wildlife care center or get a job working at a kennel or in a veterinary clinic.
- Run a dog-walking or pet-sitting business and make money while you get experience working with animals.
- Take advanced biology classes in high school.

thing I do when I get in is check on the cases that had surgery maybe the day before. Then the other surgeons and I get together with the technicians and the overnight people. I have appointments until about lunchtime, and I have a technician or two that help me restrain animals, take temperatures, take Xrays, and stuff like that.

In the afternoon we do surgeries. We have real operating rooms with real tables and anesthesia monitoring, just like for people. It's the same thing . . . it just looks a little different because everything is a little smaller. The surgery we do is mainly for cases we saw that morning. Usually I get home anywhere from six thirty to nine p.m., when all the work is done. I usually do some work at home on the computer at night, depending on what happened that day.

That's what my day looks like four days a week. On Wednesdays I'm home, and the other surgeons and I share weekend "on-call" duty with other vets at the hospital, because there always has to be somebody on call at night or on the weekends.

THEN TO NOW

1992: Graduated from Ludwig-Maximilians University, College of Veterinary Medicine, Germany

1994–1997: Residency in small animal surgery, University of Pennsylvania veterinary teaching hospital

1997–1998: Lectured at the University of Pennsylvania teaching hospital

ME: It seems that there would have to be a sad side of your job too. How do you cope with that?

ANKE: It's hard. I think you get tougher as you get older because you have to start to separate yourself. We had a dog that passed away last night unexpectedly. He was very, very sick, but we thought he had pulled through, and then his condition took a turn for the worse. I spoke with the clinic at three in the morning and everything was fine, so I went back to bed. And this morning, he had passed away. So it's very sad . . . it's very tough. I think if you lose the ability to be sad about it, then you're not right for the job anymore, because it gives you that extra edge to fight really hard. Of course, there are situations where you just can't help the animal. Sometimes an animal has cancer, and they're going to die, no matter what you do. It's tough. I always used to take everything home with me, and I still do, but I can deal with it a little bit better now than I used to. Thankfully in surgery, our situations are always very, very controlled and it's rare that we lose an animal.

ME: Let's talk about the best parts of your job. What do you love about what you do?

WHAT IT TAKES

- A strong background in biology, chemistry, and other sciences
- A love of animals
- Good grades in college—veterinary schools are competitive to get into

1998: Certified by the American College of Veterinary Surgeons

1998–2001: Associate surgeon at veterinary surgical referral practice, northern Virginia

2001–2004: Co-owned private small animal surgical referral practice, Washington, DC

2004: Founded own private practice in Virginia

ANKE: Helping animals and helping the people that own the animals. It makes my day. I can never say no. My husband hates it—even in the middle of the night when they call and have something they need. I don't mind, I just go and do it. It feels so good to know that I put a new hip in and now this dog is going to be able to jump in the car or run again, or we'll do a surgery where the dog was three-legged lame, and now the dog can run and play Frisbee again. It's very rewarding, it really is. And most animals even seem to be thankful, which is weird.

ME: Besides the sadness involved in losing animals, are there any other challenges?

ANKE: I sometimes think that veterinarians don't get as much credit as regular physicians do, even though we went through the same training. We often put more work in, but we don't get paid nearly as much as they do. The work we do is a lot like what a pediatrician does, because like them, our patients don't talk. We have to be able to know what the problem is through other means. And the fact that there isn't always health insurance for pet owners makes it hard because you're always seen as a businessperson, so you often feel bad charging for what you do.

ME: Is what we see on Animal Planet what it's really like?

ANKE: I think Animal Planet paints a very realistic picture of veterinary medicine, at least the hard-core work in the ER. But

---

INTERESTED IN BEING A VET? HERE'S ANKE'S ADVICE

Don't give up. It's very hard work and it's very hard to get into vet school. So persist, and work really hard to get good grades. It's a very rewarding, wonderful career, so just go forward and try it out.

there are lots of people who work as veterinarians in other fields like research, in administrative forms, at universities, or in the private sector.

In the Field

FIVE MORE CAREERS WORKING WITH ANIMALS

ANIMAL TRAINER Animal trainers not only teach dogs to sit, stay, and come, but some train wild animals, from grizzly bears to elephants. Anytime you see a movie or TV show with a wild animal onscreen, you can be sure that an animal trainer is just outside the shot, coaching the animal's "performance."

ANIMAL CONSERVATIONIST Some of the most interesting animals on the planet—rhinoceroses, gorillas, tigers—are endangered. Conservationists work in zoos, research facilities, on nature preserves, and in nature to find ways to protect these species and bring attention to their plight.

ZOOKEEPER If you want to get up close and personal with cool, exotic animals and don't mind spending a lot of time on your feet, then check out this career. Zookeepers meet the zoo animals' nutritional and physical needs, as well as get to know the animals so they can monitor their behavior and emotional state.

PET THERAPIST Everyone knows that cats and dogs are like therapy in the form of a furry companion. But what about when the pets themselves need a little couch time? Pet therapists deal with behavioral issues affecting pets, like separation anxiety, by using their background in animal behavior or psychology.

SERVICE DOG TRAINER Have you ever seen a young dog wearing a harness and a vest that says "Dog in Training"?

This dog was learning to be a service dog to work with blind or other disabled people. Service dog trainers get the dogs ready to start their new "jobs," as well as show the new owners how to work with their canine companions.

YOU NEED TO KNOW ABOUT

The Association for Women Veterinarians (www.vet.ksu.edu/AWV/index.htm) is a national organization dedicated to supporting women veterinarians and encouraging more women to enter the field. Here you'll find resources, info on the history of women in veterinary medicine, and a list of must-reads for girls interested in being a vet.

For more careers in medicine, check out the physical therapist profile on page 416 and the nurse-midwife profile on page 279.

lunch break

HOW TO RESEARCH
YOUR DREAM JOB

Since we have access to pretty much any information at our fingertips, it's possible to become an expert in just about anything. I truly believe that when it comes to career exploration and job hunting, the more information you can get your hands on, the better. Here are some of my top research tips:

- Read the trade magazines for your industry. Trades are magazines geared at professionals, and just about every industry has one. For example, I used to work in children's television, so I read trade mags *Broadcasting & Cable* and *Electronic Media* every week, just to stay up-to-date on any news in the television industry.

- Google people you're going to be meeting with or want to approach about an informational interview. The more you can find out about that person, on both a personal and professional level, the better. When I worked at Cartoon Network and took meetings with animators, I'd always be impressed if someone came in and knew a little bit about me—it showed me that they'd done their homework!

- If there's a company or organization you're interested in learning more about, visit their website. You can usually read their mission statement, read recent press releases to learn about the kinds of work they're doing, read bios for top employees, and maybe even find out how to apply for a job.

- Do your own market research! If you're interested in pursuing a certain career, or maybe even starting your own company someday, do your own e-mail survey. With a quick post on Facebook or Twitter, you can instantly crowdsource valuable feedback from tons of people about your ideas or goals.

- Read anything and everything you can get your hands on that concerns your interests, from articles to autobiographies.

HOLLY McPEAK

Professional Athlete

The Facts

WHAT? A professional athlete is anyone who gets paid to compete as an athlete. In the United States, women are pro athletes in sports like soccer, golf, basketball, tennis, and of course, beach volleyball.

WHERE? They can live just about anywhere, although sometimes it's determined by their sport. For example, in season, WNBA players live in the city where their team is based. Professional beach volleyball players like Holly have to live on the beach (sounds tough, huh?).

Holly McPeak,
Professional Beach
Volleyball Player

HOW? There are no educational requirements, but pro athletes must have great natural athletic ability, passion for their sport, and a willingness to work hard.

$$$: It depends on the sport. WNBA players earn an average of $55,000 to $80,000 a year, while a tennis pro can make over $100,000 in one match. Many athletes supplement their income with sponsor bonuses.

DRESS CODE? Athletic gear. Holly's work outfit is a bikini!

STRESS FACTOR: On a scale of 1 to 10, a 2 when training and a 6 when competing

i had the chance to interview three-time Olympic beach volleyball player Holly McPeak in Hermosa Beach, California, where she lives and "works," staying fit and training to be the best beach volleyball player she can be. We grabbed a drink at Coffee Bean on a sunny California day. Here are some highlights of our conversation.

ME: What were your career dreams as a teen girl?

HOLLY: Growing up, I knew that it was important that I do well in school, because I really wanted to earn a volleyball scholarship. Volleyball was my passion, and I knew it was also my vehicle to get into a good school and get a good education. I was able to get a scholarship, and I started at the University of California at Berkeley and graduated from UCLA. I got a good education, and my volleyball paid for it. My original plan when I started college was to be an attorney. I didn't think sports would actually become my career.

"I love the fact that you get out of it what you put into it, because no one's going to train harder than me."

ME: So when did you realize, "Hey, wait a minute . . . I can actually earn a living by playing volleyball"?

YOU ASKED . . .

"Were the sacrifices you made for your career worth it for the success you've achieved?" **—FALLON, AGE 18**

HOLLY ANSWERED . . .

"That's funny, because I don't necessarily feel that I made any sacrifices. I worked my butt off, but I know that that's what it takes to succeed. Yes, I have to travel. Yes, I miss people's birthdays and things like that, but it's all part of the process of doing what I want to do to achieve my goals. So I don't feel like I made any sacrifices—I've just worked hard and stayed focused and followed my dreams."

7:00–8:30 A.M.: *Wake up, make breakfast for my husband, and take the kids to school.*

8:30–10:00 A.M.: *Work out at the gym.*

10:00–10:30 A.M.: *Grab a snack!*

10:30–1:00 P.M.: *Volleyball training, comprised of hard drills and repetitive training on the beach with usually three other people or a coach and my partner.*

1:30–4:00 P.M.: *Shower and do other errands, like grocery shopping, picking the kids up from school, dentist appointments . . . whatever I need to do in the afternoon. I use these couple of hours to do my "normal person" stuff— pay bills, clean the house, do laundry, that kind of thing.*

4:00–5:00 P.M.: *Slip in another hour of cardio workout.*

5:30 P.M.: *Shower and make dinner, or get ready to go out . . . whatever is going on that night.*

9:30 P.M.: *I'm physically and mentally exhausted and I'm ready to go to bed.*

HOLLY: I think it was my senior year at UCLA. I had just finished playing as a collegiate player, and I started to train on the beach. I had played beach volleyball my whole life, but never professionally. And I just fell in love with it. I love the fact that you get out of it what you put into it, because no one's going to train harder than me. I studied the game, and as soon as I started playing, I was hooked, and it just took over my life. I loved it. It was something that challenged me in every aspect—physically and mentally.

ME: How sweet is it that what you do for your job is so good for your life?

HOLLY: Yeah, I basically get paid to go to the gym and work out.

THE BREAKDOWN

IN MEETINGS: Rarely

ON THE PHONE: 30 minutes a day

ONLINE: 1 hour a day

SITTING: Never

READING: 30 minutes a day

WORKING SOLO: Almost 2 hours a day

WORKING OUT: All the time

I mean, I don't get paid specifically to do that, but it's a very important part of my job. I'm one of the shorter players out on the tour. I have to be fit, I have to be strong, and I have to make up for those shortcomings in other areas. So staying healthy is very important for me.

ME: So do you have a volleyball "season" or are you training year-round?

HOLLY: Basically April through November we travel internationally or all over the United States almost every weekend. After the first or second weekend in May, I don't think we have a week off until November. It's a full schedule, and it keeps us busy. One of the things that I really appreciate is being home.

ME: How do you deal with traveling so much and still being on top of your game?

HOLLY: It comes with the territory. It's taking care of yourself while traveling, hydrating, eating well, and getting a good

THEN TO NOW

1987: Played first professional beach volleyball tournament and finished in ninth place	1987: Voted NCAA Freshman of the Year at UC Berkeley	1991: Graduated from UCLA	1991: Named Rookie of the Year by the Women's Professional Volleyball Association	1993: First tournament win at the AVP Phoenix Open	1996: Came in fifth at the Atlanta Summer Olympics with partner Nancy Reno

night's sleep. Those are all really important to me. I know I've done the work to train and I'm in shape. I just have to make sure I take care of myself while I'm traveling.

ME: Can you tell me what some of your biggest challenges are?

HOLLY: I think there's obviously pressure to compete. I have to do well to make a living. If I don't do well, I don't win any money and I don't pay the bills. But at the same time, one of the lessons I learned early on is that I can't think about the money while I'm playing the sport that I love . . . I just can't. I remember in my first season, I was playing a game that was for about a thousand dollars, and I was a starving student—a thousand dollars was a lot of money. And I focused on the money and my volleyball went out the window. So that was something I learned early on. I think it's a lot of pressure when you know you have to do well to make a living.

ME: So do you have some way of centering yourself to deal with that pressure?

HOLLY: I know I've prepared the best I can. The rest is mental. It really comes down to being mentally prepared and working

WHY WAIT?

- If you're passionate about a sport, look into athletic scholarships at colleges.
- Coach a youth team in a sport you love.
- Get fit, eat well, and take care of your body!

| 2000: Came in fifth at the Sydney Summer Olympics with partner Misty May | 2004: Won the Bronze Medal at the Athens Summer Olympics with partner Elaine Youngs | 2004: Awarded Outstanding Achievement Award from the AVP | 2004: Set the all-time win record for women's professional beach volleyball tournaments (72 wins!) | 2005: First woman to break the $1 million mark in beach volleyball earnings | 2009: Inducted into the Volleyball Hall of Fame |

together with your partner. I focus on what I've trained myself to do and just allow myself to play the best volleyball I can play.

ME: It seems like there would be a lot of perks to being a professional volleyball player.

HOLLY: Yeah, there are. We get to play in front of a huge crowd of people, and it's a very fun sport. We get to travel all over the world. And then there's competing in the Olympic Games—I don't think anything can compare. And I've been able to do it three times. I've also been able to travel around the world various times and see lots of countries. I've been exposed to all parts of the world, all different cultures, and that's been great. And you get to meet a lot of amazing people.

ME: Is there any specific highlight you want to tell us about?

HOLLY: Getting on the medal stand at the 2004 Olympic Games was amazing for me. I've won seventy-two tournaments in my career, and all of those are superspecial, but to me, being on the Olympic medal stand was number one.

ME: What was it like?

HOLLY: It's a blur. It's something that I dreamed about as an athlete growing up. It was beyond. It was so special because I was up there with, in my opinion, five of the best volleyball players in the world. Two Americans who I really love, my partner who I love, and my two best Brazilian friends in the world. That was the podium. I couldn't have thought of a better podium. Except for us on top. That would have made it better. But otherwise it was a dream come true.

ME: What will you do when you're not able to continue playing volleyball competitively anymore? What's the next step?

HOLLY: There are a couple different directions I can take with my career. I can work for some of my sponsors in player relations.

And I've been in the sport so long that I have TV opportunities to be a commentator. I'd really like to do that, because I'm a credible name and I'm explaining this sport to people who don't know it.* I'd also like to help by working either

WHAT IT TAKES

- A lot of drive
- A willingness to work harder than anyone else
- Natural athletic ability

within the AVP or in some grassroots programs trying to grow the sport and reach out to people who wouldn't normally be exposed to it.

ME: Those sound like pretty great options. What are some of the pros and cons of being a professional volleyball player?

HOLLY: I think that one of the big pros of playing my sport for a living is that I get to stay healthy and fit. A lot of people who work very hard in a career are behind a desk all day working crazy hours, and fitness takes a backseat. But fitness is part of my job—it's part of what I do. On the con side, I'm out in the sun. Skin cancer's a major fear with all of us, and we have to really protect ourselves from the sun. Another challenge that's specific to our sport is the fact that we have to play in a bathing suit, and I think that freaks out 99 percent of the women. I mean, what woman wants to stand in front of ten thousand people in a bikini? That's something that I had to deal with at the beginning. And yeah, we're really fit athletes, but at the same time, we have to feel comfortable in our body. For me it's a machine. I don't think of it as a sexy thing. This is my machine. Some people think the sport takes advantage of us by making us wear bathing suits to give the sport sex appeal, but that's not the case. If I had a choice in what to wear to compete, it

---

* **AUTHOR'S NOTE:** Since the first edition of *In Their Shoes* was published, Holly has retired from competing in the sport. Today she is a regular commentator for the Pac-12 collegiate volleyball!

would be a bathing suit, because it's the most comfortable, you can move the best in it, and it collects the least amount of sand. But I think it's also been a big lesson for me in feeling comfortable in my body.

HOLLY'S ADVICE

- *Don't let anybody set limitations on what you can do. When I first started playing, nobody thought I could do anything on the professional level because I was small and I hadn't made a big name for myself in indoor volleyball. But I believed in myself, I studied the sport, I watched, I trained as hard as I possibly could, and I followed my dreams.*

- *The opportunity to play a professional sport and get paid for it is one that everybody would like to have, so treat it special, respect it, always appreciate your fans, and always appreciate your sponsors who support you and allow you the opportunity to play a sport you love and make a living doing it.*

In the Field

FIVE MORE CAREERS THAT INVOLVE SPORTS

SPORTS AGENT   Just as actors and writers have agents, so do professional athletes. Sports agents work to get the best deals for their clients, whether it be multiyear contracts or hooking them up with sponsors like Nike. They have to be great negotiators and be willing to work long hours, especially when their client's sport is in season.

SPORTS ANNOUNCER   Until recently, sports announcing had been seriously male-dominated, but today you'll find women sitting behind the anchor desk, reporting live from the sidelines, or commentating with a play-by-play. They have to become a sports specialist, tap into their journalism skills, and get comfortable being on the air.

EXERCISE PHYSIOLOGIST   Exercise physiologists specialize in knowing how exercise impacts the way the body functions. Some work in hospitals or rehabilitation centers to promote better fitness and health; others specialize in sports, and work with athletes to help them achieve the best performances they can.

COACH   Coaches are experts in their sports, and they coach athletes and athletic teams. At the school or community level, coaches might be volunteers, while others are former athletes who want to stay involved in their sport and find full-time opportunities at high schools or universities.

REFEREE   Referees enforce the rules, make calls, and assign penalties on questionable plays at sporting events. Women are popping up more and more as referees for women's team sports like basketball, soccer, and volleyball.

YOU NEED TO KNOW ABOUT

The Women's Sports Foundation (www.womenssportsfoundation .org) is a national nonprofit promoting girls and women participating in sports. The website features profiles of top women athletes, information about sports scholarships and grants, and tons more.

For more fitness-related careers, check out the yoga instructor profile on page 362.

JENNI LUKE

Nonprofit Executive Director

Jenni Luke, CEO, Step Up Women's Network

The Facts

WHAT? Nonprofit executive directors, CEOs, or presidents are the top-level execs at not-for-profit organizations, whose primary objective is to promote an issue or cause as opposed to making money.

WHERE? Nonprofits can be found everywhere.

HOW? Many nonprofit directors, like Jenni Luke, previously worked in the corporate world and decided to apply their skills to the world of nonprofit. Others work their way up or move from nonprofit to nonprofit until they reach the pinnacle, or create their own nonprofit organization.

$$$: From $40,000 to $110,000 on average, depending on the size of the organization and previous experience

DRESS CODE? Depends on the nonprofit, but generally business casual

STRESS FACTOR: On a scale of 1 to 10, a 5

step up women's network is a nonprofit membership organization dedicated to igniting women and girls to fulfill their potential. With locations in Los Angeles, Chicago, and New York, SUWN runs after-school and weekend programs that empower girls from under-resourced communities to be confident, college-bound, and career-ready, provides mentorship from career women, and more.

At the helm of this fifteen-year-old organization is Jenni Luke, who has been Step Up's CEO since 2009. Though Jenni didn't start out her career in the world of nonprofit, she knew from a young age that she ultimately wanted to make a difference in the world through her work.

"I remember watching Jesse Jackson's Rainbow Coalition speech at the 1984 Democratic National Convention (yes . . . nerdy kid). He was talking about how we're all the same and it doesn't matter where you're from—it's really about where you go. Something about the way that he worded all of that really hit me. I connected with something that I kind of already knew I cared about, but that really helped bring it to life for me.

"When I can be a fly on the wall and observe the relationships and the connections happening the way we know it does when we trust it, it's just super gratifying."

"The way that I translated that into my career was thinking that law was a great path to make a difference in social justice and equal opportunity. I was really inspired by the civil rights movement, in particular the NAACP, and the whole legal theory as a way to make change. I just thought the whole thing was just so genius."

But as it turns out, though she loved law school and felt that she graduated with a good sense of what her career as a lawyer would be like, law didn't fulfill that need to make a difference for Jenni. "I had what I considered to be a dream job right out of law school, practicing federal plaintiff litigation, and I hated it. I just hated it," she explains.

YOU ASKED . . .

"Do you think the key to success is different for everybody?"

—VIOVIO, AGE 14

JENNI ANSWERED . . .

"No, I actually think it's the same for everybody, but it might look different for everybody. I think that the key is really understanding your own personal 'why.' You know, why are you motivated? Why do you go to work? Why do you want what you want? And that can manifest in any number of different ways, and it can look different throughout your life. But as long as you understand what your touchstone is, you can navigate your life pretty beautifully. It doesn't mean it won't be hard, it's just you'll know you're on track."

"I was like, all I do all day is talk to other lawyers and talk to research librarians and talk to clerks and talk to judges. I don't talk to any people. I'm not engaged, I'm not feeling the end result of it and the impact. That's the way federal work is designed. I knew that in theory, but just being hit with it in practice was really different for me."

After three years practicing law, Jenni decided it wasn't the right fit. "I was devastated," she says. "I'd finished law school at twenty-five, and I only practiced for three years. I had to decide whether to stick with it and push through or if I was going to quit. So I quit. Then I went back to L.A., which is where I'm from, and I thought, 'Well, what does somebody who doesn't want to practice law anymore do with their law degree?' So I went into entertainment and spent five years representing writers and directors for film and television as an agent. That was just a major anomaly, but I learned a lot of great business skills."

After her time working in corporate, Jenni shifted into the nonprofit world, serving as the director of development for the Alliance for Children's Rights and then the ACLU of Southern

California before stepping into the lead position at Step Up in 2009. In her role, Jenni gets to harness all her experience from her past jobs and blend them in a meaningful way for a cause she loves. She spends her time building relationships, fostering sponsorship opportunities, and fund-raising, as well as supporting the work of the organization's staff and volunteers.

"A lot of my job is looking at what's going on in our industry and in the world in general and thinking about where Step Up fits into that picture and what partnerships we might create that make sense for us—corporate, media, community. There's a large universe of potential collaborations, and my job is seeing opportunities and then going out and creating relationships. And some of it is continuing to cultivate and bring existing relationships forward. I do a lot of that all day long.

"The first six weeks of this year were aligned a little bit differently because it was more internal. We hosted our national board retreat, our national staff retreat, and local advisory board retreats in L.A., New York, and Chicago. Getting everyone rowing the boat in the same direction is also a huge part of my job. Then I spent another week representing us at national conferences. So now it's getting back into the day-to-day, which is more of the fund-raising and relationship building and just getting it done now."

I was curious to know what makes someone cut out to run a nonprofit. Jenni's answer? Being good at consensus building and collaboration.

"When you're running

THE BREAKDOWN

IN MEETINGS: 3 hours a day

ON THE PHONE: 1 hour a day

ONLINE: 30 minutes a day

E-MAILING: 3 hours a day

SITTING: 8 hours a day

ENGAGING IN SOCIAL MEDIA: 30 minutes

PUBLIC SPEAKING: 30 minutes

READING: 30 minutes

WORKING SOLO: 2 hours

WHAT IT TAKES

- Being passionate about a particular cause or issue
- Strong organizational and business skills
- Being a good networker and fund-raiser

a nonprofit, it's not just what *you* want, it's about your community. Our goals ladder up to national and international goals for women and girls. I have sixteen full-time staff and twelve part-time staff, thousands of volunteers, fifteen people on our national governing board, and another fifty on our local advisory board. Those women have endless impact on our organization, and they're all volunteers and leaders within this organization. There's just so much ownership that happens in the community, and harnessing that is really the strength of nonprofit. When you run a nonprofit, you've got to have a strong vision and be able to lead through it, but you've got to be open to feedback and including other people's ideas. That's when it really starts to take off."

I could only imagine that there are a lot of upsides to being in Jenni's position, where she gets to spend her time supporting young women. She agreed.

"I really love the times when I get to attend an event that we do with the girls in our after-school programs, especially when it's something where they are connecting with the women that are a part of Step Up. When I can be a fly on the wall and observe the relationships and the connections

THEN TO NOW

1984: Inspired by Jesse Jackson's Rainbow Coalition speech at the Democratic National Convention

1994: Graduated from University of California, San Diego

1998: Graduated from University of Colorado School of Law

1998: Began practicing law in Colorado

WHY WAIT?

- Volunteer with a nonprofit in your community and see if you like the work atmosphere.
- Start your own organization, club, or group focusing on a cause that you're passionate about.

happening the way we know it does when we trust it, it's just super gratifying."

With responsibilities in so many different directions, I was surprised to discover that Jenni seems to have found a good job rhythm that's sustainable for a healthy lifestyle.

"The way I approach my job now is significantly different from how I did it when I started. I try to keep it to about nine thirty a.m. to six thirty p.m. every day. It works for my body. It works for me. It works for my brain capacity. With that said, I travel quite a bit, and so the energy that goes into travel and then the energy that goes into normalizing after travel definitely takes a hit in terms of how I organize my time," she explains.

I could tell from talking to Jenni that she is in a true place of "knowing" that she's in the right spot and career. But though she spent time in different careers before landing where she is today, she doesn't see any of these as a misstep. In fact, she feels that that experience, coupled with continuing to explore what ultimately fulfilled her, was the key to her journey.

| 2001: Literary agent for Broder Webb Chervin Silbermann Agency | 2005: Director of Development, the Alliance for Children's Rights | 2008: Director of Development, ACLU of Southern California | 2009: Chief Executive Officer, Step Up Women's Network |

"My personal why was really social justice, and I didn't understand that because I got caught up in what being a lawyer was. I made a choice based on that external identity versus the internal touchstone. Once I finally got back to what the internal touchstone was, it's been much smoother sailing, because I'm not fighting myself. I might be fighting some fears and lack of confidence and a lack of a skill set, and all those things, they can be remedied. What can't be remedied is not really understanding why you're doing it in the first place."

JENNI'S CAREER ADVICE

Focus on why you are interested in what you want to do, not what it looks like. I'm interested in social justice and equal opportunity and I thought that had to look like being a lawyer. But now I'm doing it as the CEO of a nonprofit with a mission squarely in the equal opportunity arena.

In the Field

FIVE MORE CAREERS WORKING AT A NONPROFIT ORGANIZATION

GRANT WRITER   The bulk of the income for nonprofits comes from grants made by foundations or corporations, but applying for and getting this money is a lot of work, including filling out tons of paperwork and extensive application forms. Grant writers specialize in applying for these grants and bringing in money for nonprofits.

COMMUNICATIONS MANAGER   How a nonprofit organization is perceived by the outside world directly relates to how willing people are to open their wallets to make donations. Communications managers are the public face of nonprofits, and they write and produce all communications material for the press as well as the general public.

OFFICE ADMINISTRATOR   Office administrators keep everything in the office flowing smoothly. They coordinate staff events, help hire new employees and get them set up, manage the office space, and make sure office supplies are in stock. In a nonprofit, office administrators play a large role because staffing is generally lean.

PLANNED GIVING OFFICER   Planned giving officers help individuals make a legal plan for donating part of their estate to an organization. For example, a wealthy woman who supports the Make-A-Wish Foundation will work with a planned giving officer to make sure part of her estate goes to the foundation after her death.

PROGRAM OFFICER   Nonprofit organizations generally have a mission, like helping underprivileged kids, or in the case of Step Up, "igniting women and girls to fulfill their potential." Program officers run the programs that the nonprofit offers, such as organizing cool activities at an after-school program for unprivileged kids.

YOU NEED TO KNOW ABOUT

The *Chronicle of Philanthropy* is the newspaper for nonprofits. It offers information on the nonprofit sector through articles and online resources, including a job board, info about conferences and events, and updates on issues affecting nonprofit organizations. Visit the paper online at www.philanthropy.com.

For more careers as an executive, check out business executive Claudia Poccia's profile on page 389.

JUNE AMBROSE

Stylist

*June Ambrose,
Celebrity Fashion
Stylist to the Stars*

The Facts

WHAT? Fashion stylists get paid to make other people look great. They work with clients to help them create "looks" for themselves, whether it is a musician doing a music video or a celeb who'll be walking the red carpet. Other fashion stylists might work on fashion shoots for department stores or ad agencies.

WHERE? Stylists can live and work anywhere, but high-profile stylists to the stars like June have to live where the action is—L.A. or New York.

HOW? Most stylists have a background in fashion and design, but it's not necessary to break into the field. What is necessary is tenacity, being extremely personable, and having an amazing sense of fashion and great networking skills.

$$$: This is a make-it-or-break-it industry, and stylists can earn as little as $5,000 or as much as $500,000 a year or more.

DRESS CODE? Cool, hip, and fashionable

STRESS FACTOR: On a scale of 1 to 10, an 8

if this book had been written twenty-five years ago, there wouldn't be a profile of a stylist because the career hadn't even been invented yet. You could say that June Ambrose is somewhat of a pioneer in the world of styling, which is a career built around helping celebrities, musicians, and other high-profile clients create their image. June was at the forefront of the field, marrying the worlds of music and style together in the early 1990s, when Sean "Diddy" Combs was first getting his start.

Though she landed an amazing job in the world of investment banking fresh out of high school, June was miserable in the corporate environment and wanted to work in a more creative field. So she quit the firm

"Who you are as a person will separate you and individualize you in this industry that's so oversaturated."

and took an internship at Uptown/MCA Records, a hip urban record label that was giving birth to all kinds of new musical talent, including Mary J. Blige. As June describes it, it was the kind of environment where if you were in the right place at the right time, you were going to get big opportunities. And she did. June tells how she broke into the world of styling.

"One day a manager for an artist walked into Uptown and said he was looking for a stylist. At the time, the fashion industry hadn't yet realized that music was a great platform to market and brand their clothing, so there weren't people "styling" musicians . . . artists kind of dressed themselves. Anyway, he said he needed a stylist, and I thought to myself, 'Oh, what's a *stylist*?' This manager knew that I was really fresh and young and he asked me if I had a 'book.' And I said, 'Of course I do, but it's at home, you know, I wasn't expecting to meet anyone today.' I was totally bluffing. It was a Friday, and he said he wanted to see my portfolio on Monday.

"I went home and called my friends and put clothes together, took pictures of my friends that I developed at a one-hour photolab, and put them in a photo album. When I

THE BREAKDOWN

IN MEETINGS: 2 hours a day

ON THE PHONE: All the time

ONLINE: All the time (on
BlackBerry)

STANDING: More than sitting

READING: 2 hours a day

WORKING SOLO: Half the time

showed it to the manager that Monday, he knew that I had thrown it together over the weekend, but he was impressed by the fact that I was so superenthusiastic about it, and he said, 'I'll give you a try.'

"I went to the shoot for the artist, and the publicist had said they wanted three different looks, so I showed up with three outfits. And he said to me, 'Is this a joke? You can't just come here with three options.' And I was like, 'How am I supposed to have options?' And he said, 'Well, girlie, figure it out. You got the job, now figure it out.'

"And I did. I found out about fashion showrooms, researched the market, started looking at movies differently,

YOU ASKED . . .

"What mistakes did you make along the way and how did you fix them?" —ASIA, AGE 14

JUNE ANSWERED . . .

"Not managing my money when I first started out was one of my biggest mistakes. When I was younger, my credit got so bad that they shut me down and I couldn't even access my account. I was a wreck. But I learned enough to get a business manager who planned my life out for me, who set up my retirement funds, who made sure that every investment I made was solid, so if I broke my leg one day and couldn't do what I did, I had a way to sustain and survive. Another mistake I've made in the past is being afraid of rejection. . . . I think being afraid has held me back in some situations. But it's like being afraid to swim—you just have to jump into the water that first time."

got every costume designer's books, read books on fabric and design and the technical trade, and I just soaked in everything there was to know about fashion and style," she explains.

In 1994 June took her business to the next level by opening her own styling company and management agency, the Mode Squad.

"I knew if I was going to excite my clients, I had to look the part and I had to reinvent myself and glamorize the work I was doing. At the time, it was this kind of grungy-schleppy job, picking up clothes and dragging them across the street, tons of hanger marks on the hands, cuts, scrapes, sleepless nights, no office, finding places to do fittings with the clients . . . it was tough. So I decided that I was going to start my own business and get my own office," says June.

The gamble definitely paid off. Through the Mode Squad, June styled a ton of music videos for big-name talent like Missy Elliott, Mary K. Blige, Jay-Z and Pharrell, Busta Rhymes, Diddy, Macy Gray, and Mariah Carey. She's also styled album covers, designed outfits for television appearances for celebs like Kim Cattrall and Kelly Ripa, and styled a slew of high-profile commercials.

And while there are now more stylists working in the industry, including some former employees whom she trained along the way, June has worked hard to build herself as a "brand," referring to herself as an "architect of style." As she says, "Who you are as a person will separate you and individualize you

WHY WAIT?
- Get the fashion mags and study them like they're homework!
- Follow Fashion Week in New York and watch *Project Runway* on Lifetime.
- Take a class on how to sketch and design clothes and start keeping your own design notebook.

in this industry that's so oversaturated. For me, it was about branding. I thought about the branding of June Ambrose from a very early time in my career."

Her vision has certainly paid off. Today June is arguably the most recognized fashion stylist in Hollywood. She's become a published author, penning the book *Effortless Style* in 2006, and more recently has become a fashion maven for reality television, working as the on-air stylist for *The X Factor*, guest judging on *Project Runway*, and even starring in her own reality show for VH-1, *Styled by June*.

I asked June to walk me through the process of how she works, from the moment a new client picks up the phone to hire her through the styling for an event. Here's how June described her job:

WHAT JUNE DOES AS A STYLIST

When a new client calls me, whether it's a celebrity client or a corporate client, they'll usually ask to see a reel or portfolio of my work. My reel is divided into categories, like commercial work, advertising work, music video stuff, and so on. Some new clients want to see my reel, and some people don't ask to see my book at all—I'm known by reputation.

Let's say Gwyneth Paltrow is a client, and say she's four months pregnant and has a premiere to go to and needs a stylist. I'll get a call asking if I can send over a reel so Gwyn can approve it. So Gwyneth looks at it, she likes it, and then

THEN TO NOW

Got a job at an investment banking firm fresh out of high school	1990: Landed an internship at Uptown/ MCA Records in New York	Styled her first video for artist MC Quashan	1996: Styled Backstreet Boys European tour	1999: Styled Diddy as cohost of the VH1/Vogue Fashion Awards

I go over and meet with her to do an interview profile. Because she's a new client, I need to know her likes, dislikes, colors, body silhouettes, complete measurements, what she doesn't like, what works for her body . . . the whole bit. If I'm styling for a TV event, my dynamic is a little different in terms of colors and patterns and textures. So I'll want to know more about the event—if it's a red carpet event, where she's going, what time of day it's taking place, what the weather will be like, and why she's going.

Then I'll have a fitting with her and we'll make "selects." We might nail down the accessories at the fitting or we might not. When I'm styling for an event, I like to have a day to fit and a day to troubleshoot before the event itself.

And that's it. When the event's over, I wrap my job up, get everything back to the showroom, figure out what was spent, tally up any other expenses, anything that was kept, and we reconcile the monies.

WHAT IT TAKES
- A lot of moxie
- Strong networking skills
- A great sense of style

Meetings with big celebs, high fashion, red carpet affairs . . . I asked June if she still got a thrill out of meeting celebs and

2003: Styled Gap commercial featuring Madonna and Missy Elliott

2004: Styled album cover for *American Idol* winner Ruben Studdard

2006: Book *Effortless Style* is published

2011: Began stint as on-air stylist for *The X Factor*

2012: *Styled by June* began airing on VH-1

being a part of that whole world. Her answer surprised me.

"In terms of the whole celebrity thing, it's never been exciting to me to meet them. If you're going to be in this industry, you're not excited about that part of it, because my approach is that I'm an artist too, and these are my peers or this is my client. So for me to be enamored just defeats the purpose. Because they're not looking for me to be that—that's what their fans are for. I'm the authority. So in order for me to be the authority and be respected, I go in with the attitude that I'm on the same level. When you're working with a client, they don't want to feel like they're working. They don't want to feel like they have to sign your T-shirt or the back of your hand. They want to feel like they're hanging out with one of their own and that you're getting a job done," says June.

JUNE'S WORDS OF WISDOM

- *Think about your career like it's the Olympics. You have your gold medal, your silver, and your bronze. Are you going to be a gold medalist? Silver? Or a bronze? I want to be a gold medalist. And that's my fight.*

- *Do an internship that will ultimately lead you into the profession that you want to be doing. Figure out what area you want to go into and connect yourself with someone who can teach you the nature of that particular business.*

- *Humbly ask and you will humbly receive. If you wear your humility on your sleeve and approach people to ask for what you want, I guarantee you that the person will receive you.*

FIVE MORE CAREERS IN THE FASHION INDUSTRY

FASHION DESIGNER Fashion designers start new trends and create the designs that ultimately end up on display everywhere from Saks to the Gap. They not only have to love fashion, but they must also know how to sew, understand textiles and fabrics, and have the skill to put garments together.

MODEL Models are everywhere—on TV commercials, in the pages of magazines, on billboards, on the packaging of products. Some do magazine and print ads exclusively, while others do runway work. Since the work is freelance, it can be irregular and the hours long, sometimes in uncomfortable work environments.

HANDBAG MAKER If accessories make the outfit, where would we be without handbag makers, who design everything from little cocktail clutches to beach bags? Handbag makers have a love of design, patterns, textiles, and sewing, and they sell their bags in their own boutiques or through larger stores like Nordstrom and Macy's.

FASHION EDITOR Fashion editors, or market editors, work at fashion magazines like *Cosmopolitan* and *Marie Claire*, where they create the fashion spreads that we flip through each month. To stay in the loop, they attend fashion shows, sample sales, and designer parties.

FASHION PHOTOGRAPHER There's more to photographing fashion spreads than snapping photos. Fashion photographers also handle all the logistics of a shoot—getting hair and makeup people on board, scouting locations, setting up lighting, and dealing with clients.

YOU NEED TO KNOW ABOUT

The Fashion Institute of Technology, otherwise known as FIT, is the number one school for anyone interested in fashion design and styling. Check out their website for information about admissions and their program at www.fitnyc.edu. If you live in the New York City area, you can even enroll in summer classes at FIT as a middle school or high school student!

KELLY McCARTHY FITZGERALD

Video Game Programmer

The Facts

Kelly McCarthy Fitzgerald, Video Game Programmer

WHAT? Video game programmers write or "code" the computer language that makes computer games run on a computer.

WHERE? Programmers usually work for game production companies, most of which are scattered throughout California, although programmers and testers can work as freelancers anywhere in the country.

HOW? Game programmers need a background in computer science and must be experts at programming the computer language of games, C++.

$$$: An average of $85,000 for someone with a few years' experience to more than $200,000, depending on the level and the product

DRESS CODE? T-shirt and jeans . . . supercasual

STRESS FACTOR: On a scale of 1 to 10, between a 2 and 3 when not on a deadline and a 9 and 10 during crunch times

i was really curious to take a peek at the life of a video game programmer from a woman's point of view and find out what goes on behind the scenes. I got in touch with Kelly McCarthy Fitzgerald, who programs computer games in Los Angeles. To get a real sense of what her days are like, Kelly kept a diary for us. Here's what she wrote about:

KELLY'S TYPICAL DAY

Today I got to work around ten a.m. and sat down in the office that I share with my lead programmer. Our studio has both cubicles and offices, with lots of windows that let in the sunshine. All around me is concept art for our game projects hanging around the public spaces for everyone to see. The atmosphere is relaxed and casual, and people dress in jeans and T-shirts and have toys and games in their offices.

"It does take a certain type of person to fit into this industry, but that type has nothing to do with being male or female."

The first thing I did at work this morning was start up my e-mail program and other computer programs that I use for my job, like Visual Studio. Then I read my e-mails, checked

YOU ASKED . . .

"What is the most difficult decision you've had to make to get where you are?" —ELISA, AGE 13

KELLY ANSWERED . . .

"The most difficult decision I had to make was at the end of my first year in college, when I still hadn't decided what I wanted to study. I had explored lots of other subjects when computer science came to mind. It sounded interesting to me, but I was afraid I would stand out and feel uncomfortable. I was really intimidated, but I gathered up my courage and attended a class one day, and found that it wasn't so bad and I really enjoyed it. Three years later I had a degree and a great job!"

out a few new websites, and perused new messages on our developer message boards to see if there were any issues that concerned anything I might be working on.

Next I buckled down to work so I could get stuff done before lunch. Today I was debugging a program I was working on, which involves analyzing what our code is doing to figure out where it might be going wrong.

THE BREAKDOWN

IN MEETINGS: 1 hour a day

ON THE PHONE: Never

ONLINE: 1–2 hours a day

SITTING: 8–10 hours a day

READING, DESIGNING, AND WRITING CODE: 8–10 hours a day

WORKING SOLO: 6–8 hours a day

When I'm debugging things, I can watch as the computer runs the game code, and stop it at any point to run it step by step to closely examine what's happening and change variables to make the game behave differently. Sometimes the problem I'm looking at is in code that I've written myself, but other times it's someone else's, which is even more challenging, because I have to try to understand what the other programmer was trying to do. Other mornings I might be helping to solve some technical issues that the designers and artists are running into or attending a project planning meeting with members of my team. Like most mornings, today there was a lot of running around between people's cubicles and offices, asking questions and viewing each other's work. Some people at work (including me!) even ride Razor scooters around the office to get from place to place quickly.

After lunch I headed back to the office, where I popped on my headphones and listened to some music. Electronic music is good for me to listen to when I'm in the zone—when

WHY WAIT?

- Start learning to program now! Start a blog or Web page and experiment coding with HTML.

- Play video games and take note of what goes into them from a design perspective.

- Try to get a position as a game tester—a lot of gaming companies hire teens for short-term testing gigs, and it's a good way to learn about the game industry environment and make contacts.

I have a plan mapped out and I know everything I need to do. It helps me to just focus and do it. Sometimes when I'm stressed out and under pressure, I'll listen to ambient music like Brian Eno or classical, which helps me calm down.

Today I needed to get down to some serious coding, which is basically writing the language of the game. Usually I come up with a plan for how my new code is going to work, and then I'll start building it, piece by piece, testing it along the way to make sure it's doing what I want. I'll end up running the game hundreds of times every week just to test it. Once I have the basics running, I'll let the designers try out what I have so far, and we'll refine the specification. We'll keep working until we get the right results.

I needed a caffeine break in the middle of the afternoon to give me a little push to get it done. I like to get up and stretch a few times during the day anyway and walk around to look out the window so my eyes can focus far away for a while. In general, though, I do okay sitting for most of the day. Our company gives us nice chairs that support us well, although a few years ago I did start having pain in my

WHAT IT TAKES

- Attention to detail
- Stamina
- The ability to sit and stare at a computer screen for long periods of time

wrists from typing all the time. But that went away when I started using an ergonomic keyboard.

Not all of my time is spent working alone in a room writing code by myself, though. As part of my job, I'm really involved in the whole creative process of game developing. That means I get to work with artists, animators, and designers as we work toward one huge creative goal.

Today I worked until seven p.m., which is pretty typical. Sometimes I'm under deadlines that require me to stay later to wrap things up. I personally prefer to try to come in early when I have a lot to do instead of saving it until the late hours of the night. I play games at night sometimes—tonight I played Kingdom Hearts 2.

While creating fun games is really cool, the reality of our business is that we're building a product for our publisher. They shell out the millions of dollars it takes to make a game, and our company commits to making it for them. Since we're essentially spending their money, they have a lot of control over what we do, and we have to meet our deadlines to deliver what they expect. And since each new game is expected to be bigger and better than the last, we are always having to find solutions to new problems. We need to meet our goals as a team, so if someone hits a roadblock, it becomes everyone's problem and we all band together to solve it. I find this very satisfying.

PAYING YOUR DUES

To start out, you'll have to land a job as an entry-level programmer, where you'll be working on small parts of the bigger game while you're learning the basics. Other entry-level positions include intern programmer, junior programmer, and game tester. Kelly, for example, interned during college at two different companies: Sunsoft of America and Black Ops Entertainment.

While it's true that women are still the minority in the game industry, it's not as bad as people think. It does take a certain type of person to fit into this industry, but that type has nothing to do with being male or female. It has more to do with possessing the knowledge, attitude, energy, and passion it takes to master the skills we use every day. It may be true that women have to prove themselves more than men do—you'll be under the spotlight and get lots of attention and people will be curious to see how you perform. As long as you can do your job, then you have nothing to worry about. The people I've worked with in the game industry are some of the most fun, interesting people I've ever met. We're smart, we're creative, and we're highly observant of the world around us. And most of us are still kids at heart.

In the Field

FIVE MORE CAREERS IN COMPUTER TECHNOLOGY

COMPUTER SUPPORT SPECIALIST Just about everyone who uses computers has technical problems at some point. Computer support specialists might work for companies like Apple or Dell and handle customer service issues, or act as in-house company support.

DATABASE ADMINISTRATOR Most companies collect electronic data, such as customer and inventory information, and keeping this data organized, secure, and accessible to the right people is the job of database administrators. They set up and design the database, maintain it, and back up information as needed.

COMPUTER SOFTWARE ENGINEER Every program on your computer, from your e-mail to your screensaver, was designed by a computer software engineer. They figure out what a new

> ## KELLY'S ADVICE
>
> *You need to stay curious and keep actively learning every day. No book, school, or person will ever teach you everything you need to know. Ask questions, follow by example, and find your own solutions to problems.*

software needs to do, and then design, code, and test the program.

NETWORK SPECIALIST Every time you connect to Wi-Fi, you've hooked into a computer network. Just about every company has a network powered by a main computer system and network specialists do everything from set-up to trouble-shooting.

IT PROJECT MANAGER If Internet technology (IT) firms were like movie studios, IT project managers would be the equivalent of producers. Project managers oversee the creation of IT systems for clients, managing the client relationship and handling the budget, schedule, staffing, quality control, and security.

YOU NEED TO KNOW ABOUT

Women in Games International was founded in 2005 to unite women around the world involved in the game industry. Sign up to receive their e-newsletter at www.womeningamesinternational.org and learn about their annual conference.

CINDY GUAGENTI

Publicist

Cindy Guagenti,
Publicist, BWR Public
Relations

The Facts

WHAT? A publicist creates and manages publicity for people like celebrities, musicians, or sports figures, or for events, like movie releases or concerts.

WHERE? Those who work with celebrities or for movie studios or TV networks are based in L.A. and New York. Some publicists work for big PR (public relations) agencies, while others might work in-house for a company or be self-employed, working exclusively with one or two big clients.

HOW? There is no one set path to becoming a publicist, although many publicists major in public relations or communications in college. Most start out as assistants or in the mailroom at a big firm and work their way up.

$$$: Average salary is $70,000, but depends on industry and location

DRESS CODE? Business to business casual

STRESS FACTOR: On a scale of 1 to 10, between an 8 and a 9

if you're a fan of celebrity mags like *Us Weekly*, then you're already very familiar with Cindy Guagenti's world. Cindy is a big-time publicist in Hollywood, and over the years has worked with clients such as Brad Pitt, Leonardo DiCaprio, Bradley Cooper, Sarah Jessica Parker, Adam Sandler, Christina Aguilera, Benicio Del Toro, and Ben Kingsley. If there's a rumor going around town about one of her clients, Cindy sets the press straight or provides a statement on her client's behalf. And there's so much more to what Cindy does, so let's get the scoop straight from the source.

ME: What does being a publicist mean?

CINDY: As a publicist, I create campaigns for my clients to publicize their projects, whether it be a TV show, a movie, or a record. That might involve things like setting up photo sessions, talking to magazines, conferring with the magazine on who the writers and photographers are, what the story is about, whether it's a "cover story," and so on. In a bigger-picture sense, we strategically plan out a client's long-term career, whether it's booking talk shows, handling personal appearances, travel, airline, hair, makeup, clothes. . . . We're involved in all facets of creating and finessing our clients' public image.

"From the outside it seems like a lot of fun, but it's a lot of work and it's really high pressure because you have a lot of people to answer to."

ME: How did you get into publicity?

CINDY: I fell into it. I was one of those people who had no idea what I wanted to do. At the time, people I knew from high school were working in the mailroom of a record company, so after two years of junior college I applied and ended up working for the president and the VP of legal affairs who, on the side, was also advising John Lennon. I built a lot of relationships and moved around in different jobs learning different sides of the business, from PR and sales to product management and

YOU ASKED . . .

"What did you do to get the life you have today?"

—WHITNEY, AGE 13

CINDY ANSWERED . . .

"I worked hard, and sometimes it's hard to have relationships with people, with men, because you're traveling so much and you're out of town. And because you're working with high-profile celebrities, sometimes people don't think they're good enough, you know what I mean? It's never really said, but I think that's what they think. Lastly, I take my job seriously, but I also always try to have a sense of humor about everything."

publicity. I ended up getting an offer at a large publicity firm as a publicist's assistant, and grew into junior publicity work. Eventually I ended up at the company I'm at now, and I've been here twenty-five years.

ME: Wow . . . twenty-five years. So you clearly love what you're doing.

CINDY: The glamour side of it really doesn't faze me anymore because I'm kind of used to it, but there are a lot of perks: parties, meeting people, free stuff by virtue of who you represent. But my greatest satisfaction is starting with someone new and growing with them and their career. For example, Adam Sandler became a client when he was in his first *SNL* movie. When we started talking to Brad Pitt, he was on a TV show for FOX, before his break in *Thelma & Louise*. I did Benicio Del Toro's Oscar campaign for *Traffic*, which was cool because he'd never really done any press before. I launched

THE BREAKDOWN

IN MEETINGS: 1 hour a day

ON THE PHONE: 6 hours a day

ONLINE: 5 hours a day

SITTING: Half the day

READING: 1 hour a day

PAYING YOUR DUES

Most future publicists start off as assistants or even in the mailroom, and they move up by working hard and showing lots of drive. Entry-level publicists will do things like answer phones, update schedules, book meetings, and other assistant duties.

Sarah Jessica Parker on *Sex and the City* back when not many people even had HBO. There are so many examples of stuff like that.

ME: It really does seem glamorous and exciting, especially the way publicists are portrayed in films and TV. Are we seeing the whole picture?

CINDY: From the outside it seems like a lot of fun, but it's a lot of work and it's really high pressure because you have a lot of people to answer to. It's a lot of strategy and a lot of planning and you don't see that side on TV. Also, unlike managers and agents, where clients pay them on commission, with publicists, our clients pay us a monthly fee, so we're always on the line. It's a tough job, but it's a great job.

ME: What are some of the biggest challenges of your work?

CINDY: The hours. When you reach the level I'm at, you're on call twenty-four hours a day, especially with BlackBerries and cell phones. When I started in this business we didn't have those. Now we're reachable all the time. And in this work we have to do press things on the weekends and a lot of late nights—premieres, parties, a lot of events that you have to be at. And it's fun on some level, but it's not a party—it's work. People look at what we do and think it's cool that we get to go to the Oscars or this or that premiere. But what they don't realize is that when we're there, we're standing in a little area where they make the publicists stand. Sometimes we don't

WHAT IT TAKES

- Being very professional and trustworthy
- Handling very stressful situations with style
- Working around the clock

have shade or it's raining and we get yelled at by the police and the fire department to get back. On top of that, you have to stand on your feet all night running around—it's work.

ME: Besides being on hand at premieres and things, could you give us an idea about the tasks you might do? Is it a lot of phone work? Juggling a million things at once? Traveling?

CINDY: It's all of that. You're constantly on the phone talking to studios, TV networks, your clients, their managers, their agents, their lawyers, the press, the hair people, the agencies, the magazines, the photo editor. For one movie launch you might have to talk to many different people at the studio—one for travel, one for a press junket, one for a premiere, one to get you money for a stylist for a magazine shoot. It's a lot of phone work. It's almost like sales—you're really selling your client, especially if you're starting out with somebody new. But you're also finessing a campaign. When you're working with a major star, it's all about their image, like what magazine covers make sense for what the movie is and making sure it's the right photographer and writer and you're putting them on the right shows. For instance, if you have somebody in a comedy, you might not want them to do

THEN TO NOW

| Attended two years of junior college | Got internship as assistant at PMK Public Relations, Los Angeles, CA | Worked at Andrea Jaffe, Inc., Los Angeles, CA |

a very serious prime-time interview. So you have to really tailor
each campaign to the client and the project.

ME: It sounds like there needs to be a lot of trust between you
and your clients.

CINDY: I just love being with somebody for a long, long time
because you end up knowing what they want to do, and you
know what they did for the last movie, what talk show they did.
You know, you become friends with them on a business level,
too. You end up hanging out a lot.

ME: What's your travel like? Are you jet-setting around?

CINDY: I've tried to cut down, but I've traveled sometimes
three weeks at a time on big international press tours. Right
now it's closer to once a month. I always try to fly when I'm supposed to be sleeping, so I don't waste time. Some people do
get private jets, but that's really high, high-profile people and
that's mostly because they can't go through airports. Plus you

WHY WAIT?

- Write a press release about an upcoming event at your school
  and try "pitching" it to a local newspaper to see if they'll write
  an article about it.

- Read the entertainment news and pay attention to how movie
  promotion campaigns work.

Joined Ryder Public
Relations,
Los Angeles, CA

1989: Ryder Public
Relations merged with
Baker/Winokur

1989: Began career as
publicist for BWR

can get in and out of anywhere really fast, especially if you're going city to city.

ME: Is there a lot of pressure in your job, knowing that in many ways you're responsible for a celebrity's public image?

CINDY: You're part of a team—there's the actor, there's the agent, and there's you. You're all working toward the same goals . . . you just have different roles. It's a very specialized job, and there's a real learning process. A lot of young girls start out and they just can't know what I know. That's why at a bigger company like ours, you'll usually start out as an assistant and you graduate to a junior publicist and then you're a publicist. By the time you're at that level, you've really learned the proper way to do the job.

ME: So paying your dues is really important.

CINDY: I believe so. I'm sure there are lots of people who are on a fast track, but I really think you have to pay your dues.

ME: Publicity as a career must attract people who think they'll get to hang out with celebs all day.

CINDY: Yeah, but you really can't be starstruck and do this job.

ME: Is there anything else you'd like to add?

CINDY: Publicity is a great job for somebody who has the right intentions and who's willing to put in the work. When I hire an assistant, she works long hours. My assistant gets there at nine and doesn't leave sometimes until seven thirty at night. She doesn't go to lunch. And she's done it for a while, too. You have to really, really, really want to do it. It's hard work, and the pay isn't great at the beginning at all, but if you really want to do it, then the rewards at the end of the day are great.

INTERESTED IN BEING A PUBLICIST?
HERE'S CINDY'S ADVICE

- *Become a good writer—it's really important in this line of work.*
- *Get an internship at a PR firm—it gives you a great feel for the job.*
- *Get involved in the community that you want to work with as much as you can. If you want to work with actors, take a drama class so you can understand better what an actor goes through.*

In the Field

FIVE MORE CAREERS IN PUBLICITY

PRESS OFFICER Press officers are often the public face of a company or organization. Their primary role is to positively shape an organization's public image in the media, and they may act as companys' spokespeople at press conferences and in interviews.

BOOK PUBLICIST Most book publishers have an in-house publicity department that is responsible for helping promote its books and authors. Book publicists might do things like write up and send out press releases to the media, arrange interviews, and come up with creative promotional campaigns, all with a goal of selling more books.

TECH PUBLICIST As the tech industry continues to grow, so does the need for publicists with technical background and experience. Tech publicists forge relationships with key players in media, including bloggers and journalists who regularly cover tech news, to maximize PR opportunities for the businesses they represent.

DIRECTOR OF TALENT RELATIONS Because of the high-profile nature of the entertainment industry, TV networks and movie studios are highly involved in managing the relationship among talent, celebrities, and the media. A director of talent relations works closely with publicity and marketing departments, as well as liaising with the public and media.

FILM PUBLICIST A film publicist works with film distributors to figure out how to best position ads and promotional efforts to not only get as many viewers into the theaters as possible, but to ensure that films are considered for awards like the Golden Globes and the Oscars.

YOU NEED TO KNOW ABOUT

The Public Relations Society of America (www.prsa.org) is the hub for public relations professionals in the United States, and the website has information about mentorships available to students.

For more on careers in Hollywood, check out the talent agent profile on page 378, the actor profile on page 433, and the movie studio executive profile on page 65.

lunch break

PAYING YOUR DUES

Many of the women I interviewed for this book mentioned how a lot of today's recent grads enter the workforce hoping, and sometimes expecting, to jump right into a big job, complete with high responsibility and a fat paycheck. They get the sense that many younger people today aren't as willing to "pay their dues."

Depending on the career you're looking to break into, paying your dues can be humbling, and yes, there can be all kinds of grunt work involved, like fetching coffee, typing up people's notes, standing over the photocopy machine for hours, and running personal errands. What makes it an even tougher pill to swallow is that many recent grads are entering the workforce more prepared than ever, because of internships and real-life work experience.

I know all about being impatient. . . . It used to be my middle name. But as I've gone through my career and paid lots of dues along the way, I can look back and see that those early, less-than-glamorous job experiences went a long way in shaping me into the person I am now.

Here are some things to keep in mind when it comes to paying your dues:

- On-the-job experience can't be beaten when it comes to learning everyday "people skills," workplace etiquette, and the how-to's for handling office politics.

- People who are promoted too quickly run the risk of not having a strong enough foundation on which to build their career.

- Being eager to do your job and showing your bosses that no task is too menial for you will go a long way toward showing people you're a go-getter. Hard work and a great attitude don't go unnoticed, so be patient—it will pay off in the long run.

HEATHER JOHNSTON

Architect

The Facts

WHAT? Architects design and plan the structure for new or remodeled buildings—anything from tiny cottages to hundred-story skyscrapers. They identify their clients' needs, come up with designs, and oversee construction through completion.

WHERE? You'll find architects just about everywhere in the country, working for large architectural firms, boutique firms, or themselves.

Heather Johnston, Principal, PLACE Architects, PLLC

HOW? Architects must have a degree from a special five-year bachelor's program in architecture or a four-year degree coupled with a master's in architecture. After graduation, they must do a formal three-year paid internship at an architectural firm before taking the Architect Registration Examination (ARE) and becoming licensed.

$$$: An average salary of $75,000

DRESS CODE? Business casual at most companies, dressier at the bigger firms

STRESS FACTOR: On a scale of 1 to 10, a 6

to find out what goes on in the world of architecture, I interviewed Heather Johnston, founder and principal of Vancouver architecture firm PLACE Architects. Heather gave me the inside scoop on her career, including busting one of the more prominent myths about architecture right away—that architects have to be great at math. Here's what Heather had to say about the "math myth" and some other misconceptions about architects.

"The whole notion that you have to be really, really good at math just isn't true. Sure, you have to do some math, but it's applied math. It's the fun stuff, it's geometry and spaces . . . it's not so scary. So I would encourage girls to be bold about that. And structural math? If you have the right attitude, it's really, really cool. I mean, in my structures class we did things like make bridges out of straws. How fun is that?

"I love being able to hang out with really smart people and hold my own."

"Another myth is that it's really glamorous and you get to jet all over the world and get paid boatloads of money. We don't. We try to dress like we do because we want people with boatloads of money to hire us. It's actually challenging—we have to have a nice enough car so the client isn't offended, but not too nice a car so they think you're charging them too much. It might seem really glamorous from the outside, but it's just not.

"The last myth is this whole idea that an architect is like an artist in a tower working alone—that we just imagine something and then it's built. It actually takes a lot of work and a lot of coordination with consultants, like mechanical and electrical engineers, to create something. There's a lot of teamwork, because we all have good ideas on our own, but when you put them together, sometimes unexpected things happen," she explained.

Heather's architecture firm, PLACE, takes on a mix of commercial, residential, and public work. At any given time they might be juggling a couple of jobs like building a new house, designing public housing, or even remodeling a garage to make it an office building. Since Heather runs the show, she oversees a staff of architects, but she is still very hands-on in most phases of a project.

"I don't do a lot of drawing anymore, maybe 10 percent or 20 percent of my time is spent drawing. Other architects here might be doing 80 percent drawing, and only ten percent management and ten percent on the phone and working things out on an Excel spreadsheet," she says. Most of the drawing Heather refers to is actually work done on a computer, although the architects still do some actual sketching at PLACE.

To get a real sense of what an architect does, I asked Heather to walk me through the whole process, from the moment a phone call comes in from a prospective client through completion of a project.

AN ARCHITECTURAL PROJECT FROM START TO FINISH

When a new client calls up and says something like "I want to put a second story on my house," the first thing I do is talk to them on the phone and make sure they have realistic expectations of what it might cost and that the job is an appropriate thing for our firm to even consider. If it is, I'll go out and meet with the client. That part is always really fun, because I'll go out with my portfolio, and we'll sit down and talk about their dream and what they have in mind, and we'll look at the house and take a bunch of pictures. Then I'll show them my portfolio and walk them through the five phases of an architecture project. If they choose to hire us, we would go through these steps to build their second story:

1. PREDESIGN is the first phase. When we get back from the interview, we'll look up the house on the building department's website and make sure that we know its exact dimensions, what the setbacks are, and what the building rules are. Also as part of predesign, we'll write a "program," which is a list of what the client is looking for, and we'll measure their house and make sure we have correct drawings to start from. Sometimes we gather conceptual information too, like if the people are interested in poetry or eclectic art or they like horses, or whatever it is. It's a lot of information gathering.

WHY WAIT?

- See if you can get an administrative internship with an architectural firm while you're still in high school or college.
- Get to know great spaces inside and out by volunteering as a docent at museums, libraries, and other architectural centers in your community.

THEN TO NOW

1983–1985:	1987–1988:	summer 1988:	1990–1991:	1991:
Interned as a carpenter at Cain Park Arts Festival in Cleveland, Ohio, during the summers	Worked various jobs as a carpenter and scene painter, Cleveland, New York, and Boston	Interned at Pei Cobb Freed & Partners, New York	Architectural intern, the Liebman Melting Partnership	Graduated with BFA, Parsons School of Design, New York

2. *The* **SCHEMATIC DESIGN** *is the phase that everyone thinks of when they think of an architect. It's where we do sketches of a design plan and we give it to the client. Then they think about it and get back to us and we sketch some more. We go back and forth with the client to develop the idea into two-dimensional finished drawings.*

THE BREAKDOWN

IN MEETINGS: 4 hours a day

ON THE PHONE: 1 hour a day

ONLINE: 3 hours a day

SITTING: Most of the day

READING: 2 hours a day

PRESENTING: Occasionally

WORKING SOLO: Half the day

3. *The next phase is called* **DESIGN DEVELOPMENT** *and* **PERMIT SET**, *where we submit for building permits as well as develop our schematic designs into detailed plans. We try to get a contractor involved in this phase, because they give us validation that we're not crazy and that our design is actually doable.*

4. *While the building department is reviewing our permit request, we put together the* **CONSTRUCTION DOCUMENTS**, *and that's when you get into all the details of what the interior will look like. When the building department comes back to us and says "Yes, go ahead and build it," we issue a set of construction documents.*

1991–1998: Interned for various architectural firms in Seattle

1998: Took summer off to be a professional bike racer

1998–1999: Worked as a project architect, Studio Jaso, Seattle

1999: Founded PLACE Architects, PLLC in Seattle

2008: Relocated PLACE to Vancouver, BC

PAYING YOUR DUES

Architects out of school begin their careers as paid architectural interns for three years. During this apprenticeship, they'll do lots of drafting, printing, copying, and helping out the architects with whatever they're doing.

5. *The last phase is* **CONSTRUCTION ADMINISTRATION**, *and it happens on-site where our contractors are building. We'll come out every week or two for a meeting and to check progress and talk about ideas, look at things that might change or whatever. Construction administration lasts six weeks to a year, depending on the project. In the end, hopefully everyone's still talking and we'll throw a party and our clients will move in.*

Like all careers, architecture has its ups and downs. I asked Heather to give me the lowdown on both.

"There's what we call 'driving the mouse,' which basically means drafting. In one construction set of drawings, there might be six hundred hours of drafting, and somebody's got to do it. It's not that bad, but it isn't necessarily glamorous. I used to say that was my job, driving the mouse. I'd just draft and draft and draft and draft.

"Another challenge is project management and dealing with clients—keeping everyone going in the same direction and moving along at the same time. Architectural design is very nonlinear—you try something, you come back, you try something else and you come

WHAT IT TAKES

- A blend of creative and mathematical talent
- Being an organized, linear thinker
- Patience (to get through the three-year internship)

back again. So people who are used to organized processes, like people who work in the software industry, or who run their own company, sometimes have a hard time with this forward-back-sideways and forward-back-sideways routine. That's the part of project management that we have to struggle with," she says.

"On the flip side, it's really awesome getting high-profile projects and saying 'Oh yeah, we built that' or, 'We're working on that.' That's cool. And I love being able to hang out with really smart people and hold my own. And then there's getting published—that's probably the most glamorous part. Getting published in *Architectural Record* was one of my proudest moments. They profiled me and my firm for the "up and coming young architects" section, and there are pictures of some of our projects and a two-page interview with me. That was awesome," said Heather.

Heather knew what she wanted to be at a young age. She did stage acting as a child, but realized by sixth grade that she'd much rather design and build a set than be acting in front of it. By the time she was sixteen, she'd figured out that she wanted to be an architect.

"I just felt like I would never get bored with it," Heather says.

INTERESTED IN BEING AN ARCHITECT? HERE'S HEATHER'S ADVICE

- *Believe in your own power and intelligence, and at the same time, be open to learning from others. Architecture is a profoundly complex field and you'll always be learning, but people will be looking to you to have a clear vision and they'll value your opinion. Keep your eye sharp and trust your instincts.*

- *Get a well-rounded liberal arts education and then go to architecture school. If you have a feel for art and the humanities, it will only enrich the work you do down the road.*

In the Field

FIVE MORE CAREERS IN ARCHITECTURE

DRAFTER   The plans created by other architects and designers for projects are often sketched, drawn out, and completed by drafters. They draw by hand or on a computer, and they lay out the different elements of a project, such as materials that will be used, where plumbing will be, landscaping ideas, and finishing touches.

INDUSTRIAL DESIGNER   These designers design what goes inside a home—everything from office furniture to kitchen fixtures—making sure it's functional, safe, and usable. While many industrial designers design materials for homes and the workplace, they might also do things like transportation and environmental design.

CONSTRUCTION MANAGER   Construction managers oversee the building of a structure, from hiring construction workers and finding the right building materials to making sure that the end product looks exactly like the architect and the client envisioned it. They must be available twenty-four hours a day and deal with any emergencies.

CARPENTER   You'll find carpenters working on-site at most building projects, and their job deals primarily with building and installing structures ranging from walls and cabinets to the actual frames of a house. Many are self-employed and specialize in a certain area.

CARTOGRAPHER   The next time you're on a road trip, consider that the map you're using to figure out your route was created by a cartographer. Cartographers create drawn or computer-generated maps, and they may work for government agencies, map companies, builders, or utility companies.

YOU NEED TO KNOW ABOUT

The AIAS, or American Institute of Architecture Students (www.aias.org), offers info on pursuing a career in architecture, a guide to architecture schools, postings about conferences and events, and links to great websites about architecture.

For more on careers that change the landscape, check out the urban planner profile on page 343.

CHRISTINE TUCKER

Commercial Airline Pilot

*Christine Tucker,
Captain, American
Airlines*

The Facts

WHAT? Commercial airline pilots jet around the country, or the world, flying millions of people to their destinations at speeds of up to five hundred miles an hour. They not only pilot the plane during takeoff, flight, and landing, but are also responsible for checking their plane prior to each flight, monitoring weather reports, and developing flight plans.

WHERE? Most pilots work out of their "home base" and fly a regular route.

HOW? Commercial airline pilots must have seven years' civilian flying or one year military pilot training with a five-year commitment under their belt, as well as having logged between one thousand and four thousand hours of flying time.

$$$: An average annual salary of $73,000

DRESS CODE? A uniform provided by the airline, consisting of pants, a top, a sweater, a tie, black shoes, and a captain's hat

STRESS FACTOR: On a scale of 1 to 10, a 5 with an occasional 8

though their ranks are rising, it's still rare to find a woman in the captain's seat of a commercial airplane. In fact, in 2010 less than 7 percent of all commercial airline pilots were women. Among them is Captain Christine Tucker, who flies a Boeing 757 or Boeing 767 between San Francisco, where she lives, and New York City, Boston, or Miami for American Airlines. Because there are so few women commercial airline pilots, especially captains, I was curious to find out how she made it happen.

"When I was younger, we lived by Greater Pittsburgh Airport. We'd see airplanes overhead all the time, so I got interested in flying at a young age. Then we moved to a street where some of our neighbors were US Air captains, and their sons were learning to fly. That's when I realized, 'Wow, I could fly a plane.' One of the sons took me up for my very first flying lesson and showed me how I could do it. I also read an article in *Parade* magazine when I was a teenager on women airline pilots. After reading that I was like, 'Okay, I can do this.' I still have that article," Christine says.

"I really like that I have a lot of flexibility in my schedule. And you know, it is still really fun to fly."

YOU ASKED . . .

"How long did you have to go to school, and did you like it?"
— **SHELBY, AGE 13**

CHRISTINE ANSWERED . . .

"To get in with a major airline, they typically want a four-year degree. My first two years I went to community college and got my associate degree in professional piloting and air traffic control. After that I went on to college in Pittsburgh and finished my four-year degree in business administration. You know . . . school's school, but the piloting courses, the flight engineer coursework . . . even the business classes, were all very interesting."

"Even today, it's still a big deal. People look in the cockpit, especially women, and say, 'Congratulations' and tell me how impressed they are with my accomplishments. *(Laughs)* I always feel bad for my male first officers because it appears no one's really paying any attention to them."

In preparing for my interview with Christine, I stumbled across this quote that some people use to describe what it's like to be a pilot: "Being a pilot entails hours of boredom interrupted upon occasion by seconds of sheer terror." Wow . . . quite a job description. So I asked her: Is it really true?

"Yes, monitoring the instruments might be viewed as a little boring, and yes, there are stresses involved, like being ready for an engine failure on takeoff or dealing with bad weather, but I wouldn't say it's necessarily 'boredom' with occasional 'terror.' That's kind of harsh," Christine answered.

So what does being a pilot really entail? What are they doing in the cockpit during a cross-country flight? How about when they're in another city between flights? I asked Christine to walk us through it.

A TYPICAL FLIGHT, A TYPICAL DAY

I get to the airport an hour before my flight, and the first thing I do is sign on to the computer so my company knows I'm there. Then I look at the flight plan from one of our dispatchers working out of Dallas–Fort Worth. He's the licensed expert who looks at the weather and talks to the other crews that have flown the route earlier so I know what kind of weather I'll have, what kind of turbulence to expect. The flight plan also includes a wind readout so I know the optimum altitude to fly in order to get the best fuel economy.

WHY WAIT?

- Look into flight lessons! You can start flying with an instructor as soon as you're physically able to manipulate the controls.
- Most commercial airlines let passengers tune in to the dialogue between the cockpit and the control tower by listening to a certain channel on the audio headset. Tune in the next time you're on a flight.
- Attend an air show near you and take a tour of a cockpit.

I also check my flight plan for things like destination weather—visibility, wind, temperature—and most important, the amount of fuel I need to safely fly the trip.

After finalizing the flight plan, I go out to the airplane and help with the "preflight." Typically, the first officer starts preflighting the airplane an hour before a flight. Occasionally I'll do the exterior preflight, which means looking at the outside of the airplane—the tires, the structure, the tail—making sure that everything's fastened and all the nuts and bolts are there and nothing is leaking or out of place. I still get a sense of awe at how large this aircraft is that I'm about to fly.

Once we get inside the cockpit, we have to program the computer with our flight plan so the navigation system will give us proper guidance. We also check which taxiway is appropriate to get to the runway. Every departure is so different. There might be five different departure routes for one runway, so you have to be prepared for which one you're

PAYING YOUR DUES

Pilots need to log around three thousand hours of flying time to get a job with an airline. Many work as flight instructors or fly night freights to earn their hours before making the switch to commercial airline flying.

going to fly. This is really critical . . . you can't make a mistake. If you've got a certain departure plan, you'd best be on it because there might be an airplane on the other runway.

I fly the Boeing 757 and 767. The cockpits of both planes are identical, but the feel of flying them is a little different. The 757 is like a sports car—it's very responsive and powerful. . . . I just love it. The 767 is more like a luxury liner, stable with even more power. There is an adrenaline rush every time you take off, partly due to the amazing performance and acceleration as you roll down the runway. You constantly have your hands and feet on the controls in preparation for takeoff. Although all of our airplanes have autopilots, I usually hand fly the airplane up to cruise altitude.

Once I'm in the air and at "cruise altitude," I'll turn the autopilot on and sit back for around five hours and monitor the instruments and navigation. The flight over most of the United States from San Francisco to New York is beautiful when looking down from six miles up. As we get closer to the destination airport, we check the weather and begin planning our approach to the airport.

WHAT IT TAKES
- Staying calm in stressful situations
- A desire to travel and see new places
- A sense of safety and responsibility

When we begin our descent, I'll hand fly the airplane for the remainder of the flight—why let the autopilot have all the

THEN TO NOW

| 1980: Began flying in eleventh grade | 1981: Started college and flew freight at night | 1984: Graduated from college and started flying bank checks in North Carolina | 1985: Hired by Air Virginia as a first officer flying metro liners |

fun? The air traffic controllers will have a planned arrival route, which is like a highway in the sky, to help keep other planes at a safe distance and flying the same direction as we are. They'll tell us what altitude to descend to and at what speed they would like us to fly. Then we'll start the approach, using an ILS or instrument landing system, which helps guide us and tells us things like if we're too high or too far left or right off course.

If I'm flying into New York, we usually get in around six a.m. In most cases we have between fourteen and twenty-four hours off-duty to enjoy the sights and sounds of the Big Apple. In New York my airline provides a hotel downtown—it's not the Ritz or anything, but it's adequate, and I love my stay in the heart of the city. I can go shopping (remember, I am a girl) or out to the theater.

Christine's schedule can be brutal, especially when she's flying across the country. Because of changing time zones (it's a three-hour difference), her body never really has a chance to catch up with her. Here's what a typical trip from San Francisco to New York and back might look like:

Fly out of San Francisco: Monday night, 10:00 p.m. Pacific
                               Standard Time (PST)

Arrive in New York: Tuesday morning, 6:00 a.m. Eastern
                               Standard Time (EST)/ 3:00 a.m. PST

1987: Was hired at American Airlines at twenty-three years old as a flight engineer on a Boeing 727

1990: Became a first officer on a Boeing 727

1996: Became a captain on Boeing 727

2002: Became a captain on a Boeing 757/767 flying domestic routes

Go to sleep in hotel:	*Tuesday morning, 8:00 a.m. EST/ 5:00 a.m. PST*
Force myself awake:	*Tuesday afternoon, 2:00 p.m. EST/ 11:00 a.m. PST*
Force myself to sleep:	*Tuesday evening, 11:00 p.m. EST/ 8:00 p.m. PST*
Force myself awake:	*Wednesday morning, 6:30 a.m. EST/ 3:30 a.m. PST*
Fly out of New York:	*Wednesday morning, 9:00 a.m. EST/ 6:00 a.m. PST*
Arrive in San Francisco:	*Wednesday afternoon, 12:30 p.m. PST*

As you can imagine, Christine is wiped out after a trip like that, which is one reason why she's worked out a schedule that gives her a chance to refresh and have quality time at home with her kids. She says it's always challenging to be away so much each month, especially because she has to make sure things at home are taken care of—the kids are set, the dog is fed, bills are paid, everything's in order. "It's not like you can just scoot back home and do something if you're flying across country. . . . You're really gone for those days," she says.

But while the schedules for commercial airline pilots can be challenging, the flexibility is also something Christine says is one of the biggest perks of the job.

"I use my vacation time as individual days instead of taking a week off at a time—that way I'm home more. I'm typically working 'on reserves,' which means that I have a guaranteed twelve days off each month, but other than that I'm on call," Christine explains. "I really like that I have a lot of flexibility in my schedule. And you know, it is still really fun to fly."

Before we wrapped up our conversation, I asked Christine to clear up any misconceptions about pilots, and she said she thinks the biggest myth is that pilots make a lot of money and are overpaid for what they do.

"We're in charge of a hundred-and-twenty-five-million-dollar airplane, we have to take medical exams every six months, we have to go through check rides, or flight evaluations, every nine months, and our job can be taken away from us if we make a mistake. There can be stress involved, with no room for error. I have two hundred twenty people in my airplane who count on me to safely get them to their destination. But I can't imagine doing anything else. Professionalism is paramount in this business, but I love what I do. I leave work every day with a sense of pride and accomplishment."

CHRISTINE'S ADVICE

- *You have to be motivated to succeed. If you're motivated, organized, and want to see new places, then you can do it.*
- *Be persistent—flight jobs are hard to find.*

In the Field

FIVE MORE CAREERS WORKING IN THE TRAVEL INDUSTRY

TRAVEL AGENT Travel agents organize, plan, and book trips for people, whether it be for business or pleasure. Their job includes everything from reserving flights, cruises, and hotels to organizing tours and providing itineraries and maps for their clients.

FLIGHT ATTENDANT While some people think flight attendants are on board to make the passengers' ride more comfortable by handing out pillows, their most important job is safety. They must ensure that passengers follow safety rules, and they assist in the case of an emergency.

AIR TRAFFIC CONTROLLER The stress meter hits a ten if you're an air traffic controller, as they monitor all the aircraft in their airspace, communicate with pilots, and make sure that all the planes are flying safe distances from one another. Those at busy airports might coordinate the landing and takeoff of a dozen airplanes at any one time.

AIRLINE RESERVATIONS AGENT Airline reservations agents take reservations over the phone for airlines and book the flights. They use a computer program to do their work and spend their whole day providing customer service.

FLIGHT MECHANIC Airplanes are checked over by flight mechanics before embarking on a trip, and they'll look over the whole airplane and use special lighting tools to look for cracks in the surface that would be invisible to the naked eye. Flight mechanics are also called in to fix any problems the pilot might sense prior to takeoff.

YOU NEED TO KNOW ABOUT

Women in Aviation International (www.wai.org) is all about encouraging women to pursue careers in aviation. At this website you'll find articles about aviation, scholarship opportunities, conference information, and links to great sites just for women interested in flying. Bonus: You can even join as a high school student!

MARY SUE MILLIKEN & SUSAN FENIGER

Chefs

The Facts

Mary Sue Milliken & Susan Feniger, Owners, Border Grill

WHAT? Chefs are professional cooks, but most do much more than just cook food. They often create the recipes and menus that are served in restaurants or private residences, oversee cooks, order ingredients, and figure out the cost involved in various recipes. Some also run restaurants.

WHERE? Chefs can work anywhere that food is served.

HOW? A degree isn't a requirement, but a college background in hospitality or culinary arts is a bonus, along with experience working in the restaurant industry. Additional training at a place like the Culinary Institute of America will open up many opportunities.

$$$: $20,000 to $40,000 for lower-level chefs at smaller restaurants; $60,000 to $100,000 or more for those in more prominent restaurants.

DRESS CODE? A chef's outfit—usually a white chef's jacket, simple pants, and a white chef's hat

STRESS FACTOR: On a scale of 1 to 10, a 7

longtime chefs and restaurant partners Mary Sue Milliken and Susan Feniger own three Border Grill restaurants in Santa Monica, downtown Los Angeles, and Las Vegas, with a fourth that opened in Las Vegas in 2014. They also own two gourmet Border Grill food trucks, and a kiosk in downtown Los Angeles, and they recently opened a location in the new Tom Bradley International Terminal at LAX. They have written several cookbooks, had two cooking shows on Food Network, have a weekly Sunday-morning radio talk show, and even had their own brand of food called Border Girls, which was sold at Whole Foods Market. So I thought, who better than Mary Sue and Susan to tell us what it's really like to work as chefs and restaurateurs? Here are some highlights from our conversation.

"The one thing you can count on in this business is that next year won't be the same as last year. The business and the atmosphere are constantly changing."

ME: You're so much more than chefs—you run three restaurants, write books, have a weekly radio show. How do you juggle it all?

SUSAN: On a typical day I might start looking at e-mails at around nine thirty a.m., something like that, and then I usually try to go into the restaurant somewhere around ten or ten thirty. I may go to Border Grill in Santa Monica, or I might get on a plane and go to one of our restaurants in Vegas. I check in with the chefs and walk through the restaurant to connect with the people there. I may end up sitting down with one of the chefs to talk or maybe going over what specials we're switching over to. Then usually right before lunch I'll taste the specials.

During the lunch service, I try to be working on the floor at one of the restaurants, either looking at the food coming out of the kitchen, which is called "expediting," or talking to customers. If it's busy, I'll jump in. Then I'll end up in meetings in the afternoon—sometimes it's kitchen meetings, sometimes it's financial meetings with the whole team. In the afternoon we might be doing an interview or a demo or a TV thing. Then dinnertime comes and I'm usually involved with the tastings, working on the floor, connecting with customers, watching food coming out, and maybe even doing office paperwork. We've got a big benefit coming up in less than a month, so right now I'm putting together auction packages and menu plans, figuring out a prep list for it, and so on. Tomorrow I'm meeting with the chef at the Beverly Wilshire Hotel to plan for the event. And then at nine or nine thirty p.m. I may meet friends for dinner at the restaurant or head out.

ME: Wow . . . that's a packed day. Is your routine any different, Mary Sue?

MARY SUE: I think I do more planning and I work a lot on the radio show, figuring out what we're going to talk about this week, writing new recipes that we're going to try out, or testing recipes. I also go to the Santa Monica Farmer's Market and see what foods are new and interesting there, research what's

YOU ASKED . . .

"Would you say that through your success, your job has allowed you to contribute something to the benefit of this world?"

—BRITTANI, AGE 16

MARY SUE AND SUSAN ANSWERED . . .

"Absolutely. One of the benefits of being in the restaurant business is that it gives us the venue and the opportunities to give back to the community in a way that many businesses can't do other than by just giving money. Giving back is a big part of our culture and our company, and it's something that we get our staff involved in so that they can see what an incredible opportunity it is.

Mary Sue & Susan's favorite charities? Share Our Strength (www.nokidhungry.org) and the Scleroderma Research Foundation (www.srfcure.org).

happening in the food industry, and do a lot of big-picture planning, like trying to figure out how we're going to sustain this business while staying true to our philosophy.

ME: I wanted to ask you about that. It seems that a lot of restaurants are here today, gone tomorrow, but you've both been very successful at keeping restaurants in business. Is it stressful knowing that your industry is so unstable?

MARY SUE: Well, the one thing you can count on in this business is that next year won't be the same as last year. The business and the atmosphere are constantly changing. We just try to stay connected to what our business and the people here need. The people who work for us are really what make the whole thing work.

ME: Besides that fact that the restaurant industry is so tough, what are some of the other challenges of being a chef and running a restaurant?

SUSAN: It's long hours, and in some ways you're always on call. If you're at the restaurant and you're planning to leave and something goes wrong, you always have to be ready to just jump in, no matter what. You also have to be able to juggle a lot of things at one time. You have to be able to handle situations that for many people would be very stressful. In one night you might have someone not show up for work, someone else give their notice, a toilet overflow, a ton of people waiting at the front door for a table, and half of your produce order doesn't arrive. You have to be able to juggle all that.

THE BREAKDOWN

IN MEETINGS: 1–2 hours a day

ONLINE: 1–2 hours a day

SITTING: 1–2 hours a day

STANDING: 4–6 hours a day

TALKING TO STAFF & CUSTOMERS: All the time

WHY WAIT?

- Many restaurants in town are hiring—if you're sixteen or older, go get a job and see if you like it!
- Take a cooking class. Many supermarkets offer free or inexpensive classes that are open to all ages.
- Cook as often as you can at home and experiment with all kinds of recipes. Start by closely following recipes and then begin adding your own personal touches.

MARY SUE: And you can look at that as a challenge, or you can look at that as an opportunity to be really creative. You'll need to figure out what kind of specials you can make with only half the produce that you were expecting, and that's actually fun in some ways. I think that's a part of what attracts people to the industry—that you get totally immersed in the job because you're so busy and there are so many challenges.

ME: What do you *love* about your job?

SUSAN: You get to wear a uniform every day—that's a great thing.

MARY SUE: That's true. *(Laughs)* You don't have to decide what to wear to work anymore—that is a big perk.

SUSAN: Plus, you know, you can have friends come in and the restaurant feels like an extended arm of your home, so that's a great thing. There's also a camaraderie that happens within the restaurant business, with staff as well as with customers that come in, and you build these extended relationships because it's a very social, giving environment.

MARY SUE: I also think a huge perk is that you get to eat. And not only do you get to eat, but you get to make recipes that you like over and over. If you love to cook at home and you make a dish a hundred and fifty times, you and your friends

PAYING YOUR DUES

Even with a degree from a culinary institute, most chefs start out working in a variety of positions—from prep cook to dishwasher—to learn all aspects of cooking and work their way up the ladder.

and family would be so sick of that dish that you wouldn't even like it anymore. But if you're cooking in a restaurant, you can make it a hundred and fifty times in the first month since you're serving it to different people, and you can really figure out how to make it better each time. So that's a huge perk.

ME: Would you say that your work is creative?

MARY SUE: Yes. It's like a puzzle every day—you walk in and see what's ready to be eaten and what's not going to be good by tomorrow if you don't figure out what to make with it, so you have all kinds of creative opportunities there. Or when you're opening a restaurant and your budget is tight . . . you have to be creative then, too. When we opened City Café, we didn't have any wine buckets and we were opening the next day, but we had no money. One of our partners found these really cool marble crocks at Pic 'n Save for $2.99 each. She bought twenty of them and we sandblasted them in the back alley of the restaurant . . . they ended up looking fantastic. So you have the ability to be creative in lots of ways—in the way

THEN TO NOW

Mary Sue graduated from Washburne Culinary Institute; Susan graduated from the Culinary Institute of America	1978: Mary Sue and Susan met while working at Le Perroquet in Chicago	1981: Opened first restaurant, City Café, on Melrose Avenue, L.A.	1985: City Café moved to larger space and changed name to CITY	1985: Opened Border Grill in old City Café space	1989: Published first book, *City Cuisine*

you create the atmosphere, in the way you create the menu. It's all a way of communicating who you are. . . .

SUSAN: . . . down to what the staff uniforms are going to be, what kind of silverware, what kind of china and glassware, how the menus are going to look—you've got all these dif-

ferent avenues besides the food where you're able to explore your own creativity. It's exciting and it keeps someone who's driven and creative really challenged.

ME: When you first got into this career, would you ever have dreamed that you'd not only be chefs and own your own restaurants, but that you would be writing books . . . even starting your own line of food?

MARY SUE: Not at all. But Susan and I were both really passionate about teaching and educating people about food, what they're eating and how they eat. So we started teaching cooking classes to people, and every time we'd teach a class people would say, "Oh, you should be on TV" or "You should be on the radio." And you know, they were right. We really do enjoy it and it came very naturally to us, which was lucky.

1995–1999: Hosted two series for Food Network (*Too Hot Tamales* and *Tamales World Tour*)

1996: Started broadcasting radio show in L.A.

1998: Opened Ciudad restaurant in downtown Los Angeles

1999: Opened Border Grill in Mandalay Bay Resort and Casino, Las Vegas

2009: Launched Border Grill food truck

2010: Opened Border Grill Downtown L.A.

2013: Opened Border Grill at the TBIT at LAX

MARY SUE AND SUSAN'S ADVICE

- *Trust your instincts, but don't be afraid to ask anyone in sight when something is baffling you. Your colleagues and role models will generously share ideas and advice that is more valuable than any education.*

- *Get in there and do the grunt work. Start as a dishwasher, be a prep cook, work in the kitchen—really try to experience it. Even though the work that you do over time might change, the hours and the commitment are the same, so you have to be really passionate about it.*

In the Field

FIVE MORE CAREERS IN THE RESTAURANT INDUSTRY

SOMMELIER   Would you believe there's a career in knowing which type of wine goes best with different meals? You might find *sommeliers* (French for "wine waiters") working in fancy restaurants, and their in-depth knowledge of wine helps them make recommendations.

HOSTESS   Hosts and hostesses are usually the first people you see when you walk in a restaurant. They have to be serious multitaskers, taking reservations, answering phones, seating people, and acting as the public "face" of the restaurant, all at the same time.

PASTRY CHEF   Many consider baking to be an art, since it takes skill and creativity. Pastry chefs might whip up delectable desserts for a French restaurant, bake three-tiered wedding cakes, or create croissants and scones for their own boutique pastry shop.

SERVER   This is one job that never gets boring. Servers have to be good at juggling information, dealing with all kinds of

people, staying cool under pressure, and multitasking—keeping
track of who wants extra butter, whose steak is too rare, and who
is missing a place setting.

LINE COOK Without line cooks, chefs' creations would never go from ingredients to finished meals. Line cooks make the food on the menu, and they must be consistent in re-creating the chef's specialties time and time again—the restaurant's reputation depends on it.

YOU NEED TO KNOW ABOUT

Women Chefs & Restaurateurs (WRC) was founded in 1983 by top women chefs with a goal of "promoting the education and advancement of women in the restaurant industry." At the WRC's website, www.womenchefs.org, you'll find information on internships, books to read, links to resources, and a free downloadable newsletter.

MELISSA BLOCK

Journalist

Melissa Block, Cohost, All Things Considered, National Public Radio

The Facts

WHAT? Journalists report the news for television or radio stations, newspapers, magazines, and websites.

WHERE? As a journalist, you can live and work just about anywhere. Many work for a specific news outlet, while others work freelance and submit stories to various media for publication or broadcast.

HOW? Most journalists have at least a four-year degree in English or journalism or a master's in journalism.

$$$: An average of $45,000 a year, depending on position and geographic location

DRESS CODE? Casual for print and radio journalists and business for on-air TV journalists

STRESS FACTOR: On a scale of 1 to 10, between an 8 and a 10 ("A bad day can be pretty stressful, but it's all relative," says Melissa.)

if you tune in to your local public radio station on a weekday afternoon, chances are you'll hear the voice of Melissa Block. As cohost of National Public Radio's two-hour news show *All Things Considered*, Melissa not only sits in the big anchor chair and introduces news pieces, but she also interviews special guests and reports on breaking news and human interest stories from the field. Since I'm a news junkie, it was exciting to peek into Melissa's life and hear about what goes on behind the scenes at NPR. Here's our conversation.

ME: The news industry seems so competitive. Was it tough to break in?

MELISSA: I don't think it was as hard then as it is now. I hunted around for a job for a bit, but found my niche at NPR, even though I hadn't worked in radio before. It just turned out to be such a great place to work. . . . Here it is nearly thirty years later and I'm still here.

ME: Did you know that you wanted to work in journalism when you got out of college?

MELISSA: I was a little torn. I got into law school but deferred for two years in a row, because by the time I got in I had started working in journalism. So part of me thought journalism was the industry for me, and part of me thought that law would be interesting. I remember having a conversation with the admissions person at Yale Law School, and when I asked her if I could defer for a third year, she said, "You know, it sounds like you're very happy doing what you're doing. Maybe you don't need to go to law school." And I realized she was right.

> "I don't necessarily need to know what the answers are—I need to know what the questions are that need to be answered."

ME: Let's fast forward to the present day. I realize your days are probably very different depending on whether you're in the studio hosting or on the road reporting. Could you walk us through what each day might look like?

MELISSA'S (UN)USUAL DAY

IN THE STUDIO . . .

I have a daughter, so my day starts with trying to squeeze in a little time with her. That's part of this whole equation—how to balance having a family and having a job that's satisfying to you. So morning time is spent with her, having breakfast, making lunch, listening to NPR's Morning Edition, as well as trying to read as much of the paper as I can. Actually, my day starts the night before, when I've gone online to read the next day's papers!

9:00–10:00 A.M.: I get to the office and I'm reading, reading, reading as many papers and websites as I can. I need to get a sense of what's going on in the world, and come up with interview ideas I'd like to do for that day's show and the week ahead.

YOU ASKED . . .

"How does what you do for a living affect other parts of your life?" —ANNA, AGE 20

MELISSA ANSWERED . . .

"I like thinking about the fact that my daughter hears me on the radio and it's just a part of her life. I like the notion that she's growing up knowing that women do this, that her mother does this, and that it's a possible career choice. It is a squeeze, though. I don't have a job where I can get in at ten and be home at five and have dinner and not have to work at night. You do bring work home with you and there's a lot that you don't leave at the office, so that's a choice. It's a choice I've made gladly and it's a wonderful thing that I'm doing, so I don't regret it. But it is a trade-off."

10:00–11:00 A.M.: We head to a staff meeting at ten o'clock every day to kick ideas around for that day's show. The best shows for me are the ones where I feel like I'm invested and have a stake in the stories and when I've brought something to fruition on the air. There's a lot of back-and-forth from all the staff in the meeting—from interns all the way up to the executive producer and the hosts—and we get some sense of what each host's assignments will be for the day.

THE BREAKDOWN

IN MEETINGS: 1 hour a day

ON THE PHONE: Maybe half an hour

ONLINE: Constantly

SITTING: Unfortunately, almost all the time

PUBLIC SPEAKING: Every day on the radio

READING: Constantly

WORKING SOLO: Half the day

11:00 A.M.–3:00 P.M.: I'm reading and preparing for interviews, doing interviews, and writing introductions to stories.

3:00–4:00 P.M.: We're doing preproduction for the show, like recording some elements that are taped in advance. We have a very early deadline. Going on the air at four p.m. is a pretty punishing thing when your day starts at nine thirty—it doesn't give you a lot of time to get things ready. There's a sort of funny acceleration. There's a point where you look at your watch and go, "Whoa, it's two thirty," and the day sort of accelerates from there.

4:00–6:00 P.M.: We go on the air. During the show I'm doing live interviews, reading introductions to reporter pieces, and handling the live broadcast of the show. Assuming we haven't made any mistakes or things haven't changed newswise, the day is more or less done after the broadcast of the show. But one of the two on-air hosts is on call until ten p.m. to update the program if stories change, or if news breaks later on. (The show is "rolled over" and updated through the West Coast feed.) Usually I can do these updates from home. But on really busy nights, when news is changing fast, I sometimes stay until ten p.m.

7:00 P.M.: I get home. Dinner with my family. A debrief of the day. And then, homework! Lots of days I bring home reading to prepare for interviews for the week to come. It might be a folder of research, a book I need to read, or a movie I need to watch.

ON THE ROAD . . .

The days when I'm on the road can really vary. Sometimes I'm working on stories that we've planned well in advance, and other times I'm responding to something that happened. For example, after Superstorm Sandy hit in 2012, my producer and I hit the road right away to cover that. Same thing with Hurricane Katrina in 2005. But other trips are well thought out and planned for a long time. For example, I went to Brazil for two weeks, and we did a whole series of stories on preparations for the soccer World Cup, deforestation, the legacy of slavery, and lots more. That was a trip I'd been dreaming about and planning for years! Sometimes I might travel to profile just one person: for example, a former NFL player who's suffering from brain injury as a result of concussions he sustained playing football. I love getting out on the road to meet and talk with

THEN TO NOW

1983: Graduated from Harvard University with degree in French history and literature

1984: Was a Fulbright scholar at the University of Geneva

1985: Started working for NPR setting up interviews for *All Things Considered* host Noah Adams

1994: Moved to NYC to report for NPR

people. And the range of stories is huge, which is partly what makes my job so great.

When I'm on the road, I go out with a producer, who does the audio recording. I'll often take photographs for our website, or post them on our Tumblr. If I'm reporting on a breaking news story, we'll file the report from the road through the Internet. Otherwise, if it's a longer-term project, we may bring hours of audio back home and spend lots of time putting the stories together here.

ME: Do you have a lot of choice over the stories you get to work on?

MELISSA: Yes. I think the feeling is that the best stories are the ones that the hosts have a natural curiosity about, which isn't to say that I'll only do stories that I pitch or that are my idea, but there's less translation involved if it's coming from me. That said, I've also done a zillion interviews that have been pitched by our staff members.

ME: How do you become an expert on all the topics you're reporting on?

MELISSA: I think the first thing you have to do is realize that you're never going to become an expert. *(Laughs.)* I see my role as a surrogate for the listener, and the listener's not an

1999: Her report investigating rape as a weapon of war in Kosovo was cited among stories for which NPR News won an Overseas Press Club Award

2003: Became cohost of *All Things Considered*

2008: Melissa's reporting on the Sichuan earthquake earned a Peabody Award expert. I don't necessarily need to know what the answers are—I need to know what the questions are that need to be answered. Obviously it can help if I'm well informed, and I certainly try to be, but sometimes the most interesting interviews come when I'm thrown into something that I haven't had a chance to really prepare for and I'm just reacting more spontaneously to. I think the main skills are being a fast reader and a quick study, having a general curiosity about things, and not being afraid to ask dumb questions, because they're probably not dumb. They're probably what everybody else is wondering and hoping somebody will ask.

ME: How do you go about booking your interviews and reporting on stories?

MELISSA: Usually the producer sets up the interviews. I'll jump in if it's somebody I know or somebody I want to establish a connection with first. But usually it's a producer doing most of the legwork. I often do a bunch of my own research, because I like digging into stories!

ME: And after you've interviewed someone and you're putting together a story, are you sitting down and writing the script for air?

MELISSA: Yes. The producer and I work pretty closely—sometimes the engineer, too—to think about structure. Usually right after an interview is the best time to talk about it because it's fresh in your mind, and often there is some moment from the interview that stands out very clearly in your mind as something to preserve. There's sort of a way that everything fits together, and the challenge is trying to figure out the most logical sequence for a story to flow. In TV news, you can rely on the pictures, but with radio, you can't. So we let the ambient sound that we record on the road do a lot of the talking for us. But the rest is in the writing, and it needs to be as descriptive as possible. I do all of the writing for my pieces.

ME: What did it feel like to hear your voice on national radio for the first time?

MELISSA: The first national piece I did was a story about a green card lottery for immigrants. It was a scary, weird thing to hear my voice on the radio. I think anyone who's ever listened to their own answering machine recording sort of does a double take and says, "That's not what I really sound like, is it?"

ME: What is the biggest challenge of your job?

MELISSA: There is a constant time pressure of being on a daily deadline with a two-hour program. That and having to juggle a lot of things in your brain at the same time. I mean, I may be doing several interviews in one day—it could be one with the US Treasury Secretary, one with an actor about her new movie,

PAYING YOUR DUES

To work in national news, many people start out at a TV or radio station in a smaller market, sometimes working as a production assistant (PA) or freelance reporter. The field of journalism is notorious for low starting salaries, but your pay will increase with your experience.

WHAT IT TAKES

- Good communication and analytical skills
- The ability to work under tight deadlines
- A willingness to pay your dues

and then maybe something light, like the guy who's grown the biggest pumpkin in Alaska. You have to keep all of those balls in the air at the same time.

ME: What do you love about your job?

MELISSA: The variety, first. Also, it's such a privilege to have access to people and to situations that a lot of other people don't have access to. You know, being in the Yankee locker room right after they've won the World Series and getting doused with champagne—that's an amazing place to be. And it's great to be able to take that and say, "Here's what I saw, here's what I heard . . . Let me tell you about this, let me take you there." I was one of the only Western reporters in Sichuan, China, during a really devastating earthquake in 2008. It was a horrible time, with so many thousands of people killed. But I was able—through radio—to reach listeners halfway around

INTERESTED IN JOURNALISM? HERE'S MELISSA'S CAREER ADVICE

- *Volunteer in your local community—jump in and do as much as you can. Whether it's for your local public radio station or community newspaper, there's nothing better than hands-on experience.*
- *Be someone nothing is lost on. Take everything in, be a good observer, and write like crazy.*
- *Keep improving your writing. Keep a journal and learn your voice.*
- *Read like crazy. Read authors whose writing you feel passionate about and figure out why their writing resonates with you.*

the world and help them understand the magnitude of what had happened, and the human toll. The best part of my job is that we connect people through the radio. It's an intimate thing, and a real privilege of my job.

In the Field

FIVE MORE CAREERS IN BROADCAST JOURNALISM

ASSIGNMENT EDITOR Assignment editors on news programs work with the staff to come up with story ideas and then assign them out to reporters, hosts, and crews. This can be a highly stressful job, since assignment editors have to keep tabs on who's working on what and make quick decisions about breaking news.

NEWS PRODUCER After assignments are handed out, news producers coordinate the production of news segments, working with a camera or audio crew and journalist to make the story happen. They research stories, find interview subjects, oversee the recording of material, and help package the story into complete news segments.

BEAT REPORTER Beat reporters are journalists who cover one aspect or "beat" for the news, usually carrying their own recording equipment for interviews, writing their own copy, and producing the final radio news segment. For example, a beat reporter who specializes in education will cover local or national education stories.

BOOKER Many TV and radio news shows rely heavily on on-air guests, and bookers are the ones who research potential guests, contact them and/or their publicists, and "book" them for an upcoming show. They might also prep the interviewer or show host, as well as prepare the guest for what to expect on the program.

NEWS GRAPHIC DESIGNER TV news uses on-air graphics—maps, diagrams, titles—in news stories. News graphic designers use their expertise and computer design programs to create these graphics. Those working for twenty-four-hour news channels like CNN might create the news crawls on the bottom of the screen.

YOU NEED TO KNOW ABOUT

The Project for Excellence in Journalism sponsors the website www.journalism.org. Here you'll find links to articles and books about journalism, an annual report on the State of the Media, resources, ideas, and job postings.

For more on careers in journalism, check out the magazine editor profile on page 325.

LAUREN FAUST

Animator

The Facts

Lauren Faust,
Animation Producer,
Artist, and Writer

WHAT? Animators make cartoons—television shows, commercials, online shorts, or even personal indie films. They do many different jobs, such as designing characters or backgrounds, drawing hundreds of frames to create the illusion of movement, or creating storyboards to plan out the action.

WHERE? While independent animators can work almost anywhere, the hubs for the industry are New York and L.A.

HOW? There are no firm job requirements for animators, beyond a talent for drawing, although a degree in animation from an art school may make it easier to land a job.

$$$: From $26,000 to $150,000 a year, depending on level of experience, the studio, and whether animating for a TV show or a movie

DRESS CODE? Can you say "cut-offs, T-shirts, and flip-flops"?

STRESS FACTOR: On a scale of 1 to 10, 5 on a good day, 8 on a bad day

animators have to be great at so many things to do what they do—be great artists; have an incredible imagination; be smart, funny, and creative; and have a unique way of looking at the world. Lauren Faust, who I met when she was an animator on *The Powerpuff Girls*, is all of the above.

The term "animator" as a job title is pretty broad, because like many fields in entertainment, creating an animated show or movie is usually a group effort. For a half-hour animated TV show, there's a whole team of people behind it—from the artists who designed the characters, to the storyboard artists who blocked out the action, to the background designer who designed the "scenery" for the cartoon, to the director who timed out the show. People in all these jobs would be considered "animators," and that just scratches the surface.

"Don't be afraid to promote yourself. People won't notice you unless you put yourself directly in their sight."

Lauren has worked for a number of high-profile shows at major networks, including being a storyboard artist on *The Powerpuff Girls*, supervising producer and story supervisor for

YOU ASKED . . .

"How long have you known what you wanted to do with your life?" —JEAN, AGE 16

LAUREN ANSWERED . . .

"I've loved drawing, art, and animation ever since I can remember, but it wasn't until I was fourteen that it occurred to me that you could make cartoons for a living. Still, at that point I only added it to the list of things I was considering for my career, along with teaching and zoology. A couple years later I visited Walt Disney World with my family, and they had an animation exhibit, which included a glimpse of a working animation studio. As soon as I saw it, I just knew that was what I had to do!"

Foster's Home for Imaginary Friends, creator and executive producer of the *My Little Pony: Friendship Is Magic* television series, and coproducer and story editor for the Disney Channel series *Wander Over Yonder*. In these roles, Lauren is involved in lots of high-level action, including story planning meetings, production meetings, and writing and storyboarding episodes,

THE BREAKDOWN

IN MEETINGS: 2–3 hours a day

ON THE PHONE: 20 minutes a day

ONLINE: 30 minutes a day

SITTING: Practically all day

READING: 1 hour a day

WORKING SOLO: 5 hours a day

pretty much all at the same time. No two days are the same, and Lauren constantly has to shift gears from one moment to the next, wearing her artist hat for one meeting and her producer hat for another, sometimes back-to-back.

I managed to cajole Lauren into keeping a diary for us for a few days. I thought it would be a great way to see what the work of a supervising producer for an animated TV show was really like. Here's a peek into her journal:

LAUREN'S DIARY ———————————————

february 13

10:00 A.M.–12 NOON: *Met with a composer to review music for a project of mine in development. It's the very first song for the microseries—very exciting!*

12:30–1 P.M.: *Quick lunch with my boss, Craig. We discussed a script outline from a freelance writer.*

1:00–2:30 P.M.: *Reread the outline we discussed at lunch to think about how to make it stronger. I felt it was very funny, but it was missing a solid character arc, and there was not enough at stake to make the story exciting.*

2:30–3:00 P.M.: Read and returned e-mails. Returned phone calls. There are several blogs and forums on animation that I check regularly to catch up on news in the animation industry. Usually when I'm checking e-mails, I do this, too.

3:00–4:30 P.M.: Prepped my own story outline for a script I am about to start writing.

4:30–6:00 P.M.: Reviewed notes for the freelance outline with Craig and another writer. We discussed our different thoughts and decided what direction to take.

february 14

9:00–10:30 A.M.: Read and returned e-mails.

11:30 A.M.–12:30 P.M.: Revised the script outline from the freelance writer. Implemented the notes we discussed yesterday.

12:30–2:30 P.M.: Had lunch and visited a friend's art show!

2:30–3:00 P.M.: Finished script revisions and turned in for approval. Craig was happy with it.

3:00–4:00 P.M.: Nap (seriously, I needed one).

4:00–6:00 P.M.: Sat down to start my own script. Wasn't able to get anything down, but I took down some notes and did some drawings of ideas for possible gags and sequences. Hopefully they'll fit into the final script.

february 15

10:30–11:00 A.M.: Got in late today. Ran into an old friend I worked with on Powerpuff Girls who had been working in Europe for the past two and a half years. Besides

WHY WAIT?

- Talent counts for more than experience, so hone your skills—take drawing and writing classes as often as you can.
- Draw all the time!
- Rent DVDs of great animated movies like *Toy Story* and *Cinderella* and watch the extra features for the behind-the-scenes scoop on how the films were made.

PAYING YOUR DUES

Most animators start as production assistants or storyboard clean-up artists, and they stay in these positions for one to two years. They'll be expected to do things like make copies and scans, organize artwork, hand out memos, prepare materials for artists, and implement story or drawing notes made by a director.

saying hello and catching up, Craig and I wanted to gauge his interest in writing scripts for us. Hopefully we can secure him—we've always liked his work!

11:00–11:30 A.M.: *Turns out I was locked out of my office! I had to wait for someone to let me in. Talked about Disney movies with the other writers while waiting.*

11:30 A.M.–12:15 P.M.: *Read and returned e-mails and phone calls. I was hoping to receive notes on the outline I sent to my bosses in programming. It has been three days and I haven't heard back from them. They usually send the outline back right away if they like it, so I'm worried they will have heavy changes. Unfortunately, worrying about it is giving me some monster writer's block for my own script.*

12:30–1:30 P.M.: *Lunch with friend I ran into earlier, Craig, and our producer.*

2:00–4:00 P.M.: *Sat in on editing session with Craig. Episode was slightly too long. I made some suggestions to help cut down.*

4:00–5:30 P.M.: *Met with a development exec from the network and a coworker to discuss an acquired property from Japan I've been asked to help develop as an animated series. Good meeting. There are plans to meet with a cowriter next week to proceed with the bible, which is basically a proposal or summary of a show.*

7:00–9:30 P.M.: *Dinner with a former colleague. Discussed the animation biz.*

WHAT IT TAKES

- A great imagination
- Natural artistic ability
- Being comfortable working solo

february 16

10:00 A.M.–12 NOON: *Read and returned e-mails. Also, an animator came by with a question about a scene. I finally got word from programming on my outline. It was approved! In fact, they were quite happy with it and had only one minor adjustment. Turns out my boss had approved it on Tuesday, but the e-mail did not get through to any of us. I've been worrying for the past two days for no reason!*

12:30–2:00 P.M.: *Lunch.*

2:00–6:00 P.M.: *I was supposed to be writing, but the writer's block has continued, even though my outline was approved. I wrote some things I was unhappy with and put aside. Then, in hopes of stirring up some inspiration, I spent some time drawing some new characters I have to introduce in this episode. Sometimes that helps me to figure out how to write for them. Not much luck. I have a lot of drawings, but very little writing to show for it.*

february 17

9:30–10:30 A.M.: *Read and returned e-mails.*

10:30 A.M.–12:30 P.M.: *Supposed to be working on my script, but I still have that nasty writer's block.*

12:30–2:00 P.M.: *Lunch.*

THEN TO NOW

| 1992–1994: Attended California Institute of the Arts | 1993: Layout artist, Rough Draft Studios | 1994–1996: Animator, Turner Feature Animation | 1996–1998: Animator, Warner Bros. Feature Animation | 1999–2003: Storyboard artist/writer, Cartoon Network Studios |

2:00–3:30 P.M.: *Story meeting. A freelance script was turned in a few weeks ago, and I felt it needed work, but Craig was much more unhappy with it. The writer is going to be revising it, so we discussed our plan of attack to fix it.*

4:00–6:00 P.M.: *I spent the end of the day suffering with more writer's block. The fact that it's late afternoon on a Friday isn't helping. I sure hope I have better luck next week!*

writer's block update

In the following two weeks, I managed to write forty-six pages of the eighty-eight-page script. Thankfully, the first half of this one-hour special was approved with very minimal notes. Sometimes a couple of days of letting my brain breathe does the trick . . . that and the all-encompassing fear of missing a deadline!

In the Field

FIVE MORE CAREERS IN ANIMATION

IN-BETWEENER Because animation is literally bringing inanimate objects to life, each frame of an animated project has to be either hand-drawn or drawn on a computer so that the movement we see on our TV is smooth. In-betweeners are the people who do all the drawings in between key poses to make the transitions smooth.

2003–2007: Supervising producer/story supervisor, Cartoon Network Studios

2004: Nominated for an Emmy Award

2005: Nominated for an Annie Award (the highest honor for excellence in animation)

2009–2011: Creator and executive producer *My Little Pony: Friendship Is Magic*

2012: Began working as coproducer and story editor for *Wander Over Yonder*

BACKGROUND ARTIST   Live-action shows are filmed on location or on a set, but the background of an animated project has to be designed from scratch. Background artists look at photographs, art, and movies to get inspiration and then draw and paint the background, giving animated characters a "world" to live in.

CHARACTER DESIGNER Whoever your favorite animated characters are, behind their cool look is a character designer. Character designers are responsible for designing all of the animated characters in a show, making sure that the design is consistent with the creator's vision and the show's style.

ANIMATION TIMER   Bringing characters and objects to life is part of an animation timer's job. They act out what their characters will be physically doing and make notes on timing sheets on how many seconds each movement should take. This tells the in-betweeners how to translate the desired action through the drawings.

STORYBOARD ARTIST   Before any film, TV show, or commercial is produced, a storyboard is created to visually plan out what the end product will look like. In animation, a storyboard artist draws out each scene, detailing the action, sound effects, and dialogue. When it's finished, a storyboard might resemble a graphic novel.

YOU NEED TO KNOW ABOUT

Animation World Network, or AWN (www.awn.com), calls itself "The Hub of Animation on the Internet." This site has everything from interviews with leading animators and job postings to animation business directories and thousands of links to animation resources, as well as a free monthly online magazine called *Animation World* magazine.

lunch break

PROFESSIONALISM
101

When you're applying for an internship or job, being professional—in the interview, in your correspondence, in your life—is critical. That's because being *unprofessional* is a major turnoff, and it's the fastest way to take yourself out of the running for an open position.

Don't get me wrong—I'm not saying you need to be super formal or that you need to act like somebody you're not in order to land a job. It's possible to maintain your kick-ass personality while still presenting yourself in a way that's professional and appealing to prospective employers.

Here are some strategies to get you started:

Begin and end e-mails using appropriate salutations and closings. Dear Ms. _____is probably the safest choice, while if you've built up a rapport, opening an e-mail with "Hi (or "Hello") _____" is probably fine. Avoid using words like "Hey" as they feel too familiar, and on the flip side, don't go too formal and impersonal ("To whom it may concern"). For signing off, stick with something standard like "Sincerely," "Best regards," or the abridged, "Best."

Use "buffer" sentences. Always open and close your e-mails with a "buffer sentence" before launching into what you need or abruptly ending your note. An example of an opening buffer sentence would be, "It was a pleasure to talk with you on the phone last week" or "I hope this e-mail finds you well!" A closing buffer sentence might read, "I appreciate your taking the time to read this" or "I look forward to hearing from you soon."

Just say no to emoticons and abbreviated text speak. Use full words, with their correct spelling, all the time.

Keep follow-up correspondence brief and to the point. Whether it's a thank-you, a check-in e-mail, or a response to a request for more information, edit your message so it doesn't overload the recipient with unnecessary information.

Don't place demands on people. Be sure to phrase your follow-up or inquiry for more information as a *request*, not something you expect or demand a potential employer to provide to you. Nothing turns people off more than being told what to do.

Send a thank-you note. Always follow up an interview with a thank-you note to everyone you met with. Short, sweet, and to the point works fine (a handwritten note will earn you bonus points).

Proofread before hitting send. Be sure to read over (at least once, ideally twice) your e-mails and letters before sending them out into the big wide world to catch any spelling or grammar gaffes.

Clean up your digital media profile. You don't have to eliminate all traces of the real you online, but see if anything potential employers have access to contains content that could be seen as offensive or cause them to look unfavorably on you. If so, get rid of it or hide it using privacy settings. In additional to cleaning up traditional social media channels, Google yourself to find out what comes up (both text and picture), since you can be sure hiring managers are going to do the same.

SUSANNAH GRANT

Screenwriter

The Facts

Susannah Grant,
*Screenwriter and
Director*

WHAT? Screenwriters write the screenplays or movie scripts for every film that gets released, as well as for thousands of movies that never actually get made. They might adapt novels or other stories, or come up with an original concept to write about.

WHERE? Screenwriters can work anywhere, although many choose to live in L.A. or New York to be closer to the action.

HOW? Writing ... a lot! According to Susannah, "No one cares where you studied, if you studied, or whom you studied with. All they care about is whether or not you have something to say and can say it in a way that's either artistically accomplished or (more likely) commercially promising."

$$$: Anywhere from $5,000 to more than a million dollars a year

DRESS CODE? Anything they want

STRESS FACTOR: On a scale of 1 to 10, wildly and unpredictably between a 1 and a 10 (according to Susannah)

i know there are lots of aspiring screenwriters out there, so I wanted to profile someone whose films we've seen and who's work we really connect with. I was lucky enough to hook up with Susannah Grant, an extremely successful screenwriter whose writing earned her an Oscar nomination for *Erin Brockovich*. Susannah also wrote the screenplays for *Ever After* starring Drew Barrymore, *28 Days* with Sandra Bullock, and *Charlotte's Web*, starring Dakota Fanning and Julia Roberts.

"I try to focus on the things that are harder for me before I indulge in the stuff that's easy."

I talked with Susannah about how she got into screenwriting, what it feels like to work in Hollywood, and what she loves about her job. Here's our conversation—in screenplay form, of course.

INT. DEBBIE'S OFFICE IN SEATTLE. LATE MORNING.

Debbie dials Susannah's number and waits as the phone on the other end rings. She checks the clock to make sure she's calling on time.

After three rings, Susannah picks up the phone.

INT. SUSANNAH'S OFFICE IN SANTA MONICA, CA.

Screen becomes split screen so we can see both Debbie and Susannah talking.

DEBBIE

Hi, Susannah! It's Debbie Reber calling.

SUSANNAH

Hi, Debbie!

DEBBIE

Is this still a good time to talk?

SUSANNAH

Yes, it's perfect.

DEBBIE

Great. Do you mind if I put you on speakerphone so I can record our conversation?

SUSANNAH

No problem.

Debbie pushes the orange speaker button on her phone and gently sets the handpiece down in its cradle while pushing "record" on her tiny handheld recorder.

DEBBIE

All right . . . we're set! I would love to start by hearing in your own words what exactly you do as a screenwriter.

YOU ASKED . . .

"How have you managed to keep going and believing in yourself and your dreams even if other people gave up on you and stopped believing in you?" **—MANDY, AGE 18**

SUSANNAH ANSWERED . . .

"It's difficult working in a field where people are judging you on some level. And it's easy to think that if they don't like the writing, then there's something wrong with you. So before I expose my work to anyone else, I decide for myself how I think I've done. And if I don't think I've done as well as I could, then I don't turn in the script yet. Once I get to the point where I can look myself in the mirror and say, 'I did a good job this time, regardless of whatever anyone else thinks,' then I put it out there. It's a very conscious thing I do, because you can make yourself crazy hoping for validation from others."

THE BREAKDOWN

WRITING: 60 percent of the day

PHONE CALLS WITH AGENTS,
PRODUCERS, STUDIO PEOPLE:
40 percent of the day

SUSANNAH

I try to create and communicate stories through the
film medium that move
people, that make them
think, that challenge their
ideas of who we are. I
spent a lot of time watching films when I was growing up, and
it always felt like it was a positive force in my life. Now I like to
write stories that will have the same impact and comment on
the world around us.

DEBBIE

What is it about films that you love so much?

SUSANNAH

I think there's something really powerful about sitting in the
dark with a couple hundred people and having a significant
emotional experience. There's something that happens in the
air when you're all laughing together or you're all moved at the
same time. I like to be a part of creating that for people.

DEBBIE

What are some of the movies that really inspired you when you
were a teen?

THEN TO NOW

| Graduated from Amherst College with BA in English literature | Worked as a fact checker for *Rolling Stone* magazine | Attended American Film Institute (AFI) | 1992: Was awarded the Nicholl Fellowship in Screen-writing | 1994: Staff writer on *Party of Five* for FOX | 1998: Wrote the screenplay for *Ever After: A Cinderella Story* |

The one that really rocked my world was *Network*. I watched that when I was thirteen or fourteen and it just blew my mind. But it was always more about the experience than the movies. (*laughs*) My friend and I created the "dreadful movie club," and the two of us would pick the worst movie in the paper and go and see it and have a fantastic time.

DEBBIE

So did you know you wanted to pursue a career in screenwriting after you graduated from high school?

SUSANNAH

No. I majored in English in college. After college I thought I would be a journalist or an actress, so I lived in New York and pursued both for a while. Along the way I tried to write a screenplay, but I just couldn't quite figure it out. Eventually I reached a point where I looked ahead and I just couldn't see a career in journalism or acting working for me. So I abandoned both and I moved out of New York. I ended up in San Francisco, where I had a job I didn't like very much and a boyfriend who I really liked a lot. When he finished law school, my boyfriend decided to travel around the world for a year, so I asked him if I could borrow his computer. The plan was I would meet him in Paris in six months. I tried writing a screenplay again, and for some reason, it all came together nicely

2000: Wrote the screenplay for *28 Days*

2000: Nominated for an Oscar for her screenplay *Erin Brockovich*

2006: Wrote the screenplay for *Charlotte's Web*

2007: Made directorial debut with her original screenplay *Catch and Release*

2009: Wrote screenplay for *The Soloist*

2011: Became executive producer and writer for CBS series *A Gifted Man*

and I had so much fun doing it. And then I went to Paris to meet up with the guy and he had met a Swedish model in Thailand and fallen in love with her. So our relationship was completely kaput, but I had a screenplay and a passion that I really liked.

DEBBIE

Can you break down for us how the process of writing a screenplay works for you, from the seed of the idea through the completion of the movie?

THE SCREENWRITING PROCESS ────────────

THE PITCH *The first step is getting a job and signing on to write something. The ideas for your screenplays will either come from you as a writer or they'll come from somebody else who has an idea. The screenwriter articulates the idea so that somebody who's going to be paying you to write it can get a sense of what they're paying for up front. That's called "pitching." It's going into a room and saying, "Here's the movie I want to make with you," and then talking them through it, trying to give a sense of how the movie will feel. And ideally they say, "That sounds great, let's go ahead and write the script."*

WRITING THE SCRIPT *They pay you half your fee up front and the other half when you deliver the first draft, and you contractually get three months to write that first draft. I usually take one month to just think and make notes and an outline and stuff like that, and then the rest of the time will be writing it. But I don't just sit down to write it until I know what I'm going to be writing. During the writing you're pretty much alone and doing your own thing. . . . I really love doing the first draft because then it's just mine. Usually you do a second draft and often a third. If everything goes smoothly, after a couple of drafts we'll have something that everyone feels* good about, and then it becomes the studio producer's job to turn it into a movie.

MAKING THE MOVIE   The writer's involvement in this stage varies. Sometimes turning in a final script is the end of your involvement, but more often than not I get what's called "meaningful consultation" in the production. I can't approve or disapprove anything, but if somebody suggested a director or actor who seemed completely wrong for the project, I would at least be listened to. But that's something that comes with a certain amount of experience—early on in your career, it's not going to happen. Once a director's on, you tend to do more work on the script with the director, because getting it ready to shoot is different from getting it ready to just be read. Once they start shooting, if you had a good relationship with the director, you're often welcome on the set, and that can be fun and it can also be very tedious. Making a movie is a lot of long hours with nothing happening, but it is fun to watch it initially.

POSTPRODUCTION OF THE MOVIE   After the filming, which takes about three months, the producers create a "rough cut" or rough edit of the movie, and if you've been intimately involved with the director, sometimes he or she will bring you in to consult on the cuts of the movie as it gets edited, but that's not a given.

MOVIE IS RELEASED   The movie comes out and you go to the premiere, and that's fun. And then you read the reviews and sometimes they're good, sometimes they're not. I try not to read the reviews; instead, I make sure that by this time I'm writing something else.

TIMELINE   In a fast-track scenario it can take two years from when you first decided to write something to it being on the screen. Sometimes it can take decades.

WHAT IT TAKES

- A love of writing and the movies
- Extreme self-motivation
- Good networking and people skills
- No shortage of good ideas

DEBBIE

You've had such a successful screenwriting career. What's your secret?

SUSANNAH

I've had really good luck and I've worked extremely hard, and writing only gets better the more you work at it. There's no point at which working more on a script is actually damaging. The easiest thing for me is writing dialogue that reads well, so I try to focus on the things that are harder for me before I indulge in the stuff that's easy. And I think that level of rigor has probably helped me professionally.

DEBBIE

Do Hollywood takes on screenwriting portray a true picture?

SUSANNAH

It's true that screenwriters are sort of the low woman (or man) on the totem pole. But on the flip side, screenwriters are the only people in the film industry who don't need someone else's permission to work. So for example, if you've gotten into a position where nobody thinks you can write anything but silly comedies, all you need to do is write a drama and prove

everybody wrong. You can write yourself out of any professional hole if you're willing to work hard enough.

DEBBIE

Do you need to have an agent in this biz?

SUSANNAH

Yeah, you really can't get your ideas in front of studios without
an agent.

DEBBIE

What would you say is the best part about your job?

SUSANNAH

Since I've had children, I'd say that the best thing is the flexibility and that I can work when I want to—it's the biggest luxury
you can imagine. Also, if you get a certain amount of success,
it's a job that pays really well. I really like working with funny,
creative, crazy people and there just don't seem to be as many
rules as there are in other professional environments. Lastly, I
get to work on something that I love—movies.

DEBBIE

What film are you most proud of?

SUSANNAH

Obviously *Erin Brockovich* is the one that people have
responded to most strongly. I really do like that work—I love
the person, I love the movie it ended up being. I have a real
fondness for the ones that fail, too. But my favorite one is
always the next one I'm working on.

DEBBIE

Do you do a lot of research when you're writing a movie?

Perfect note to end on. Thanks so much for letting us peek inside your world, Susannah. Bye!

SUSANNAH

Thanks for including me in the book! Good-bye!

Susannah and Debbie both hang up the phone. Screen goes black.

SUSANNAH'S ADVICE

If you're a teenager interested in becoming a screenwriter, the most important thing I can tell you is this: Don't write screenplays. Not yet. The screenplay form is so full of mechanics that it's almost impossible to find your voice as a writer within it. And all that matters as a screenwriter—as any kind of writer—is voice. So write something else, anything else—poems, letters, stories. Write lots of them. Eventually you'll feel your way to who you are as a writer. You'll notice where your sensibilities lie, what you're good at, what you need to get better at. The more rigorous you are in discovering what you have to say in this world, the greater the odds are that once you write a screenplay, (a) it will be time well spent, and (b) someone will buy it.

In the Field

FIVE MORE CAREERS WORKING AS A WRITER

NOVELIST Novelists create amazing worlds in their heads and write about them in ways that keep the readers glued to the page. Like screenwriting, writing fiction books takes a lot of self-discipline—novelists do most of the work all alone, hunched over a computer or typewriter and transferring their ideas and thoughts onto the page.

PLAYWRIGHT While screenwriters write for celluloid, playwrights write for the stage. And whether it's a one-act skit or an opera, playwrights take into consideration the venue of their play and create material that will translate well in a theater.

TECHNICAL WRITER As computers and technology become a larger part of everyday life, the technical writing field continues to boom. These writers might write brochures about new products, directions on how to use computers and software, or press releases and articles explaining complicated concepts in ways that the layperson can understand.

FREELANCE WRITER Freelance writers usually work from home, and they might write anything from magazine articles to marketing materials for a big company. Like most self-employed people, freelance writers are always looking for their next job, even as they're working on a dozen projects at once.

COLUMNIST Columnists don't get paid to report the news objectively, but rather present their strong opinions and perspectives to the public. Well-known columnists might be syndicated in major newspapers all over the country, while others might have a monthly column in a magazine.

YOU NEED TO KNOW ABOUT

Creative Screenwriting is a magazine aimed at screenwriters, with great articles about the trade, interviews with screenwriters, resources, and updates on news relating to the biz. Check it out at your local bookstore or read more about it online at www.creativescreenwriting.com.

For more on writing in Hollywood, check out the TV show creator profile on page 1.

MICHELLE GRANDY

Nurse-Midwife

The Facts

WHAT? Nurse midwives are nurses who've taken additional coursework to become certified as a midwife, which means they specialize in overall women's health care and caring for pregnant women, delivering babies, and providing postnatal care.

WHERE? Most midwives work in hospital settings, while others are at birthing centers or start their own practice.

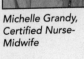

Michelle Grandy, Certified Nurse-Midwife

HOW? Nurse midwives need a four-year bachelor's degree in nursing or a related field, as well as a master's degree from a certified nurse-midwifery program.

$$$: An average salary of $90,000

DRESS CODE? Casual to business casual while in the office or clinic, and scrubs while delivering a baby

STRESS FACTOR: On a scale of 1 to 10, between a 6 and an 8 (depending on the day)

i wanted to interview someone in the medical profession for this book, and I just loved the idea of talking with a midwife, because unlike many jobs in medicine where people are responding to an emergency, illness, or disease, midwives are dealing with something that's positive—pregnancy and childbirth.

Michelle is a certified nurse-midwife who works out of Northwest Hospital in Seattle. I met with her in her office at the clinic.

ME: How does a midwife do things differently from a doctor?

MICHELLE: Midwifery focuses on a holistic view of pregnancy and childbirth. I think a lot of times medical professionals see pregnancy as more the physical piece of it, and some of the other pieces get left behind. But pregnancy, the birth, and parenting changes everything about a woman—it changes every relationship she has, including the one she has with herself, it changes her emotional state, her spiritual state. And so for a lot of women who have normal, healthy pregnancies, the physical piece is small in comparison to this whole other journey that's happening.

"Everything can be total chaos around me, but I can see my way through the logical steps to get us to where we need to be."

Physicians see high-risk pregnancies all the time and so they're kind of expecting that at any moment a pregnancy can become a problem. And of course that's true, but why would you spend your energy thinking about that when it's 80 percent or 90 percent likely that everything's going to be totally fine? And while as midwives we always have in our mind all of the high-risk things that can happen in a pregnancy, if a woman presents to me as normal, my expectation is that she is normal and will continue to be normal through this journey, unless she shows me something different. In which case we'll take those other paths to find out what's going on.

ME: How do you help women through this "other journey" they're on?

MICHELLE: Part of it is giving them time—I have twenty to thirty minutes for each appointment. And I think the other part is being "open." When I sit down with a pregnant woman, the first thing I say is "Hi, how are you?" And then I say, "Tell me what questions or concerns you have." And then I just wait in silence for those to come forth. And if she says, "I don't know . . . everything's fine," I might give another open-ended question, and then wait. I'm leaving the space open for her to talk. And if she truly is fine and she truly doesn't have anything to say and everything's totally cool, which happens a lot, then I always have an agenda of things to talk about, based on where she is in the pregnancy, and things to check in with her about. But I'll always give her the space to talk first.

ME: What is it like when you're actually with a woman who's in labor and about to give birth?

MICHELLE: I have the ability to remain calm in very stressful situations. I think that tends to be the characteristic of lots of

YOU ASKED . . .

"How have you pushed past all the problems and obstacles life has thrown at you to be where you are today?"
—JOANNE, AGE 15

MICHELLE ANSWERED . . .

"My biggest obstacles centered around financing my education. My family didn't save any money for me to go to college, so I had to go off of loans and scholarships and whatever I could get. Getting good enough grades so that I could qualify for whatever monies were being given out by the school was really important. I stayed motivated by being passionate about the work and feeling like I could make a difference."

medical providers. Everything can be total chaos around me, but I can see my way through the logical steps to get us to where we need to be. Although a woman who's having a normal labor is not "chaos," for her it's very intense, it's very painful, and the sensations are very strong in her body. I'm also keeping an eye on everything that

THE BREAKDOWN

IN MEETINGS: Several times a month

ON THE PHONE: 1 hour a day

ONLINE: Half hour a day

STANDING: Half the day

PUBLIC SPEAKING: Occasionally

READING: 1–2 hours a day

WORKING SOLO: Almost never

could go wrong, and signs that problems might be coming down the road. Is the baby doing okay? Is it doing well enough that I think it's going to be okay for the next hour or two or three or however long I think it's going to take us to get to the end of this journey? That's always something I'm tracking. How is the father of the baby doing? Has he eaten lately? How's his energy store? And whoever else is in the room supporting her, are they getting what they need? At the same time, I also hold positive energy and confidence in the woman's ability to deliver the baby—"I know you can do this."

ME: When did you know you wanted to be a midwife?

MICHELLE: When I was in college, I was studying to be a nurse,

THEN TO NOW

1987: Graduated from Seattle Pacific University with BS in nursing

1987–1989: Worked as a nurse at the Veteran's Administration Medical Center in Seattle

1989–1995: Worked as a nurse in labor and delivery, postpartum, and the nursery, Northwest Hospital

WHY WAIT?

- If you have a close friend or family member who is pregnant, see if you can attend the birth as an observer.
- Contact a local birth center or women's health clinic and ask about observing a midwife for the day.
- Read books about midwifery, like *Baby Catcher: Chronicles of a Modern Midwife* by Peggy Vincent.

and I had a semester on obstetrics nursing with a great professor, and the idea that pregnancy is a "normal process" connected with me. There are few types of ways to work in medicine where you're actually dealing with healthy people, so I liked that a lot. Then, when I was working as an OB nurse, I'd be giving women in labor great support, being right there with them and coaching them, and then I'd have the physician walk in at the last minute, catch the baby, and get all the money and all the glory. I thought, *I'd like to do that.*

ME: What's the reality of the job that girls should know about if they're interested in being a midwife?

MICHELLE: It involves happy, fun experiences most of the time. But there are lots of times when it's hard and stressful, too. And there are times when things don't go well or the baby dies. I mean, that

WHAT IT TAKES

- Staying cool under pressure
- A nurturing nature
- Being a good listener

1996: Received master's in nursing from University of Washington

1996–2003: Worked as a certified nurse-midwife at Providence Everett Medical Center

2003: Began working as certified nurse-midwife at University of Washington Medical Center

2003: Joined faculty at University of Washington School of Medicine does happen. It doesn't happen a lot, but a lot of people say, "Oh, how wonderful to be a midwife," and on my good days I say, "Yes, it is wonderful." But you do get those life-and-death moments, those scary moments where the woman is bleeding and you're the one standing there and trying to manage it. You have to be able to think ahead really fast.

MICHELLE'S (UN)USUAL DAY

There are two different kinds of days in my work. One is a "clinic day" where I'm scheduled from eight thirty a.m. to five p.m., with an hour break in the middle of the day. I have clients scheduled every half hour during that time, unless it's a new client, and then I see them for an hour. With each client, I go in, spend twenty to thirty minutes with them, then come out and do some charting, which is writing down everything that happened during a visit on that client's chart. Then I move on to see the next client.

Typically, things happen—people are late, somebody talks a little longer, somebody has more extensive problems— and then things back up. When things get backed up, that can cause some stress. So sometimes a lunch that is supposedly an hour is really only fifteen minutes, or I'm supposed to be out at five p.m. but things got busy, and I didn't have a chance to do my charting, so now I have to do that at the end of the day. That happened more when I was new—I would take too long because I couldn't think as clearly about problems. Now that I've been a midwife for eighteen years, it happens less and less.

On my "call days," I'm on call for twenty-four hours, so I will be with anyone in our group who is in labor. We usually have between twenty and thirty women due to deliver a baby each month in our practice, and they don't come one a day. I'll have one twenty-four-hour shift where not much is happening, and then I'll have another where I have three women in labor and I'm kind of going from room to room to be with them.

During a labor, I'll come in and out of the labor room depending on where the woman is in the process and what she needs. If she has three or four people in there all attending to her every need and she's coping really well, at a certain point during her labor I'll be there less. And as the labor progresses and things get more intense, I'm there almost constantly. After the birth I usually stay until the baby starts breastfeeding and everybody seems settled, and then I'll leave because the nurses will take over and get the woman everything she needs—food, a shower, a bath for the baby. Then one of the other midwives or I will see the woman every day that she's in the hospital and talk about going home—what to expect and any concerns she might have.

In The Field

FIVE MORE CAREERS IN HEALTHCARE

CHIROPRACTOR Chiropractors study the spine and nervous system and look at their impact on overall health. Unlike doctors, chiropractors approach healing from a less "medicalized" perspective, and they use healing tools like massage, electrotherapy, and ultrasound therapy.

PHYSICIAN'S ASSISTANT Physician's assistants, also known as PAs, work closely with doctors in hospitals, clinics, or private practices doing different procedures that a doctor might typically do. They might take medical histories, perform physical exams, draw blood for testing, give shots, dress wounds, and make diagnoses.

LAB TECHNICIAN Hospitals never rest, and lab technicians work around the clock in hospitals, testing blood, tissue samples, and body fluids to help doctors diagnose their patients.

ER DOCTOR Doctors who specialize in emergency care have to be ready, willing, and able to handle any problems that come through the emergency room door, and they never know what illnesses or injuries their next shift might bring.

ANESTHESIOLOGIST These medical doctors specialize in administering anesthesia to patients. Much of the work of anesthesiologists involves putting people "under" for surgery, and then monitoring the patient throughout the operation to ensure that they are stable and pain free.

For more careers in health and medicine, check out the nurse profile on page 128 and the physical therapist profile on page 416.

DEENA WEISE

Dental Hygienist

The Facts

WHAT? Dental hygienists specialize in oral health care and help their patients by cleaning their teeth, performing oral examinations, and offering preventive health care.

WHERE? Dental hygienists almost always work in a dentist's office

HOW? You'll need at least an associate's degree in dental hygiene and to pass a licensing exam, as well as do continuing education to stay on top of new trends and techniques.

Deena Weise,
Dental Hygienist

$$$: A median annual salary of $70,000

DRESS CODE? Medical scrubs

STRESS FACTOR: On a scale of 1 to 10, a 4

if you've been to the dentist (and let's hope you have . . . regularly!), you've interacted with a dental hygienist. While you may think of these specialists solely as the people who clean your teeth, their job is really about helping their patients work toward the most optimum dental health possible.

For this profile I interviewed Deena Weise, who's been a practicing dental hygienist in her hometown of Oley, Pennsylvania, for more than twenty-five years. I happen to know for a fact that Deena not only loves her job, but she knew she wanted to be a dental hygienist from a very young age. (I know this because she's one of my closest childhood friends!) But I'll let her tell you about it in her own words.

"When I was in middle school, I had braces, and it was probably at that point, when I started to go to the orthodontist, where I started to be fascinated by teeth and the mouth and a career that works with the public. Because I would go to that office and they would always be so nice and cheerful—it seemed like a happy place to go. So I researched all the jobs in the dental field, and it seemed like dental hygiene was a good fit. At the time, I didn't want to go to a four-year college. So dental hygiene was

"I love that I can be one-on-one with a patient, and that's why I picked dental hygiene over dental assisting. My patients have taught me so many things along the way."

a great fit for me because it was a two-year associate degree program, and then I was able to be licensed to practice and come out in the working world and become a dental hygienist right away," she explains.

DEENA'S TYPICAL DAY

When I first get to work, I look at my schedule and see how many patients I have that day, to see who is coming in and exactly what services they're going to need. Then I get my room cleaned and ready and set up my trays of instruments (either sterilized or disposable).

Usually I see my first patient at eight a.m., so I bring them back to my room and interact with them. And when I say I interact with them, I actually just stop, make eye contact with them, and just connect and talk with them. "How's your last six months been? Have there been any medical changes? Is there anything I need to know?" It's really important that I connect with my patient and get them comfortable.

Next, I usually put my mask and my glasses on. I either have to take Xrays or I just get right into the dental cleaning, and I clean their teeth, of course talking to them a little bit during that period. After we're all done, we'll discuss if there's anything different or new that I need them to do in the next six months to get a better result in their mouth. Or if they're doing really well, I might just tell them to keep up the good work.

Next, the doctor I work for will come in and check my patient, and when he's done, I'll make their appointment for their next checkup and say good-bye.

And it kind of just flows like that throughout the day. Usually I have forty minutes for an adult, and thirty to forty

YOU ASKED . . .

"Have you ever wished you chose a different career?"

—MADDY, AGE 14

DEENA ANSWERED . . .

"Yes, there were times throughout my twenty-five-year career where I felt like, what do I want to do when I grow up, even though I was in this amazing profession and I loved it. But I think those are natural life observations. I think it's okay to think that you want to do something else, but I just continued with my love, and that was dental hygiene. Do I think that someday I'll do something else? Well, I don't know. I am very happy and content in what I'm doing now."

minutes for a child. It just depends. I see patients from three years old to one hundred years old. So there's a wide variety in my day.

Because there are many people who have anxiety about visiting the dentist, I was curious to know more about how Deena deals with patients who are less than happy to be sitting in the dentist's chair. She explained that being a good dental hygienist is more than just being an expert at the technical side of the job—being warm, personable, empathetic, and able to connect are very important.

"I am very individualized in dealing with my patients. Even if it's somebody that I've seen and I already know, I still connect with them in the beginning—so many things can happen in their lives in that six months. So I take that first five minutes of the appointment to see what their mood is. Maybe they had a death in the family. They may have gotten married. They may have had a baby. So you just kind of observe and go from there.

THE BREAKDOWN

ON THE PHONE: 30 minutes

SURFING THE WEB: 30 minutes

SOCIAL MEDIA: 30 minutes

E-MAILING AND INSTANT MESSAGING: 30 minutes

SITTING: 30 minutes

STANDING: 6 hours

READING: 1 hour

WORKING SOLO: 6 hours

THEN TO NOW

1989: Graduated from Northampton Community College with AA in applied science in dental hygiene

1989: Became registered dental hygienist

1990–1999: Worked as dental hygienist for Dr. Dennis Petricoin, DDS

WHY WAIT?

Be proactive about your own dental health and pay close attention when you go to the dentist for your regular checkups.

Do I have to be more sensitive during the appointment? Do I have to distract the patient a little bit more? I individualize for each patient, especially with kids or if they have special needs. I'm definitely emotionally and physically exhausted by the end of the day, because I'm very in tune with my patients and try to make them feel comfortable in the chair," Deena explains.

I could tell from talking with Deena that her patients are her passion. I asked her if working with people is the part of her job she loves the most.

Deena answered, "Yes, I love that I can be one-on-one with a patient, and that's why I picked dental hygiene over dental assisting. My patients have taught me so many things along the way. I have patients who are runners. I have patients who are doctors. I have patients who are moms. There's just such a wide variety of people you meet along the way, and it's fascinating most of the time. I'm always anxious to hear their stories, and it's made me a very good listener.

"I have this one patient who came into our office with a mouth that, let's just say he never wanted to smile. He could've used orthodontics earlier in his life, but he had some other problems, including missing teeth, plus he was in jeopardy of

1999: Worked as dental hygienist for Dr. David Causa, DMD

2000–present: Dental hygienist with Dr. Damon Tomeo, DMD

losing more of his teeth. He had a long dental road ahead of him. When he first came in, he didn't really want to talk or smile. I took my time with him and said, listen, if you stick with us, trust us, and you do what we tell you to do, you're going to end up having more longevity, and you're going to want to smile a whole lot more in the end. And between me

WHAT IT TAKES
- Patience
- Being outgoing and an extrovert
- Being a good listener
- Good people skills
- Flexibility
- Being okay working with saliva, bacteria, splatter, and other bodily fluids

getting him into better dental health and the dentist doing a whole bunch of dental work . . . you should see that man smile. His whole personality changed. It was a really fun transformation."

But as with most jobs, I knew that there had to be parts of the job that were more challenging than others. As it turns out, the same thing that Deena loves—working with people—can also be the part that is difficult. Sometimes patients are cranky or unfriendly, and Deena can bear the brunt of that negative energy. And sometimes it's just being "on" all day in an effort to connect with each and every patient.

"By the end of the day I'm exhausted," she explains. "It's kind of like being a hamster on a wheel. It can be a little bit monotonous, because you're setting up for a patient. You're bringing a patient back. You're connecting with that patient. You're cleaning that patient. It's pretty much the same thing every appointment. And it takes a lot of energy to be 'present' that whole time. There's definitely some decompression I have to do after work. Sometimes it just takes a car ride. Sometimes I need an hour or two. For me, refocusing on my family is usually what brings me out of it, whether it's coming home and cooking dinner or it's going to one of their sporting events. Or sometimes I'll run."

But if you ask Deena, she wouldn't have it any other way. Dental hygiene has been the perfect career for her life and lifestyle. It's enabled her to be available for her busy life as a mom raising two daughters, and still find time to practice self-care.

"One of the best parts of this job is that you can, for the most part, make your own schedule. You can work five or six days a week. You can work one day a week. And the majority of dental hygiene jobs are not on the weekends. They're not at night. They're not on holidays. So it's just very conducive while you're raising a family, for sure," she says.

Not only is dental hygiene flexible, but it's also stable. In fact, career projectionists list it as one of the best-growing careers in the coming decades. That's one of the reasons why Deena has never looked back after choosing to go down this career path so many years ago.

"Like anything, it's had its ups and downs. But I've never in twenty-five years experienced a drought of jobs. It's a well-paying job, there is job security, there are usually health and retirement benefits. Dentistry is becoming much more preventive, so everyone is taking really good care of their teeth, they're going to the dentist, and people have dental insurance. So people are keeping their teeth, which means I will always have a job, because there'll always be teeth to clean!"

DEENA'S CAREER ADVICE

Keep your options open—don't feel like you need to decide right away what to do for your career. Major in something general and then, as you get older, you can decide what to do as you start to experience life a little bit more.

In the Field

FIVE MORE CAREERS WORKING IN DENTAL HEALTH

DENTIST Hopefully you're very familiar with what a dentist does, because you see your dentist twice a year for checkups. General dentists provide preventive and maintenance dental care, doing everything from cleanings and fluoride treatments to filling cavities, pulling teeth, and performing more complex dental procedures such as root canals.

ORTHODONTIST If you've ever worn braces, you already know what orthodontists are all about. These specialists focus on jaw alignment and position of the teeth and spend much of their time working with children and adults to give them the smile they want.

PERIODONTIST A periodontist is a type of dentist whose focus is on gum care, tending to patients with gum disease, dental implants, and more. Periodonists are required to have an additional three years of education beyond dental school.

ORAL SURGEON When a patient requires surgery on the mouth, jaws, or facial bones, they are often referred to an oral surgeon, who specializes in these types of operations. Oral surgeons might do anything from standard wisdom teeth removal to jaw reconstruction surgery.

DENTAL LABORATORY TECHNICIAN When people lose teeth, they often get replacement teeth so they can do things like chew, talk, and eat normally. Dental laboratory technicians use their technical and artistic expertise to create realistic teeth implants based on molds of the patients' teeth.

YOU NEED TO KNOW ABOUT

The American Dental Hygienists' Association (ADHA) is a peer-based community supporting dental hygienists by ensuring access to quality oral health care, promoting dental hygiene education, licensure and reach, and more. Their website—www.adha.org—has an extensive section on career planning and development for would-be dental hygienists.

AMANDA KOSTER

Photographer

*Amanda Koster,
Freelance
Photographer*

The Facts

WHAT? Professional photographers are paid to take photographs—from wedding and editorial photos to magazine photos and fashion shoots.

WHERE? They might work for magazines or companies as in-house photographers, while many are self-employed and work out of their own studios as freelancers.

HOW? There are no strict educational requirements, although most photographers take classes to learn about lighting, development techniques, and other skills. Most photographers work as an assistant or apprentice to an established photographer to learn about the job.

$$$: An average of $25,000 to $65,000 on up, depending on the kind of photography

DRESS CODE? Casual

STRESS FACTOR: On a scale of 1 to 10, a 5

it's taken her several years, but photographer Amanda Koster has found herself in the enviable position of having created her ideal work situation. While she spent much of her early career doing freelance editorial work for magazines and newspapers, over the past ten years, Amanda has been able to focus much more on her personal passion of telling stories of real people, human rights, cultural diversity, and global equality through her work. In addition to taking powerful photographs, she runs the digital storytelling organization she founded, SalaamGarage, creates multimedia content for clients like the Bill and Melinda Gates Foundation, *Newsweek*, and the *New York Times*, teaches storytelling at the university level, writes books, and presents at TEDx conferences. Talk about a multifaceted career!

"In many ways it has been my tenacity that has led me to where I am today."

Since Amanda splits her time between her separate work worlds, she shared her journal with us for two very different days in her life. Here are her entries.

AMANDA'S JOURNAL

april 25, seattle, wa

Today I woke up at five thirty a.m. I have an assignment for Sunset magazine, so I'm heading to Dungeness National Wildlife Refuge on the Olympic Peninsula, an amazing park near where the subject lives.

Like any morning before a shoot, today I did my normal rush around the house to gather all of my gear and information. For this kind of shoot I travel light with portable gear, my favorite way to work. Photographing outside feels the best to me, and though the morning is hectic, I look forward to meeting my subject and working outside today.

My assistant arrives around six a.m. She knows exactly how my gear should be packed and does a double check.

We laugh about how early it is, have a little tea, and load up the car, heading north on I-5 by six thirty. We have to race to catch the ferry and just make it by three minutes. Once we are crossing Puget Sound on the ferry, the view of the Olympic Mountain Range is beautiful. . . . It felt great to be out of the city.

Our subject, Gordon, was waiting for us at the park when we got there. I usually like to talk with people before we start shooting to get an idea of how comfortable they are with being photographed, if they've done this before, and if they have any ideas. I also like to do some location scouting by walking around with my assistant and finding good spots to photograph, keeping in mind the direction of the light, everything that's in the background, and how busy the location is. Today we discovered the perfect spot.

We photographed Gordon for about a half hour. I tried

YOU ASKED . . .

"When did you decide that this is what you wanted to do with your life?"   —KAYLA, AGE 12

AMANDA ANSWERED . . .

"I was studying to be an anthropologist, and I thought that taking pictures of my research would be a great way to get myself ahead as an anthropologist. When I graduated from college, a friend of mine asked me to come to Ethiopia with her. I'd never been to Africa before, and I went and took all of these photos of kids in Ethiopia, brought back the photos and showed them to people, and no one believed I had actually been there. Everybody said, 'I thought everyone in Ethiopia was starving to death. These kids aren't starving—they're wearing winter jackets, and they're smiling and they have chubby cheeks.' When I realized how powerful photos were as a way to teach people about the rest of the world, that's when I knew what I was meant to do."

THE BREAKDOWN

(AN OFFICE DAY)

IN MEETINGS: 2 hours a day

ON THE PHONE: 2–8 hours a day

ONLINE: 3–6 hours a day

SITTING: All day

READING: 2 hours a day

WORKING SOLO: All day unless assistant is in

(SHOOTING DAY)

IN MEETINGS: 1 hour a day

ON THE PHONE: 30 minutes a day

ONLINE: 2 hours a day

STANDING: Most of the day

READING: 1 hour a day

photographing from many different angles, since things in any shoot—the light, the conversation, and the energy—are constantly changing. I also have to be very sure that Gordon is comfortable at all times in order to get the best results.

While I was shooting, my assistant was taking meter readings, making sure bugs didn't crawl into my camera bag, that the drizzle didn't touch my gear, and that no hikers ran over my lenses.

We wrapped up the photo shoot and were on our way home by noon. My assistant drove so that I could make phone calls, write lists . . . just think. We stopped for lunch, caught our ferry to the mainland, and dropped the film off at the lab to be processed on our way back to the studio.

We're in my office by three o'clock. We listen to Youssou N'Dour's amazing album Egypt, while my assistant works on some scanning and Web design and I return a few calls, check my e-mails, and get back in the office groove. It seems as though there are always twenty e-mails to compose and fifteen calls to make at any given moment.

By five thirty, my assistant heads out, while I stick around to finish up a few more things. I've always got e-mails coming

WHY WAIT?

- Start taking pictures now! Photograph things that interest and excite you.
- Take a photography class in your school if it's offered.

in from people in other time zones, so I handle them as well. E-mails from Western Europe and New York usually get me up early, while those from other countries keep me going late into the night. It doesn't bother me at all—I like to feel connected to the planet.

As I walk home, it's like I can feel the entire time zone unwinding. The sun is setting and there are fewer cars on the streets. People are smiling more, moving a bit slower. The cats are out, eyes closed, very still. I love this time of day.

After I make dinner, I sit at my kitchen window, eat, and do some journaling, still seeing traces of daylight in the sky. An airplane flies by and I think of Saturday, when I will leave for Morocco and I, too, will be on a plane that high.

april 29, fès, morocco

Today I am in Morocco. This is one of seven days where I am photographing a project called "Moroccan Women's Music Project: Voices of Women in Islam." Our goal is to create a CD of musicians performing, as well as a multimedia collection of photographs, video, and sound for an exhibition that will tour with the CD release.

I woke up around five a.m. to pack up my gear before

THEN TO NOW

1993: Graduated from Southern Connecticut State University with BS in art history, anthropology, and religious studies	1993: First traveled to Ethiopia	Took photography courses at International Center of Photography, New York	1995: Established own company, Amanda Koster Photography

breakfast. Our team was leaving right after we ate, driving to the town of Taroudant, six hours away. With me was the production team—a videographer, my photography assistant, a producer, a sound engineer, two musicians, a coproducer, a linguist, a translator, and a fixer—as well as our driver.

I first got involved in this project while attending a panel discussion about traditional Moroccan music in Brooklyn, where I encountered Zeyba Rahman, the chairperson of the World Music Institute. I was so inspired that I approached her with an idea for a photography exhibition that could travel with the CD release and concerts. I thought it was important that people had the chance to see the women they were hearing.

Luckily, Zeyba saw the merit in my idea and asked me to be a part of the project. Looking back, I can see that this is how much of my work happens. In many ways it has been my tenacity that has led me to where I am today.

The musicians were waiting for us when we arrived in Taroudant, dressed in their traditional clothing, smiling and chirping amongst themselves. After nearly a year of preparations, it felt amazing to be there with them. The women were wearing the most amazing blue-colored jellabas (Moroccan women's outerwear). Underneath the jellabas they were wearing their traditional clothing, which we thought would preserve all aspects of this particular tradition for the photos.

2001: Launched body image project called "This Is Beautiful"

2005: Went to Kenya as a mentor and instructor with Bridges to Understanding

2007: Founded Salaam-Garage

2008: Amanda's book *Can I Come with You?* is published

2010: Gave her first TEDx talk

We got set up and the women started performing their music with a simple chant. The chant began to build on itself, the rhythm speeding up and new instruments being introduced. The music creates a sense of contemplation and divine focus, and as a result, I found myself in a contemplative state, which made photographing interesting. I found that the more I invited this feeling in, the more I was able to follow the music, the chanting, and the exchange going on among the musicians. This kind of connection is important for my work. Whether I'm photographing the CEO of Microsoft, a woman who was widowed by HIV/AIDS, or a Moroccan musician, the connection must be there.

We had some technical challenges today, because the musicians perform inside dark rooms and they are constantly moving, so I had to push photography to the limit with the ASA, motion, depth of field, and focus. I have the feeling focus will suffer throughout this project because there was always such limited light. However, over the years I have learned to just let go and appreciate what I get.

The women I was photographing were awesome. I tried to remember when certain things would happen in the various songs so that I could anticipate a movement to photograph. For example, there was one woman whaling on a small clay drum. I wanted to make sure I could shoot underneath her because the action was wild and her expression was so intense. The drummer knew what I was doing, and when she

PAYING YOUR DUES

Many photographers spend several years working as a photographer's assistant, which is basically a paid apprenticeship. Photographer's assistants are the right-hand person to a photographer, and they learn the ropes while doing things like running errands, booking photo shoots, making copies, managing portfolios, and answering the phones.

hit the drum, she smiled, like she knew I wanted to capture that. Once we established that, we collaborated and I got the shot. The best part about it was none of us skipped a beat. The music stayed on course, the song continued, and no one even realized the silent conversation that had occurred.

WHAT IT TAKES

- A keen creative eye
- Excellent networking skills
- Passion and a clear vision

We wrapped up recording and shooting around six o'clock and worked together to load everyone's gear into the van. Then we went to one of the women's homes for dinner, where we hung out in a typical Moroccan living room— very long and narrow with couches and cushions along the perimeter of the room and tables in the middle. We all (musicians, musicians' family, and crew) sat together, sipping our tea and eating our dinner, laughing, singing, talking a little . . . mostly just attempting any form of communication.

After dinner it was time to go. We all stalled a bit—no one wanted to say good-bye. I hugged every woman good-bye, hugging Amineh, the one I connected with the most, last. I saw her tears and next I felt mine. She affected me. I appreciated her and she appreciated me.

After the crew said good night, we were quiet—we have all been affected by the women of Taroudant. Sometimes after an experience like that, there really are no more words. We quietly waved one another off to our hotel rooms, and Maggie and I settled in. We cleaned up for bed and talked a little about the shoot, but were very silent inside. As I lay down and began to fall asleep, I thought about Amineh's tears welling up in her big black eyes . . . a picture I will never take. There are millions of photos to take, but the ones I remember the most are the ones I see without a camera.

These are the photos that I experience, I feel. These are my favorite photos of all.

In the Field

FIVE MORE CAREERS WORKING IN THE FINE ARTS

GALLERY DIRECTOR Galleries are like small museums that showcase works from various artists, except unlike pieces in a museum, the items in a gallery are generally for sale. Gallery directors look out for new talent to showcase in their spaces and play a key role in executing and promoting an exhibition.

PORTRAIT PAINTER Painted portraits used to be a familiar sight hanging over fireplace mantels, and while they're not as common today, business-savvy painters who specialize in this

---

INTERESTED IN PHOTOGRAPHY? HERE'S AMANDA'S CAREER ADVICE

- *I see a lot of people freaking out when they try to take pictures for the first time. They're really worried about whether or not the pictures are going to be good enough before they even take one. So why not just take the pictures? I guarantee you'll find pictures that you love on that roll of film.*

- *Come up with a mission statement. When I got back from my first trip to Ethiopia, I realized what my mission was as a photographer: to use photographs to teach people about the rest of the world.*

- *Make sure you always listen to your instincts and follow your heart. No matter what job you have, you have to deal with your finances, the phone . . . everything else. So why not pick a job that you absolutely love, so when the phone rings you really look forward to answering it?*

artform can make a living doing their craft, since many businesses, organizations, and families still commission portraits.

STAINED-GLASS ARTIST While many of us think of churches when we hear the words "stained glass," a boom in historic home renovation has created a resurgence in jobs for stained-glass artists. People who specialize in stained-glass artistry can make their living designing custom windows and other decorative fixtures for clients.

ILLUSTRATOR Those looking to make a living as an illustrator might find work at newspapers or magazines, or in advertising or children's book publishing. Whether you're drawing cartoons or illustrating a short story for a magazine, this career can offer flexibility and variety, since many illustrators work as freelancers.

PRINTMAKER A printmaker creates a template or "plate" for a piece of art, usually on some sort of material like a piece of wood or glass or even stones, and then prints the art from these plates. Printmaking is a specialty craft, and the possibilities for creating unique works of art are unlimited.

YOU NEED TO KNOW ABOUT

The American Museum of Photography (www.photographymuseum.com) is a virtual museum where you'll find tons of information about the history of photography, the development process, virtual photography exhibits, and much more.

For more on careers in art, check out the animator profile on page 257 and the museum curator profile on page 110.

ERIN OSBORNE

Public Relations Specialist

Erin Osborne,
Public Relations
Account Director

The Facts

WHAT? Public relations specialists help to foster and promote positive public images for the individuals, organizations, or companies they represent.

WHERE? Some PR specialists are housed within a company or organization, while others might work for a public relations firm or be their own boss.

HOW? You'll want to get a BA in a liberal arts major, such as journalism, marketing, public relations, or English.

$$$: An average annual salary of $55,000

DRESS CODE? Business casual to business, depending on the work environment and clients you serve

STRESS FACTOR: On a scale of 1 to 10, a 7

careers in public relations have been around for many years, but as the world of social media continues to explode and evolve, this industry is doing the same. In fact, PR is considered to be one of the hot career tracks in the coming years, with the number of available jobs growing more than 12 percent.

To find out what this industry is all about, I talked to Erin Rubino, an account director for Green Rubino in Seattle. I asked Erin to fill us in on what exactly she does and what makes her job so great.

ME: PR as an industry seems to get a lot of buzz, but there also seems to be a lot of misunderstanding about what exactly public relations is. Can you set us straight?

ERIN: It can be confusing, because in PR we're very behind-the-scenes in helping to tell the story of our clients in a compelling way. Basically, we find the audience a client wants to reach, figure out a story angle to reach that audience, and then figure out a media channel that can endorse that story.

"I've always loved to write, so I took journalism classes in college, but I didn't really think journalism was for me. Then I took some broadcast classes, which again wasn't really for me. But then I took an advanced PR class, where you work with a real client on a real PR campaign, and I loved it."

ME: Got it. So you're trying to control or shape the way your clients are perceived.

ERIN: Yes. We're figuring out what's unique about a client. That's one reason it's helpful to come at this position with a journalistic background. Anybody could write about a hotel opening and how many rooms there are and these are the amenities and this is the technology. That's just news. I think a PR person's job is to continue the story past the opening to find interesting things journalists are going to want to write about or cover for their news outlets.

ME: Can you give us an example to bring that concept to life?

ERIN: At Green Rubino we work with a lot of travel and hospitality clients. So one type of client we often support is a new hotel that's opening. We are typically retained six months before the hotel opens, as construction is wrapping up. We will meet with all the people involved in the creation of the new hotel, like the general manager and the sales manager, and try to figure out what's new and interesting about the hotel and how we can differentiate it from its competitors. Once we come up with that story, we take that information and put it into a press kit, which is basically media-friendly documents that help tell the story. The kit includes story angles or fact sheets and other documents that can be shared with media.

ME: When did you figure out that you wanted to go into public relations as a career?

ERIN: I've always loved to write, so I took journalism classes in college, but I didn't really think journalism was for me.

YOU ASKED . . .

"Do you have advice on how to start pursuing a career like public relations while in school, besides an internship?"

—KYLE, AGE 17

ERIN ANSWERED . . .

"I had one class where we were encouraged to go out in the community and help a real business with all the PR brand work. I don't see why that couldn't be done on a volunteer basis, like for a nonprofit group. If you have some of the skills that you've learned in school and you feel like you could bring value to an organization, probably a smaller nonprofit that didn't have a PR department, that can help build your portfolio. But it's a tough question, because I think the only way to get your foot in the door in the PR world is to have an internship—you need that experience."

Then I took some broadcast classes, which again wasn't really for me. But then I took an advanced PR class, where you work with a real client on a real PR campaign, and I loved it. Once I did my internship at a PR firm, it became increasingly clear that it was what I wanted to do.

THE BREAKDOWN

IN MEETINGS: 4 hours

ON THE PHONE: 1 hour

SURFING THE WEB: 30 minutes

SOCIAL MEDIA: 30 minutes

E-MAILING: 2 hours

SITTING: 3 hours

PUBLIC SPEAKING: 30 minutes

READING: 30 minutes

WORKING SOLO: 1 hour

NETWORKING WITH MEDIA AND BUSINESS LEADERS IN THE COMMUNITY: All the time

ME: I know most PR specialists either work in-house at a company or organization or they work for an agency, which is the route you chose. How did you decide on your path?

ERIN: I wanted to stick with an agency early in my career because I thought I could try a lot of different things, and then ultimately move into an in-house position. But I'm still working in an agency. I've found a good niche that I like in travel and tourism. And being at a midsize agency like mine, you definitely have your hands in a lot of different pots. I think an agency is a really good place, because you can grow from being an intern to entry level to midlevel. And by the time you are midlevel, you're much more attractive to being brought in for an in-house position.

ME: Can you tell us about the rhythm of your workday?

ERIN: Sure. Today I got in at eight thirty a.m. and got ready for a conference call that I had at nine o'clock with a travel-and-tourism-related client. This client has a wine event coming up in February,

WHY WAIT?

- Join the advertising and promotion committee for various school events and come up with creative ways to promote the activities.
- Notice and become aware of how organizations, businesses, and even causes and movements use public relations to spread their message.

and we've been working to get some wine and travel writers over to the region to experience the wineries and the hotels and then write about it. So this was a planning call for that event. Next I was on the receiving end of a presentation from a company that was selling us a software database we use for gaining information about potential influencers like journalists and social media. So I listened to her presentation about content marketing, which was interesting. Then I had a team meeting. I manage four managers, so throughout the week I have internal meetings with each of them to talk about what they are working on and help them with hurdles they've encountered throughout the week. Then it's noon, so I am talking with you and simultaneously trying to monitor Twitter for one of our hotel clients. At one p.m. I have a conference call with a spa we are working with to talk about a grand opening event they have at the end of March. Then I have another internal meeting and then a few more conference calls.

ME: Wow . . . that's a lot of meetings. Is that typical? Is it unusual for you to be in the office all day?

THEN TO NOW

| 2003: Interned at the Juvenile Diabetes Research Foundation | 2004: Interned at Hill & Knowlton | 2004: Graduated from Gonzaga University with a BA in public relations | 2004–2006: Senior associate, Stearns Johnson Communications | 2006–2008: Account manager, Richmond Public Relations |

PAYING YOUR DUES

Most people do an internship at an agency while in college, and then find an entry-level position once they have their degree.

ERIN: It totally varies. Last week I was out quite a bit. And we also have client meetings, as well as quite a few after-hours events. It's definitely not a nine-to-five job.

ME: What might an after-hours event be?

ERIN: Things like media dinners at restaurants, which target food writers and food bloggers. Some agencies may say if you have an after-hours event, you can come in late the next day. But even with that, it's not a forty-hour workweek. You're always on. You are basically the middleman between the media contact and your client, and the media have crazy deadlines, especially if there's breaking news. You're that first line of defense, so you pretty much always need to be available.

ME: How about clothes . . . What's the dress code like?

ERIN: The fun thing about working at an agency is it's a creative agency. So we have designers that come in flannel shirts and jeans every day, because they typically don't have client meetings. In the PR department, we are business casual, business professional, because we are more client-facing.

2006: Began volunteering with the Make-A-Wish Foundation

2008: Took job as account manager, Green Rubino

2011: Promoted to senior public relations account manager, Green Rubino

2012: Promoted to account director, Green Rubino

ME: What do you love most about your job?

ERIN: I love working with businesses and helping them tell a cool community story, especially small businesses. Helping small businesses and small agencies gain their own voice and grow is really great.

WHAT IT TAKES

- Strong writing skills
- Good interpersonal communication skills
- Being comfortable with public speaking
- Good at building relationships

ME: And how about the challenges . . . What's difficult about it?

ERIN: The hardest part of our job is that we are always the middleman, often between a journalist on a deadline and a client who either doesn't want to give the information or doesn't have the information the journalist needs. So we need to run interference.

ME: It sounds like it takes a kind of "sixth sense" to be successful in this career—you have to understand how to make the connection between your clients and stories that will resonate with the press. Almost like you need to have the "X factor" but for PR.

ERIN: Yes. It's definitely a personality type. And it's not just a type. You have to like connecting people. You have to be good at solving those puzzles. I love working with destinations, especially smaller communities, because I get to go in there and talk to basically everyone in town. I do a tour through the town, and I figure out what's interesting about it and find the different stories within different communities. Then I get to go back and share those with media. Maybe they had never even thought about exploring the region before. So basically I get to go on a trip, experience and explore a region, and then come back and share with people all the cool things I learned. So it's like that puzzle again. I think about which press would be interested in this experience that I just had, and then I encourage them to go do it themselves and write about it.

ERIN'S CAREER ADVICE

Make the most out of every opportunity you get, even if it doesn't seem like a place that you want to be. I think relationships are huge. And so forge relationships with anyone you can, or your employer. You never know how that person is going to help you out or how you might help out that person, and that can come back to you.

In the Field

FIVE MORE CAREERS WORKING IN PR, COMMUNICATIONS, AND MARKETING

DIRECTOR OF MARKETING Marketing encompasses advertising and public relations, and professionals are big-picture thinkers who try to figure out the best ways to "market" a company's products, brand, or ideas. Directors of marketing come up with strategies to expand their company's market and make the company more profitable.

CORPORATE COMMUNICATIONS MANAGER Corporate communications managers deal primarily with internal communications within a company, creating brochures, in-house websites, and other communications materials about the company business and philosophy for employees, shareholders, or the public relations department.

EVENT MARKETING SPECIALIST Event marketing specialists create events that allow brands or companies to interact with the public in a way that will positively influence how these brands or companies are perceived. These specialists might handle all aspects of these events, from planning and organizing to managing venue logistics, hiring talent, and more.

PUBLIC AFFAIRS SPECIALIST Very similar to PR specialists, public affairs specialists work on behalf of government agencies and nongovernmental organizations, keeping the public informed about the activities of these organizations by holding press conferences, issuing press releases, and spearheading public affairs campaigns.

COMMUNITY RELATIONS MANAGER If you've ever been to an author event at your local Barnes & Noble, it was probably organized by a community relations manager. These professionals work for local organizations and businesses, managing how the public interacts with them and organizing community outreach efforts.

YOU NEED TO KNOW ABOUT

PR Week is a print and online trade magazine focused on public relations professionals, though you don't have to be one to take advantage of their online content. Through weekly online editions and monthly print editions, *PR Week* covers breaking news, analysis, and opinion related to the public relations world of work. Check it out online at www.prweek.com/us.

lunch break

STANDING OUT IN A TIGHT JOB MARKET

It's no secret that upon receiving their diploma, most graduates won't be greeted by an eager recruiter waiting to welcome them into the perfect entry-level position at an ideal company. (Oh, that it would be so easy!)

The reality you're likely all too aware of is that the job market is rough, and landing a gig can be a highly competitive endeavor. The good news? There are ways to stand out in a field of applicants, which boosts your shot at getting the offer of your dreams. Here's how:

Be authentic: Don't try to be the candidate you *think* you should be. . . . Be the candidate you *are*. Employers know when they're getting sold a bill of goods, so keep it real and totally you throughout the whole interview process. The bonus? When you do land a job, you'll know it's probably a good fit. After all—they wanted the real you!

Be bold: If you identify your dream job, don't be shy about pursuing it. Put yourself on the line and let the company or organization know that working for them is *exactly* where you want to be, that you will work your butt off in the position, and that they won't regret giving you a chance. Instead of passively waiting to hear about next steps, take the initiative to follow up with the hiring manager or your would-be boss by sharing one or two original ideas about how you would add value were you to be hired.

Take risks: Some people have done crazy things to get hired, including taking out Google ads to get the attention of an employer and offering a foot massage in exchange for a job. You don't have to go that far, but you could consider doing something unconventional to pique an employer's interest. Finding an original and creative way to present your résumé, picking up the phone instead of e-mailing when it's time to follow up, or designing a unique and customized thank-you note will all get more notice than people doing the same old thing.

Be professional: In a crowded job market, unprofessionalism is the quickest way to get your application tossed into the recycle pile. Be courteous, gracious, and professional in any and all communication throughout the interview process and you'll already have an edge on the competition.

Be persistent (but not pesky): The hiring process can take a while, and sometimes after time has passed with no word, job seekers assume a job has been filled and move on. Don't be afraid to regularly follow up on a job lead until you get definitive word that the position is closed—you just might outlast the other contenders. But don't go overboard—a once-a-week phone call is appropriate (daily e-mails or texts are not).

Be specific: Customize your résumé and query letter for every job you're applying to. The more specific you can be in how you relate your experience to a company's needs, the more easily they'll be able to see you fitting into that role. Generic is out. . . . Custom is in.

Over-deliver: Sometimes job candidates are asked to provide samples or create something original as a way to show an employer how they would approach a work task. If this comes up for you, treat the assignment like it's the most important project you've ever done. Don't just give them exactly what they expect—put in that extra 10 percent of value to wow their socks off.

Know your stuff: When you have an opportunity for a phone or live interview with a company, do your homework ahead of time so you can speak intelligently and naturally about what the company does. Being knowledgeable about a prospective company shows you're taking the opportunity seriously.

Be remarkable: Marketing guru Seth Godin writes about being "remarkable" as a way to be noticed, or as he describes, to be the purple cow in a field of black-and-white Holsteins. Being remarkable is about doing the unexpected, being unique, going above and beyond, and truly "showing up" to anything you do by letting your passion pour through. Find your own way to be remarkable and you'll be noticed—guaranteed.

BARBARA BOXER

Senator

Barbara Boxer, U.S. Senator, California

The Facts

WHAT? U.S. senators serve in the Senate, which is one of the two chambers of the U.S. Congress. There are two senators for each state, and their job is to write and vote on bills, ultimately making decisions about what will be signed into law.

WHERE? Senators spend much of their time working and living in Washington, D.C., although they work out of home-state offices as well.

HOW? Senators need to be at least twenty-five years old, have lived in the United States for a minimum of nine years, and be a resident of the state they are hoping to represent. Most senators have a background and experience in law and/or local or federal government, and they must run to be elected every six years.

$$$: An annual salary of $174,000

DRESS CODE? Business professional

STRESS FACTOR: On a scale of 1 to 10, between a 5 and a 10, depending on what's happening in the Senate

when it comes to having a successful political career, Senator Barbara Boxer of California is an expert. After a brief stint as a stockbroker when she first graduated from college, Barbara made the switch to politics and hasn't looked back. She's been working in national government for more than thirty years, first as a member of Congress from 1983 to 1993, and as a senator ever since. When she was elected for her third Senate term in 2004, more people voted for her than any other senate candidate in the history of the United States!

As you can imagine, Barbara is an extremely busy woman, as she divides her time between her offices in Washington, D.C., and northern California, and she focuses much of her time and energy working toward improving the quality of public education and health care, as well as championing environmental and crime-fighting efforts. And that just *"My job is more of an honor than glamorous."* scratches the surface. Barbara took the time to answer these questions about her job and life:

ME: What were your career dreams when you were younger?

BARBARA: When I was a little girl, I wanted to be a ballerina. When I was in high school, I decided I wanted to be a stockbroker.

ME: What kinds of tasks might you do on any given day?

BARBARA: In Washington, D.C., a typical day might consist of meetings with constituents* to find out their issues of concern, meetings with staff to plan legislative and communications strategy, committee hearings to fulfill my responsibilities as a committee member, press conferences to communicate issues of concern and action plans to address those issues, and Senate floor statements to discuss pending legislation and

---

* THE LINGO: A **constituent** is someone who lives in an area represented by someone who's been elected. In this case, it's a citizen of California.

YOU ASKED . . .

"How many times have you fought to keep your head above water?"
—MYKAILA, AGE 15

BARBARA ANSWERED . . .

"I have been in elected office since 1976. There have been more times than I could possibly recall where I felt a heavy load on my shoulders. But each time, I had a skilled staff, a supportive family, and an optimistic belief in the future, and therefore I was able to come out of those dark moments with even more experience and dedication to my work."

other issues. In California, a typical day might consist of meeting with constituents and groups, meeting with state staff, visiting various cities and counties to see firsthand the needs of the people of California, connecting with elected officials in the state, holding press conferences to bring the issues to the hometown press, and giving speeches on topics ranging from foreign relations to flood control to education. Also, I often present certificates of merit to those Californians doing outstanding work in the fields of education and environment.

ME: How many hours do you work per week? And what are your hours, as in, what time of day or night?

BARBARA: I have no set hours—some days start at eight a.m. and end at one in the morning; some start at nine a.m. and end at seven p.m. It all depends on the schedule of the Senate.

THEN TO NOW

1962:	1962–1965:	1972–1974:	1974:	1976–1982:
Graduated from Brooklyn College	Worked as a stockbroker	Served as associate editor, *Pacific Sun* newspaper	Became a congressional aide	Elected as member, Board of Supervisors, Marin County, CA

ME: What's the first thing you do when you get to work in the morning?

S
E
N
A
T
O
R

BARBARA: It depends on the day. Sometimes I have break-fast meetings with constituents, other days I go straight to a committee hearing—there is no predictable schedule for me on any given day, except for our Tuesday mornings, when we have our Senate Democratic Leadership meetings.

ME: What is the last thing you do before you go home? And how much work, if any, do you take home?

BARBARA: There is no one thing I do each night before I go home—sometimes votes run very late into the evening. But almost every night, I have a large package of material from my staff to go through for the next day. I review drafts of letters to constituents, informational memos on legislative

WHY WAIT?

- Run for student government at your school and see what it's like to be part of a campaign.
- Volunteer in a local political campaign. There is always plenty of work to be done, like stuffing envelopes, making phone calls, and handing out flyers.
- Get a politician to come visit your school—part of their job is community outreach. When they get there, don't hesitate to ask questions!

| 1983: Elected as a member of the House of Representatives, California | 1993: Elected U.S. Senator representing California | 1997: Authored a Patient's Bill of Rights | 2010: Elected for fourth term |

issues, talking points, testimony and statements for committee hearings, as well as press clips from as many as fifteen newspapers and transcripts of radio and television interviews.

ME: Your job appears so glamorous and exciting from the outside. . . . What's the reality?

BARBARA: I think you can already tell from the description of my work that on an everyday basis, there is not much glamour in the Senate. My job is more of an honor than glamorous.

ME: What is the travel like? Do you split your home life between two cities?

BARBARA: Travel is a major part of my job, because I have family on both coasts, and my work is on both coasts.

ME: What's the best part of your job?

BARBARA: The best part of my job is helping people.

ME: The most challenging aspect?

BARBARA: The most challenging aspect is bringing an issue across the finish line—it takes skill, determination, and enormous focus to get that done.

ME: Any advice for a teen girl hoping to succeed as a politician one day?

BARBARA: The best advice I can give any young person is to find an issue that you care about deep in your heart. If the issue is children, then map out a way to build coalitions to help our children. If the issue is the environment or help for

our seniors, the same applies. Once you build coalitions, show
leadership by bringing everyone in and not being afraid to say
what you think. Your skills will be noted, and eventually you
will become a natural candidate for public office—starting at
the local level. Another recommendation is to volunteer in a
campaign for someone you believe in. Work hard, be part of a
team, and again, your leadership skills will be noticed.

In the Field

*FIVE MORE CAREERS IN GOVERNMENT AND
POLITICAL SCIENCE*

LOBBYIST Lobbyists use their political savvy and powers of
persuasion to try to convince voters—be they politicians or the
general public—to make a decision that benefits their cause.
They might work for private corporations or on behalf of nonprofit agencies.

PRESS SECRETARY Powerful politicians like Senator Boxer
have the equivalent of their own private public relations
department. At the head of this is the press secretary, whose
job is to handle all media issues surrounding the politician's
work, including holding press conferences and issuing statements on behalf of the politician.

CAMPAIGN MANAGER For major political races, campaign
managers work tirelessly behind the scenes, handling all the
details involved in running a bid for election. They might work
for up to two years prior to an election, and they do things
like manage thousands of volunteers, hire political consultants,
and plan big fund-raisers.

SPEECHWRITER Government officials at high levels deliver a
lot of speeches, and speechwriters work behind the scenes to

write them, tailoring the speeches to the specific audience and using persuasive writing skills to convey the content in the way the official intended.

POLITICAL POLLSTER   Political pollsters run frequent polls to get a pulse on where the public stands when it comes to a political candidate or issue. Then they analyze that information and work with campaign managers to address the concerns raised.

YOU NEED TO KNOW ABOUT

Young Politicians of America (www.ypa.org) is aimed at getting students ages fourteen to twenty-two interested in politics. YPA is not associated with a political "party"—its goal is to raise awareness of political discourse among teens and get teens involved in their own communities.

SUSAN SCHULZ

Magazine Editor

The Facts

Susan Schulz,
Magazine Editor

WHAT? An editor in chief manages the content for a magazine and is ultimately responsible for the people who come up with ideas, assign and write the articles, and design and lay out the magazine. Making sure the advertisers are happy with the placement of their ads is also part of the job.

WHERE? There are thousands of magazines across the country, although the hub for the industry is definitely New York.

HOW? Most editors in chief started out like Susan did, as an intern, and then work their way up, position by position.

$$$: From $60,000 to more than $125,000, depending on the size of the magazine

DRESS CODE? Business casual is the norm.

STRESS FACTOR: On a scale of 1 to 10, between an 8 and a 9 (Susan says, "It's always stressful, but it's usually an exhilarating stress.")

i've always pictured magazine bigwigs working in interesting old buildings in Manhattan, dressed in the lastest fashions, surrounded by lots of young, hip colleagues oozing energy, drive, and creativity. Well, I wasn't disappointed when I went to New York City to meet with magazine exec Susan Schulz.

Susan has a coveted job working for Hearst, one of the largest magazine publishers in the world, so I wanted to find out how she did it. How did she get there? What does it feel like to work there? And most important, is it really as cool as it seems?

"I always wanted to be a magazine editor," Susan admitted. "When I was a teenager I read *Seventeen* magazine and ate it up, just died when it came in the mail. So I went into college as a journalism major, but switched to become an English major with a journalism minor. That switch just broadened my horizons. I totally loved reading, so it was a great major for me.

"When I graduated from college, everybody was freaking about what they were going to do and if they were going to get a job. But I didn't stress out about it. I was sort of like, 'Well, I'm going to graduate and I'm going to look for a job in magazines.' I just kind of had a belief. I decided to talk to anybody who could help me get in. I wasn't expecting to graduate and start out working for *Vogue*. I just wanted to go and be somebody's assistant. I was like, 'Please, somebody, let me answer your phones. I just want to be there, I want to learn, I want to help you.' That was my approach, and I think that's really what got me in.

"I wasn't expecting to graduate and start out working for Vogue. *I just wanted to go and be somebody's assistant. I was like, 'Please, somebody, let me answer your phones."*

"I started out at *Redbook* and then went to *Good Housekeeping*. But when I went to *YM*, that's when I started to realize that what I loved wasn't so much just writing articles and things, it was the idea of helping teens. When I got to *YM*, I realized I loved that age group so much and that's when I thought, 'I've found my passion.'

"When it came to moving up the ladder, I always took the approach that I'll get there when I get there and I'm going to work as hard as I can and do as good a job as I can. I've worked hard my whole life, I've gotten noticed for it, and it's worked for me. So I kept doing what I did, and luckily, I was in certain right places at certain right times. Plus, I always really liked what I was doing, and I think in a way that helped me," explains Susan.

While there is a certain amount of being in the right place at the right time in anyone's career success, there is also a lot of hard work, dues paying, and persistence, especially when it comes to the world of magazines. Susan worked her way up from the bottom as she moved around from magazine to magazine, and she landed at *CosmoGIRL!* when it was first

YOU ASKED . . .

"In order to achieve your success, what did you have to give up along the way, and was it truly worth it?"

—MALLORY, AGE 15

SUSAN ANSWERED . . .

"Definitely, it was worth it. In my second job as an associate editor, I probably worked until ten o'clock at night for two years, and then I became a senior editor and probably worked until nine o'clock every night. When I first started at CosmoGIRL! as deputy editor, I was working until ten o'clock a lot. So, I sacrificed a lot of 'going out with my friends.' But I think you have to want it enough that it really is your main priority, and that's what it is for me. I didn't mind those late nights so much, because if you like what you do, you're happy doing it and you're not thinking about what you're missing out on. It sounds so cliché, but the hard work does not go unnoticed."

THE BREAKDOWN

IN MEETINGS: 5 hours a day

ON THE PHONE: 1–3 hours a day

ONLINE: On and off throughout the day

SITTING: Almost the entire day

STANDING: Never . . . unless running from meeting to meeting

PUBLIC SPEAKING: Occasionally

READING: Constant, ongoing

WORKING SOLO: 4 hours a day

launched, where she was the deputy editor, overseeing and nurturing the junior editors on staff. When the editor in chief left the magazine two years later, Susan moved up one step closer, becoming the number two at the magazine.

"At the time, I thought, 'Oh my God, can I be the executive editor? I don't know.' And the new editor in chief said, 'Of course you can. There's like two more tasks that you haven't already been doing that you'll need to do,'" Susan relates.

Susan loved being the executive editor, but then things changed again. When Atoosa Rubenstein, then editor in chief of *CosmoGIRL!*, moved over to run *Seventeen*, she recommended that Susan pitch herself to management to be the new editor in chief.

"My response was, 'I don't think I can do that. Editor in chief . . . that's so huge.' But I couldn't say no, because Atoosa really believed in me. So I wrote up a proposal, and when I was doing it, I realized that not only *could* I do this . . . but I *wanted* to do this. So I got the editor in chief job, and it was so surreal. I don't think my adrenaline came back down for literally a few months."

I asked Susan to tell us what really went on behind the scenes of a popular teen magazine.

I get up pretty early in the morning to read because as the EIC, I'm still just a cog in the wheel that is this entire magazine. You know, there's the art department and the editors and the production department and the research department . . . and if I don't turn first, then none of the other cogs turn. I do a lot of reading between seven thirty and nine thirty a.m., so that when we start work at nine thirty I can pass out a bunch of stuff that can then be fielded out to the different departments.

At nine thirty I meet with my managing editor, who deals with the schedules and budgets. So she'll come in and say, 'Oh, there's an issue with so and so,' like maybe there's a staff issue, or she'll say, 'Okay, the advertising department got an ad page and we have to figure out where we're going to put it.' For example, if we have a two-page story and we want to stick an ad in between it, we need to make sure it's going to look good. Maybe I need to ask the art department to do a redesign on that story so we can put the ad in between those two pages.

After that meeting, I'll often have a meeting with my deputy editor or my executive editor to talk about story ideas and the progress of certain stories.

Every day at eleven thirty I meet with my art director and my creative director and I look at the magazine layouts. Once they're approved, the copy or manuscript can be put into

PAYING YOUR DUES

The best way to break into magazine publishing is to do an internship while you're in college. You'll be doing lots of grunt work, but you'll also be in the mix at a very exciting atmosphere. Interns who prove their passion are often rewarded with assistant jobs upon graduating from college.

the layouts and cut to fit, because usually when you write a manuscript, you write it much longer than will actually be on the page. At some point, the layout and the copy have to be married together by the production department, and then the editor goes back and cuts down the copy, and then I end up seeing it again and then one more time.

Then it's lunchtime, and I usually have a lunch that I'll go to, like today. Dove held a photo contest for their self-esteem campaign, so I judged the contest and they had a big luncheon for the winner today. Or the other day for lunch I met with a relationship therapist who might be an expert on one of our future stories.

In the afternoon, I usually have more meetings. Sometimes at four o'clock we'll have a lineup meeting, which is basically where we plan the next issue and figure out what stories are going to be in what sections of the magazine. The whole staff will be in those meetings. Other times we'll have a staff meeting where we'll go over a previous issue and talk about what we liked and what we could do differently in the future.

I try to have all my meetings over by five because

WHAT IT TAKES

- A willingness to work long hours
- The ability to handle tight deadlines
- Being able to work well with others
- Having great writing skills

THEN TO NOW

| Graduated from Loyola College in Baltimore | Started magazine career as editorial assistant at *Redbook* magazine | Became assistant editor at *Good Housekeeping* | 1997: Made her move into teen mags as associate articles editor at *YM* magazine | 2000: Joined *CosmoGIRL!* as deputy editor |

WHY WAIT?

- See if there is a teen writing organization in your community where you can learn how to sharpen your creative skills.
- Many local newspapers have a teen page that is produced by teens, for teens—that's a great place to get some real-world experience.

with one meeting after another, I can get pretty fried. But usually at five o'clock or so, my design director may come back in and show me a few more layouts they've been working on, or the managing editor might come back in and say, 'This is what happened today,' or 'What's your decision on that?" and that kind of thing.

Then sometimes I have events at night. Not that often, but sometimes it will be a charity event that I'll go to with my publisher. So those are the events where I'll have to wear a ball gown and I'll get my hair and makeup done. I always find those events are sort of fun, but it's also sort of weird. It's like getting ready for the prom and then not getting to go with your friends because you're working.

Just hearing about Susan's busy day made my head spin. I also knew that she was running late for a meeting, since her assistant buzzed in a few times during our conversation. Before

| **2003:** Appointed editor in chief of *CosmoGIRL!* | **2005:** Won a "Do Something" Award from the Alliance for Eating Disorders Awareness | **2010:** Became editorial brand director, Cosmopolitan/ Hearst Magazines | **2011:** Appointed foundation president, NY Women in Communications |

we wrapped things up, I asked Susan to share some of the highs and lows of being an editor in chief of a magazine.

"The politics of the job is the hardest part for me, because it's like playing a chess game where you have to think three steps ahead. Like, 'If I do this, then this, this, and this are going to happen.' So if you can think that far ahead, and that's not the result you want, you've got to go back to square one. And sometimes the best decision that you can make for one part of the business is literally the opposite of what would make somebody else happy."

She adds, "On the flip side, the thing that makes me happiest is knowing that the magazine is selling really well. That's a really good day because I know it makes the company and everybody happy. Or when we get a really good celebrity for the cover. . . . Just the anticipation of a good sale is also great. Today is a good day, because I announced three promotions, and I love when I can reward hard work. I rarely have a bad day, because even when something bad happens, I know that this magazine helps so many girls, and that really feels good."

SUSAN'S CAREER ADVICE

- *Don't sell yourself short. Yes, there is competition out there and there are many other people going for the same position, but that doesn't mean that you're not going to be the one selected. Focus on your strengths, what you can do, and sell yourself as the best person for the position.*

- *Aim to be as helpful as you can be—think of the job as "here's what I can do for you" as opposed to "here's what I want to get from this job." If you focus on what you can offer a company, it puts you in the right frame of mind that no job is too small, and if you devote just as much energy and thought to a small task, you will perform well and get noticed.*

FIVE MORE CAREERS IN MAGAZINE PUBLISHING

FACT CHECKER   A magazine's reputation is only as strong as the material printed on its pages, so fact checkers go through articles and any other written material for the mag and make sure that every single word is correct, like making sure names are spelled correctly and ensuring that statistics and resources quoted in an article are true.

ART DIRECTOR   Art directors oversee how the text and images of a magazine are presented, laying out the pages and making sure the design is clear, cool, and true to the magazine's brand.

ADVERTISING SALES MANAGER   The price you pay for your subscription to a magazine doesn't cover the cost of creating, printing, and distributing it. Advertisers pay big bucks to have ads for their products in magazines, and every magazine has a sales team that finds new companies to advertise and keeps their current advertisers happy.

COPY EDITOR   When the written content for a magazine article is turned in, a copy editor goes through the material and cleans it up, making sure there are no grammatical errors, rearranging things to make the text flow better, or sometimes cutting pieces to make it fit into the layout.

PRODUCTION MANAGER   Production managers at a magazine are responsible for the production aspect of printing a magazine—overseeing paper stock, colors, typesetting—and they make sure the finished product looks as great as the publisher intended, not to mention completed on time and within the budget.

For more on careers in journalism, check out the journalist profile on page 246.

YOU NEED TO KNOW ABOUT

TeenInk is a magazine, book series, and website devoted entirely to teenage writing, art, and photography. Through the website, you can submit your writing to be considered for publication, read tons of articles and reviews, as well as participate in their Writers' Workshop Forums. Visit them online at www.teenink.com.

LUPE VALDEZ

Sheriff

The Facts

Lupe Valdez, Sheriff, Dallas County, TX

WHAT? The sheriff is the head law enforcement officer in a county. Sheriffs typically oversee all the police departments and jails within a county.

WHERE? There are more than 3,500 sheriffs offices across the United States—nearly every city and county has one.

HOW? In most states and counties, the sheriff is an elected position, and sheriffs typically have extensive experience working at different levels of law enforcement, as well as an educational background in criminal justice.

$$$: An average salary of $85,000 a year

DRESS CODE? A sheriff's uniform, usually made up of pants, a button-down shirt, a hat, shoes, and badges

STRESS FACTOR: On a scale of 1 to 10, between an 8 and a 10

for someone who is in charge of one of the largest jails in the country, Sheriff Lupe Valdez of Dallas County has broken through a lot of barriers. Not only is Sheriff Valdez the first woman ever to be elected sheriff of Dallas County, but she's also the first Hispanic sheriff in the county. Lupe has an impressive career background in law enforcement, most recently working as a special agent with the Department of Homeland Security before being elected as sheriff in 2005.

I had a chance to talk with Lupe about what it's like to be in her shoes, and believe me, they're big ones to fill. Here is our conversation.

"What is the old saying? 'A woman has to work twice as hard and gets half as much credit.' "

ME: I've never met a sheriff before. Can you explain to me what you do?

LUPE: Dallas County is the ninth largest county in the United States. We have the seventh largest jail in the United States, and I have almost two thousand employees, so it's a pretty big organization. I don't think there's any other female who's got this much authority in law enforcement, so it's pretty much a frontier for women. I have at least thirty-five sections in the department reporting to me, from the jail to patrol to criminal investigation to courtesy patrol. We also have our own cooking facility, which takes a lot of management. Basically, I run a little city of eight thousand prisoners every night and at least five to six hundred officers on duty at all times, as well as another two hundred to three hundred patrol officers. There's no such thing as leaving it without any attention, so people are always here, working holidays and doing all sorts of things—criminal investigations, victims' assistance, transporting two hundred to three hundred prisoners a day.

ME: Do you find that there are special challenges being a woman in this job?

LUPE: What is the old saying? "A woman has to work twice as hard and gets half as much credit." Because I broke so many barriers, I really have to prove myself. There hasn't been a Democrat in this office in forty-two years, and there's never been a minority sheriff here. There are some people who want you to succeed and there are some who want you to fail. So I think the difficulty comes in keeping your head above water and doing the things that are right for the department and keeping those other things out of the way.

ME: That sounds very stressful—how do you deal with it?

LUPE: For a while I wasn't dealing with it very well, so when I noticed it was having an effect on me, I started trying to catch a movie here or there or get together with friends more. And every year or so I schedule a trip to a monastery where they practice silence, and I'll go for three or four days where I can meditate and just totally be with myself and catch up with what's going on with me and my body. But there is a lot of stress. Recently I've noticed that I've been having problems with it, so

YOU ASKED . . .

"What were your motives for getting involved in this career, and have they changed since you've started?" **—SARAH, AGE 18**

LUPE ANSWERED . . .

"I got into law enforcement by accident, and I've always taken the approach of, 'Okay, now that I'm here I'll do the best I can, and maybe I can get to the next level.' There's nothing wrong with having goals of being four or five levels ahead, but that wasn't me. I gave up a good job with the federal government in order to run for sheriff. I had come to the conclusion that being somewhere where I could mentor, where I could make a difference, and where I could influence for the better was important enough that even if I lost, it would have been worth trying."

I actually built a little room in my home that I call my "sanctuary room," and I just go in there every two or three days and sit for five to ten minutes and let my spirit catch up with me.

ME: Can you tell us a little bit about how you actually spend your day?

LUPE: This office essentially hadn't been given any attention for about ten or twelve years before I got here, and a lot of things that were needed were not even here to run a normal department. So right now my job is a lot of restructuring. I end up having a lot of meetings. The main thing for me is that I'm holding people accountable. That didn't happen before. If you were in a position before, you were there because somebody liked you. It didn't matter if you could do it or not. And now, if you can't do the position, then you don't belong there. Unfortunately, in situations like that you have to spend a lot of time getting to know people to figure out who would fit best in that position. For my first year as sheriff, I was literally working seven days a week, sixteen or seventeen hours a day on weekdays and seven to eight hours on the weekends. But there was so much that had to be redone. There was also a lot

PAYING YOUR DUES

Before you become a sheriff, you'll need to spend time working in law enforcement, most likely as a police officer, and then work your way up the ladder.

THEN TO NOW

| Graduated from Southern Nazarene University, Oklahoma, with BS in business administration | Graduated from University of Texas at Arlington with MA in criminology and criminal justice | 1976–1986: Captain in the U.S. Army National Guard & U.S. Army Reserves | 1978–1980: Correctional officer with the Department of Justice, Federal Bureau of Prisons | 1980–1983: Special Agent, GSA, Office of Inspector General |

WHY WAIT?

- This might seem obvious, but don't get in trouble with the law! If you're interested in being a police officer, you'll want to have a clean record when you apply to the police academy.
- Do volunteering in your community, where you'll have an opportunity to show your dedication to serve.
- Check with your local police or sheriff's department to see if they offer any special programs or classes for high school students.

of backstabbing and working against each other in the department before I was elected. And I've been trying to change that mind-set to, "We are a team, we're going to work together."

ME: When do you feel the most satisfaction in your job?

LUPE: I know I'm making some good changes that are going to last.

ME: I know that you were elected into office. How well were you received into the department?

LUPE: I didn't come up through the ranks. When I won the election, the newspaper headline said something like, "Five Strikes Against Her and She Still Won." Well, one of the strikes was that I did not come up through the department. My opponent's supporters were putting up charts of what was going to happen to the people in the department if my

1983–1987: Special Agent, U.S. Department of Agriculture	1987–2003: Special Agent, U.S. Customs	2003–2004: Senior Special Agent, Department of Homeland Security	2005: Elected sheriff of Dallas County	2008, 2012: Won reelection bids

WHAT IT TAKES

- Dedication to the job
- Being able to handle office politics
- A fair and disciplined nature

opponent didn't win, like people being fired and demoted. So of course when he lost, the people who had done this were scared about what I was going to do. When I started, I had a two-hour interview with all captains and above, and they literally came into my office shaking. I would say, "Why are you shaking?" and they would say, "I don't know what you're going to do to me." So I said to them, "I'm going to give you the opportunity to be the best officer that you have ever been."

ME: Are there any misconceptions about the field of law enforcement?

LUPE: A lot of shows glamorize things that don't exist. No department has the money to spend on testing everybody's DNA. It's never going to be like it is on TV. Women leaders in law enforcement have to be way above the norm and have to work a lot harder and prove themselves much more than their male counterparts. Hopefully, ten years from now that won't be the case, but it is right now. When I came in, there wasn't a single female on the whole executive staff except for a secretary. Out of fifteen on the executive staff, there was one minority. So that is changing. I'm trying to make the department look like the face of the community. You know, the community is not all white males, and we need to change things so that people can start identifying. I don't think we'll ever get to the point where the community totally trusts law enforcement, but we can get to the point where they can feel that they're being treated fairly.

ME: What would you have said if someone told you when you were a teen that you'd become the sheriff of Dallas County in 2005?

LUPE: I would have said you come from cuckoo land or outer space. I grew up extremely poor. My family were migrant workers. And there was a time in Dallas when Hispanic people were not allowed through the front door of restaurants. So the idea of ever being a sheriff was just so far out from where I was at. I happened to get into law enforcement by accident, but I always remembered that I wanted to make a difference, and I think this job provides the most opportunity for me to do that.

INTERESTED IN WORKING IN LAW ENFORCEMENT? HERE'S LUPE'S ADVICE

Go for it! We need more women working in law enforcement. We need more people who are not concerned about their egos. When you go on official duty, you no longer represent yourself. It's not about you—it's about the whole department. And I think that women have a tendency to think that way— we're nurturing, so we think about the whole instead of just about "me."

In the Field

FIVE MORE CAREERS IN LAW ENFORCEMENT

PAROLE AGENT When offenders have been released from jail, they are often on parole and must check in with a parole agent at regular intervals. Parole agents might arrange for drug testing of the parolees or interview them about their living arrangements and job search, as well as offer support and direction to ex-offenders.

DETECTIVE Detectives are in the business of investigating and solving crimes, from petty thefts to murders. They research the crime scene, search for clues, interview witnesses, and interrogate suspects, usually working around the clock until the crime is solved.

BOUNTY HUNTER Bail bondsmen hire bounty hunters to find fugitives who skip out on bail, so they can get their bail money back. They then give a percentage of the bail to the bounty hunter as payment. In most states, bounty hunters can carry guns and go on people's property without a warrant in order to do their job.

POLICE OFFICER Police officers are the members of the law enforcement community most visible to us. Their primary job is to protect people and enforce the law, and they might be doing deskwork in the squad or driving around on patrol with their partner.

DISPATCH OFFICER Whether they're looking for information or have an emergency and need a police officer immediately, people calling the police department reach the dispatch officer. They're based in the squad room and they keep tabs on where all the officers out on patrol are and what calls they're responding to.

YOU NEED TO KNOW ABOUT

The National Center for Women & Policing (www.womenandpolicing.org) is an organization dedicated to increasing the number of women in law enforcement. On the website you'll find great information about how to become a police officer, articles and downloadable publications about the status of women in law enforcement, job links, and much more.

For more on careers in law enforcement, check out the district attorney profile on page 36.

ANNE CORBETT

Urban Planner

The Facts

Anne Corbett, Project Director at Vision McMillan Partners

WHAT? Urban planning, also known as city planning, deals with how cities are developed and shaped. Urban planners figure out what buildings and businesses should go where, and how the public transportation of a city should work to have the best impact on the community.

WHERE? Every city and regional government has a planning division that deals with things like transportation, real estate development, and historic preservation. Urban planners might also work for special interest groups or nonprofit organizations.

HOW? Urban planners typically get their undergraduate degree in urban or city planning, but to advance in the field, they'll need a master's degree.

$$$: An average salary of $68,000 for urban planners with a master's

DRESS CODE? Casual to business casual

STRESS FACTOR: On a scale of 1 to 10, an 8

there is actually a job shaping the cities of tomorrow. In researching urban planning, I discovered Anne Corbett. Until recently, she was the executive director of Cultural DC, a small nonprofit in Washington, D.C., that aims to make sure that artists and art organizations in the city have affordable spaces that support their art—from theaters and art galleries to housing for artists. Though Anne is now directing the creation of a new community at a historic landmark in D.C., our interview covers her job with Cultural DC. Here's our conversation.

ME: Urban planning sounds like such an interesting concept, but I'm not sure I get what you actually do. How do you spend your days?

ANNE: On any given day I might be sitting down to meet with a real estate developer or landowner who has a particular project they're looking to build. It might be a big office building where the developer also wants to have art space on the ground floor, or because of the city rules, they are required to have some sort of art space included. So my organization would help them think about that art space and come up with something that works well, given the other things that will be

"A lot of times my work and leisure time are the same thing."

YOU ASKED . . .

"What is the most rewarding aspect of your career?"

—REBECCA, AGE 16

ANNE ANSWERED . . .

"A lot of times we're dealing with rundown buildings that have been vacant for a really long time, so seeing the before and after of a building that was maybe boarded up and covered with graffiti, and then seeing it totally refurbished and people doing arts activities and things that they love there—that transformation is really pretty magical."

THE BREAKDOWN

IN MEETINGS: 4 hours a day

ON THE PHONE: 2 hours a day

ONLINE: 3 hours a day

SITTING: Most of the day

PUBLIC SPEAKING: 30 minutes
a day

READING: 1 hour a day

WORKING SOLO: 2 hours a day

GUIDING STAFF AND
REVIEWING THE WORK OF
OTHERS: 3 hours a day

in the building and what else is going on in the neighborhood. So I spend a lot of time getting to know people who have property, projects, and buildings that they're planning.

At the same time, I might spend part of my day meeting with different people who work at arts organizations. Like this morning, I got a phone call from an organization of actors that is getting evicted from their space. They told us what their needs are, and we put the information in a database so that when we find people with buildings who have space, we can put the two together. That's really my specialty—having in my head a sense of things going on all over the city. When something is happening in the arts world as far as real estate goes, I'm the "go-to person" and can help broker those relationships.

Another thing I might be doing is sitting in a meeting with architects and talking about the design of a housing building, making sure that the apartments are big enough for the artists who live and work in them and that they've included the kinds of amenities that are important to artists—high ceilings, good windows with natural light, a freight elevator or heavy-duty electrical requirements. We help the architects figure out how to design it and then we come up with a plan for marketing those units to artists in our area, schedule open houses, and put ads in the paper.

ME: It sounds like you have a very full job. How do you squeeze it all into a workday?

ANNE: I used to come to work at nine or nine thirty a.m. and be here until seven or seven thirty p.m., and then go to events in the evening. A lot of my job is who I know, and I have to keep building relationships with as many people as possible, so I spend time going to business receptions and arts events like gallery openings or theater events. Other nights I might be going to a community meeting where a project is being presented to the community so they can give their input. I used to work more than ten hours a day, maybe fifty to seventy hours a week. And I love what I do, so usually I didn't have a problem with that. But now I have a child. He's sixteen months old and he's in day care, but he can only be in day care until six p.m., and he has to be picked up regardless of what's going on at work, so either my husband or I have to get up and walk out of our office and do that. It's a very different balance for me. Now I spend more time at home on the computer, anywhere from half an hour to two or three hours at night after my son's gone to bed so I catch up. I can't go to all of the nighttime things that I used to—I really have to pick and choose. And that's good and bad. Most times I would rather be at home with my son than at a reception making small talk with building developers. But it makes it harder for me to do my job when I'm not able to put in all of that networking time.

THEN TO NOW

1992: Graduated from Wake Forest University, North Carolina, with BS in mathematical economics	1994: Quit Taco Bell to pursue urban planning	1996: Interned at an economic development consulting firm	1997: Received master's in community planning, University of Maryland	1997: Was inspired by hearing Kennedy Smith speak on downtown revitalization

WHY WAIT?

- Volunteer or intern with an organization that interests you, especially as it relates to planning and running community events.
- Get involved with what's going on in your community by reading the paper and notices about community development or revitalization projects.

ANNE'S "AHA" MOMENT

When I graduated from college in 1992, there weren't a lot of jobs to be had, and I also didn't have a very good GPA coming out of school. So I ended up taking a job for [a corporation that owns fast food restaurants]. I was literally running restaurants, running the drive-through, and managing all of the people in it. After a couple of years I started helping them plan new restaurants. They would assign me a new restaurant that hadn't been built yet, and I would work with the contractors, start planning the marketing of the new store, hire all the people, and do everything to get the store open and ready. But I didn't think that the way the corporation was going about the whole process was very thoughtful—they never seemed to talk to the community or ask people what they wanted. So I started asking the people I worked for about trying to build in a community process, and they just didn't understand what I was getting at. I just kept hitting brick walls. So I literally had an "aha" moment where I

1998: Began working at Cultural Development Corporation (CDC)	**1998:** Published the book *Arts in a Living Downtown*	**2000:** Promoted to executive director, CDC	**2012:** Became project director at Vision McMillan Partners

realized that this was not how communities should be shaped. It shouldn't just be private companies trying to figure out how to make the most money—there's gotta be something more. So I started doing research and found the field of urban and community planning and decided I would get a graduate degree. I quit my job, went back to bartending and waiting tables, and went back to school and got a degree in community planning.

ME: So between work and being a mom, how do you find the time to recharge?

ANNE: Well, I go to the gym, I take my son to the park, I go to the movies. I think my personality is really driven—I'm incredibly centered around my job and I'm ambitious. And a lot of times my work and leisure time are the same thing—if I have to go to an art gallery opening because there are people there that I need to see, I can look at that as not just work, but as leisure time as well.

ME: What would you say is the most challenging part of your job?

ANNE: Because we're a nonprofit, we have to raise money for everything that we do. Sometimes people are paying us for our services, but not in the same way that most private companies work. Usually the projects we're doing can only partially pay for themselves, so we have to go to foundations, corporations, or individuals and ask them for the funds—make a case and tell them why what we're doing is really important. And when you're trying to run a project at the same time you're trying to raise

WHAT IT TAKES

- Creativity
- Thriving in a fast-paced environment
- Being open to constructive criticism
- The ability to think on your feet and handle pressure

money, it makes for a stressful situation. Sometimes you wish that you could just focus on doing a project and doing it right, and it would be nice if it could just pay for itself.

ME: But you really seem to love your job, despite the challenges and long hours. What makes it all worthwhile?

ANNE: When you negotiate a really great space or a project that provides great space for different people and the community is really happy, that makes it worthwhile. Say there's a new dance studio in a neighborhood. The people who run the dance studio are really happy because now they have a place to teach the classes and rehearse their dance stuff. The owner of the building is really happy because his building has a dance studio in it and it turned out to be much better than he thought it might be. That's really, really rewarding when you see all of those different things come together and everybody feels like their neighborhood is much better than it was before.

INTERESTED IN URBAN PLANNING? HERE'S ANNE'S CAREER ADVICE

- *Since you need a master's degree in city or urban planning, study whatever interests you in undergrad and try to do well in it.*

- *Get to know the city or community that you're in, and spend time paying attention to how a city runs—that might be seeing what your neighborhood association has going on or attending community meetings around big development projects.*

FIVE MORE CAREERS WHERE YOU CAN HELP SHAPE YOUR CITY

CITY MANAGER   You might not think of cities as "businesses," but they need to be managed as if they are. Think about it . . . cities have huge budgets, lots of staff, and a million details all needing attention at the same time. City managers report to the mayor and are in charge of managing the day-to-day "operations" of a city.

LANDSCAPE ARCHITECT   Landscape architects plan what the landscape of public spaces—from courtyards and malls to playgrounds and zoos—will look like, figuring out how to incorporate trees and bushes, flowers, grass, fountains, benches, and walkways. Most are hands-on in putting their plan into action.

NEIGHBORHOOD WEEKLY NEWSPAPER EDITOR   Most communities, big and small, have a weekly newspaper. These weeklies cover the local scene, including news, events, arts, and music, with a goal of bringing the community together. Editors at these weeklies assign stories and shape the tone and content of the paper.

DIRECTOR OF TOURISM   Most cities employ a director of tourism, who promotes businesses and events in the city with the goal of bringing in money to the community through tourism. Even small towns need tourism directors to promote attractions like the world's largest ball of paint in Alexandria, Indiana, or Lucy, the sixty-five-foot-high elephant statue on the Jersey shore.

COMMUNITY EVENTS COORDINATOR   Street fairs, Halloween parades, Christmas tree lighting ceremonies—these are the kinds of happenings that a community events coordinator might organize. No matter how big or small, community events coordinators are always looking for ways to bring people and businesses together to build community.

YOU NEED TO KNOW ABOUT

The American Planning Association (www.planning.org) is the go-to source for all information on urban, suburban, regional, and rural planning. Through this organization you can find out about conferences, read publications about planning, research schools with planning degrees, and learn about student chapters of the APA.

For more on careers that change the landscape, check out the architect profile on page 219.

MICHELLE CARTER

International Development and Relief Worker

The Facts

Michelle Carter,
Country Director, CARE
International in Lesotho
and South Africa

WHAT? An international development and relief worker works for a government agency or an NGO (nongovernmental organization) to provide emergency relief or development support to countries and regions in need.

WHERE? Development and relief workers can be found in all corners of the world.

HOW? Getting into development and relief work is competitive—many relief workers have a master's or doctorate in international relations or other specialties that directly relate to the work they do, as well as a strong track record of volunteerism.

$$$: $20,000 to $50,000 a year or more, depending on the agency and position. Most agencies also provide a stipend to cover housing and food costs of staff living abroad.

DRESS CODE? Casual, but may be inspired by the country (like having to wear a skirt or veil in certain countries, not showing arms or legs in others)

STRESS FACTOR: On a scale of 1 to 10, a 9

fresh out of college, I worked for a relief and development organization called CARE. While working for CARE, I had a chance to travel to Africa, and I came back with an immense amount of respect for the relief workers who worked "in the field," sometimes in seriously difficult and even dangerous conditions.

I knew I wanted to profile a relief and development worker for *In Their Shoes*, so I decided to go back to my career roots. CARE put me in touch with Michelle Carter, who has worked in Haiti, Rwanda, Mozambique, Burundi, Lesotho, and South Africa. Michelle was wonder-

"Somehow, no matter how well I plan things, I end up with urgent issues at the end of the day that have to be handled immediately."

ful enough to share some writing about what her life as a relief worker in the heart of Africa is like.

MICHELLE'S WORK

I always knew I wanted to do something to help others, and that's probably why I studied psychology in college. Growing up, my father was in the military, so I had the privilege of living in Thailand and Europe, as well as visiting North Africa and Asia on family vacations. I loved traveling.

After college I took a year off and started thinking about being a diplomat, or finding a job where I could work on issues facing poorer countries. As I started researching these types of jobs, I realized that I needed a master's degree, so I applied and got into graduate school, where I focused on international economics and Sub-Saharan Africa. While in grad school, I figured out that it wasn't politics or international business that I was interested in—it was trying to find a way to make things work better for poor countries. I remembered traveling as a young girl and seeing the brown drinking water in Thailand or the incredible poverty in India and other places. I also loved the idea of working in a job where I would have the freedom to see the world and learn about Africa, a place where my ancestors came from many years ago, but I knew very little about it beyond the mostly negative portrayals in the media.

And now here I am. I'm doing exactly what I dreamed of. I work for a great international relief and development organization, CARE, and I'm living in Africa.

I work with a team of specialists to design, plan, and implement the projects to help the people in need, as well as send reports on our work to the donors who fund our projects.

My hours are long. I'm usually up by five or five thirty a.m. to check e-mails on my laptop and see if there is anything I need to know about going on in the world or at CARE headquarters in the United States. There's a seven-hour time difference between where I live and headquarters,

YOU ASKED . . .

"How did you get to where you're at without getting distracted or drawn in by the peer pressure around you?"

—KRISTIN, AGE 16

MICHELLE ANSWERED . . .

"Like all teenagers, I was very influenced by my friends. However, I was also lucky to have a strong family who instilled in me the basic values of not hurting myself or others. My father would always say to me when I went out, 'Remember who you are.' I think my family's faith and trust in me built up my confidence to remain focused on doing well and not get distracted by drugs, drinking, boys, or not doing well in school. I know that I'm one of the lucky ones to have a strong family and role models around me, but I think that even if someone has a tough home environment, we all need to be able to look at ourselves in the mirror and make sure that we're okay with who we are."

so getting up early gives me a chance to communicate with people there if I need to. Then I'll eat breakfast, shower, and drive to the office, which isn't too far from my house.

THE BREAKDOWN

IN MEETINGS: 3 hours a day

ON THE PHONE: 30 minutes a day

ONLINE: 4 hours a day

SITTING: Not very often

PUBLIC SPEAKING: Occasionally

READING: End up reading at night

WORKING SOLO: Rarely

My job itself changes from day to day. If I'm in the office, a lot of my work is about the projects I'm involved in. Sometimes I'm having planning meetings with staff, writing and editing proposals and reports to describe CARE's work in the field. I make sure our projects are high quality and will have the positive, long-lasting impact that we're hoping for. Sometimes I'm meeting with donors to see if they're interested in funding some of our projects. I often have meetings with the local government or other NGOs to talk about CARE's programs, discuss policies, or to talk about how we can work together. Then there are days when I'm dealing with not-so-exciting but also important financial reports and budgets. The meetings and organizational part of my job isn't so glamorous, but it's an important part of what I do.

When I can, I try to grab lunch with folks from other organizations in the area to hear about their projects and work—it's a nice break from staring at the computer.

Somehow, no matter how well I plan things, I end up with urgent issues at the end of the day that have to be handled immediately. I try to leave work by six thirty p.m. or so. The hours are long, but the work really keeps me inspired, so I never really feel tired. When I get home, I usually warm up some dinner and then relax with a book or watch TV to catch up on the latest events. Sometimes I get on the Internet

WHY WAIT?

- Gain experience by volunteering in your community.
- Learn other languages, such as French, Portuguese, Spanish, or even better, Arabic, Russian, and Kiswahili!

to send e-mails or chat or call my family and friends. Other nights, there might be some cultural event going on in town—a dance, art exhibition, or something else that I go to.

My favorite part of my job is going out to the field to see our projects, which I try to do as often as possible. On those days, I get up really early (usually around five a.m.) and drive in a four-by-four or pickup truck long distances over bumpy roads to get to where I'm going. I always wear a long skirt in respect of the culture, where rural women do not wear pants. When I'm in the field, my primary interest is getting a better sense of how the projects are helping the poor. For example, one of the projects we have is to help women's associations increase their peanut production so they can make more money. Then we teach them different ways to save monies for difficult times, like if there is a drought or a family member gets sick with malaria or HIV. So when I'm in the field, I take a look at how these programs are running and think about what can be improved.

Most of the time, the CARE staff in the field knows the community members really well, and they also speak the local

THEN TO NOW

1993: Graduated from Smith College with a BA in psychology, minor in international relations	1996: Graduated from Georgetown University with an MS in foreign science	1995–1996: Interned at USAID	1996: Was a CARE Fellow, CARE Haiti	1997–1999: Assistant regional director, CARE Haiti

language, so they translate for me. When I'm in the field, I also try to meet with local government officials and let them know what CARE is trying to do to help their communities and discuss any concerns there might be. It's always good to hear them thank CARE for the work we're doing to help people address their problems.

The last part of my day in the field involves the CARE staff. Usually we'll grab a sandwich and talk about what's going on. I'll let them know what I think can be improved, and I'll share my deep appreciation for the hard work they do in very challenging environments. I'll always leave time for the staff to share with me any concerns they might have, because they are our connection to the communities.

The work isn't easy. Poverty is very complex, and sometimes I get depressed because I know the world is unfair and that there are always going to be winners and losers. But then there are great moments too, like when I'm speaking with a woman who tells me that a project has changed her life—that she can provide more for her family and everyone's healthier, better educated, and empowered to make changes in their lives.

One of the best perks of my job is getting to live

WHAT IT TAKES

- A strong sense of integrity
- A willingness to live in less-than-comfortable environments
- A sense of adventure

1999–2000:	2002:	2002–2004:	2004–2009:	2009–2012:	2012–present:
Project manager/sub-office team leader, CARE Rwanda	Promoted to assistant country director for program, CARE Rwanda	Deputy regional director for East & Central Africa, CARE Atlanta	Assistant country director for program, CARE Mozambique	Country director of CARE Burundi	Country director, CARE Lesotho and South Africa

in another country, and I try to take advantage of all that it has to offer on the weekends. Some weekends, I travel around. Others I might go to the beach, enjoy conversations with the locals, and learn a lot about the interesting culture, like art, dancing, and great African music. I'm very interested in their culture. This is all part of the big adventure that I'm on.

In the Field

FIVE MORE CAREERS WORKING OVERSEAS FOR A RELIEF AND DEVELOPMENT ORGANIZATION

COMMUNICATIONS OFFICER A big part of the work at relief organizations is getting information to the donors—the people who contribute money to the organization and its programs. Communications officers deal with the media and act as the face of the organization.

PEACE CORPS VOLUNTEER People interested in a career in international development sometimes start with the Peace Corps. Peace Corps volunteers help people in a developing country, doing anything from building schools and better plumbing systems to educating and counseling.

RELIEF DOCTOR Relief doctors often work with organizations such as Doctors Without Borders (Médecins Sans Frontières) and use their expertise to aid people in regions where access to health care is limited.

LOGISTICS MANAGER When working in relief situations in other countries, there are often a lot of logistical details—transportation, a shortage of gasoline, bad roads, security, and safety issues within the community. Logistics managers figure out how to work safely and efficiently within a village, city, or country.

MISSIONARY Associated with an organized religion, missionaries commit their lives to sharing their faith in the hope of converting others. While they don't have to work overseas, many missionaries live in developing countries and center their work on humanitarian efforts while spreading news of their religion.

YOU NEED TO KNOW ABOUT

Cross-Cultural Solutions gives teens ages fifteen to seventeen the opportunity to volunteer abroad in a developing country like India, Ghana, Tanzania, and Guatemala. Service trips happen over the summer and focus on projects like working with local children, planting gardens, and beautification projects. Find out more at www.crossculturalsolutions.org.

lunch break

THE POWER OF MENTORS

Having a mentor in your corner has never been more important than it is today. Navigating the world of school, college, and work can be more than a little confusing, and mentors are the ideal people to give you tips, strategies, and support so you can breeze through (or at least make figuring it all out more fun).

Here's what you need to know:

WHO THEY ARE

Mentors are people who advise, guide, and support their mentees in areas like school, relationships, college, career, and life. Mentors do what they do because they like passing on their knowledge and helping others get through things they may have already overcome.

At its core, mentoring is a relationship between two people—the mentor (the person providing the guidance) and the mentee (the person receiving the guidance). And for the record, lots of people have them, even business execs at the top of their game and big-time celebrities. Famous mentoring pairs include Oprah (mentor) and Dr. Phil (mentee), Madonna (mentor) and Gwyneth Paltrow (mentee), and Tom Cruise (mentor) and Jeremy Renner (mentee).

In their most basic role, mentors are there to offer advice, perspective, and insight to their mentees about everything from handling small challenges to making major life decisions. Depending on the relationship a mentor and mentee have agreed on, mentors might also find themselves doing things like:

- Reviewing an essay or job application
- Writing a recommendation for college admission
- Being available for quick answers and advice
- Being open to sharing personal experiences
- Teaching a specific skill (writing, public speaking, computer programming, etc.)
- Sharing names of connections and resources within their network
- Leading by example

WHERE TO FIND THEM

There are different kinds of mentoring relationships: informal and formal. Informal mentors might be people like teachers, tutors, an older student, or a coach—someone who's in your life and does the things a mentor does, but without an explicit understanding that they are mentoring you. In fact, sometimes mentors might not even know they're seen as a mentor—they may simply be leading by example and helping a mentee see what's possible. Formal mentoring relations are typically brought together by an organization that screens mentors specifically with the purpose of connecting them with mentees.

Are you looking for a mentor? Visit Mentoring.org (www.mentoring.org) and search by zip code for opportunities to meet a mentor through an organization near you.

MIRIAM KRAMER

Yoga Instructor

The Facts

Miriam Kramer, Yoga and Movement Instructor

WHAT? Yoga instructors help people practice yoga either through classes or one-on-one instruction.

WHERE? They usually work at yoga studios, in gyms that offer yoga classes, vacation resorts that offer spa and yoga services, or in their own private practice.

HOW? Yoga instructors generally apprentice with a mentor to learn different skills and methods, as well as practice yoga for years themselves. There is no formal yoga certification requirement, but taking workshops or classes in different disciplines is important.

$$$: $40 to $80 dollars an hour

DRESS CODE? Cool, comfy, and casual yoga wear . . . lots of loose cotton

STRESS FACTOR: On a scale of 1 to 10, a 3

have you ever practiced yoga? I do it from time

to time, and I really enjoy it. There's something about yoga that just makes you feel good—body, mind, and soul. Yet I know that for real "yogis" it's about so much more—breathing, tuning in . . . connecting. As a result, there's definitely something unique about yoga instructors. They have a certain energy and calmness that is really motivating and inspiring.

I got in touch with Miriam Kramer, a yoga and movement instructor in Los Angeles. I wanted to find out what being a yoga instructor was really like, beyond my perspective as a student. First things first: I asked Miriam how she got involved in becoming a teacher and to explain yoga and the lifestyle that goes along with it.

"In a career field where you're being a healer or a giver, the hardest part is making sure to recharge yourself so that you can be a giving person."

"I went to UCLA under their dance program, and I just fell in love with dance. I thought that every day was so joyful and was just about playing with the body. It was always something new. But I injured my foot when I was eighteen years old, so one of my teachers recommended I take Pilates to stay fit while my foot healed. When I graduated from college, I decided to go to New York and study with the master Pilates teacher Romana, got certified, and ended up teaching Pilates full-time and dancing professionally. A few years later, just for fun, I started going to the Iyengar Yoga Institute in Los Angeles, and once I took one class I knew it was my calling. I instantly fell in love with the process of yoga, and I haven't left since. I realized that the teaching of yoga was going to carry me throughout my life . . . it is a whole philosophy of living, and I could relate it to everything I did.

"In terms of what yoga is, the word 'yoga' means 'union.' And it's not just the union of the body and the mind, but it's the union of the individual self with the universal self, as well as the union of the body, the mind, the emotions, and the intellect. So people go to yoga classes to learn how to 'practice' yoga on their own and in their life. Our yoga teachers talk about how when we're going outside, we'll see what the weather is like. So for example, if it's cold, we'll wear pants and a big sweater. In yoga, we do that for our body—we ask 'what is the weather of our body and our mind and our emotions today?' From there we tailor the practice to what's going on inside of us.

"To be a yoga instructor, you have to be very flexible, body and mind, have a high amount of energy, and you can't be rigid in your ideas of what you're going to be doing on a daily basis, because you never really know who's going to be in front of you to teach. You also have to be willing to take time to build up your practice. It's not the kind of thing where you get certified and then suddenly somebody knocks on your door and offers you a fifty-thousand-dollar-a-year job. You have to be willing to start slow and ease yourself into it," Miriam explains.

The job scenario for yoga instructors is certainly different from many other more traditional careers. Most yoga instructors aren't full-time employees at a yoga studio unless it's their

YOU ASKED . . .

"Has a loved one ever said something that made you feel like giving up?" —REBECCA, AGE 12

MIRIAM ANSWERED . . .

"I think the only person who's ever told me I can't do something is really myself. I've been my harshest criticizer, my own worst enemy, and I think that's the biggest challenge in this type of career. But what yoga really teaches you is to be true to yourself and the essence of you. So anytime anyone, myself included, says something that makes me feel like giving up, I remind myself of what I'm most passionate about. If you don't love having your job really be a part of your whole life, then it's probably not the right fit for you. You have to keep digging for that place."

own studio—more typical is the path that Miriam has taken. She works at a variety of jobs to create what would be the equivalent of one full-time job. She teaches several yoga classes a week, does private Pilates instruction for about ten clients a week, and runs the creative movement program at a private ele-

THE BREAKDOWN

ON THE PHONE: 10 minutes

ONLINE: 10 minutes

SITTING: 10 minutes

SOME FORM OF MOVING: 3–6 hours a day

WORKING SOLO: Only in own yoga practice

mentary school, where she teaches improvisational dance and movement to pre-K through sixth grade. On top of all that, Miriam practices yoga every day for one to two hours. As you can imagine, all of these different pieces keep her fairly busy. I asked Miriam to tell us about the realities of the lifestyle.

"The lifestyle can be somewhat restricting because you're at the whim of other people's schedules, but at the same time there's a lot of flexibility, too. Since most people work eight to five, most yoga classes are either early in the morning or late at night. So oftentimes you may be teaching two classes a day—one at night and one in the morning—and then you'll have your day free to do your practice or any other endeavor that may interest you. Your 'job stability' is also very dependent on your performance, and if you get injured and it's serious enough that you can't teach, you can't work," she says.

I wanted to get a better sense of what a day in Miriam's life might look like, so she broke it down for us.

MIRIAM'S (UN)USUAL DAY

I wake up around five thirty a.m. and feed the cats, and then I do my yoga practice for about an hour and a half. Next I eat breakfast. And by the way, I always eat three meals a day. People who are dancers and movement and yoga teachers

WHY WAIT?

- If you don't already, start practicing yoga now—it's never too early!
- Attend yoga workshops that are open to the public to learn about various yoga techniques.

eat a lot. I get dressed and get ready to go—leggings and a T-shirt or some other kind of exercise clothing. Then, depending on when I'm teaching, I'll leave for work. Let's say I have a class at eight a.m. I'll leave by 7:40 and I'll start teaching at eight, and I'll teach for about an hour and a half. Then I'll have a short break and then maybe I'll teach a couple of private classes.

Next I take a lunch break. Usually I'll have some soup and toast and cheese and bread. My afternoon is generally pretty open, and then I'll teach another class in the evening, often a six o'clock to seven thirty p.m. class. Then I come home and have dinner and relax. Oftentimes before I go to sleep I'll do another breathing yoga practice, and then I'll go to sleep at around ten p.m. By the end of the day, my body is usually very, very tired. I try to be relaxing in bed by eight or nine p.m.

Hearing about her day made *my* body tired. It's exhausting enough doing one yoga class a day. Miriam is doing several, plus dancing and Pilates, not to mention her own yoga practice

THEN TO NOW

Graduated from UCLA with BA in dance performance and choreography

Received certification in Pilates from the Pilates Studio of New York

2000: Completed three-year teaching training at the BKS Iyengar Yoga Institute of Los Angeles in the morning and evening. I asked her if she found the pace tiring.

"In a career field where you're being a healer or a giver, the hardest part is making sure to recharge yourself so that you can be a giving person. Because

WHAT IT TAKES
- A love of yoga and a belief in the philosophy behind it
- Being good at inspiring others
- A calm personality
- Being very disciplined

you're putting out energy all the time, you need to make sure that you go to class to recharge yourself and continue to teach yourself. I get body work sessions on myself—at least twice a month I'll get a massage or something like that, so I can really feed myself and get recharged," she explains.

But I could tell that the payoffs of the career are worth it for Miriam. Her love for her work came through as we spoke, and it was obvious that she has found a career that allows her to have a perfect "union" between work and life. I wrapped up our interview by asking her what she loved most about her job.

Miriam answered, "I love when I'm looking out at my students and I feel a genuine joy coming from them toward me. It's an unspoken message we're sharing that this isn't just about movement or healing their aching back—it's about this greater process of discovery that we're all in together. I may have a day where I'm teaching and it's not my best class—maybe I wasn't watching my students as closely as I wanted to or giving

2000: Started as Pilates teacher/ apprentice at Drago's Gymnasium

2005: Became yoga teacher at Iyengar Yoga Institute of Los Angeles them the right correction—but I realize that they look at it as a lifetime process that they're interested in experiencing themselves. Those are my favorite moments."

INTERESTED IN BEING A YOGA OR MOVEMENT INSTRUCTOR? HERE'S MIRIAM'S ADVICE

- *You have to "do." Yoga is a life of action and it's really about integrating your whole life around a yoga lifestyle and listening to your inner self.*

- *There's so much more to this life than just making a certain amount of money—there can be so much fulfillment in doing a career that maybe isn't a big moneymaker.*

- *The joy of this type of work is acknowledgment that you do not have all the answers and there is always room for personal and spiritual growth. Don't allow others to dissuade you if you believe being a movement instructor is your true path. Stay focused on your desire, and the life practice of this art form will be your teacher and companion*

In the Field

FIVE MORE CAREERS IN FITNESS

PERSONAL TRAINER   Personal trainers usually work at fitness centers or are self-employed, and they work one-on-one with clients to help them reach their fitness goals. They create training programs and often actually go through the fitness regime with their clients, acting not only as a fitness expert, but also as a supporter and motivator.

NUTRITIONIST Nutritionists specialize in creating nutritional plans for their clients, whether it's with a goal of losing weight, recovering from an illness, or simply eating a more balanced, healthy diet. They might cook for their clients, teach them how to food shop, or provide them with healthy recipes and monitor their diet.

WELLNESS COACH   A career that has become more popular in recent years is a wellness coach. These coaches view their clients more holistically than personal trainers, and they provide guidance for healthy living not only with regard to fitness and nutrition, but also emotional, mental, and spiritual well-being.

GYM MANAGER   Gym managers not only run the business side of a gym, but they also work to bring in more clients. They make sure the atmosphere of the gym is a positive one; develop ideas for fresh, new classes; and offer promotions and place advertisements to boost membership.

PILATES INSTRUCTOR   Pilates involves what's called "contrology," defined as the "complete coordination of the mind, body, and spirit." Pilates instructors are trained in this technique and use a variety of exercises involving repetition and coordination of the body so people can be physically, mentally, and spiritually balanced.

YOU NEED TO KNOW ABOUT

Yoga Journal is both a print magazine and an online journal you can find at www.yogajournal.com. Check it out for tons of articles about yoga, information on yoga poses, a directory of classes around the country, and resources for training.

For more fitness-related careers, check out the professional athlete profile on page 175.

ULLIKA PANKRATZ

Visual Merchandiser

Ullika Pankratz,
Visual Merchandiser
and Display Designer,
IKEA

The Facts

WHAT? Visual merchandisers design product displays for stores and boutiques, figuring out where products should be sold within a store and designing displays that showcase the merchandise in ways that will maximize sales.

WHERE? Many, like Ullika, are freelance and work exclusively with one or two big clients, while others work for department stores, chains, and small boutiques.

HOW? Most visual merchandisers have a four-year degree in visual design or merchandise, as well as experience working in retail.

$$$: $25,000 to $55,000 or more, depending on experience

DRESS CODE? Casual to business casual, depending on whether they're building displays or going to meetings

STRESS FACTOR: On a scale of 1 to 10, a 4

when i think of ikea, I think of affordable furniture, cool designs, an enormous building, and the most delicious Swedish meatballs around. When Ullika Pankratz thinks about IKEA, she thinks about how to design a product display within one of their stores around the world.

Ullika is a visual merchandiser and display designer, and for the past twelve-plus years she has been working with IKEA, traveling around the world to design and set up mini "shops" within the stores. Ullika's travel schedule is intense: six weeks at a store anywhere in the world, two weeks home, and then back out to the next store for another six weeks, and so on. I caught up with Ullika while she was on a break between gigs at her home in Portland, Oregon.

ME: What does being a visual merchandiser entail?

ULLIKA: I do the interior setups and inside decor for IKEA, from space planning to visual merchandising to graphic setting and things like that.

ME: And so when you say you do the "inside decor," what exactly does that mean?

ULLIKA: I do anything from setting up the racking that is needed for the goods to be laid on, to doing podiums, decorations, displaying the products. Let's say we want to remodel a shop inside of IKEA. I'll do the whole floor planning with displaying and figuring out what we're going to do with each product. I specifically work in displaying the original merchandise, the little shops within IKEA, like the cook shop or the home organization department.

"You have to like taking a drill in your hands, you have to like to hammer, to paint, get dirty, get on your knees, get a ladder. . . . You have to be a very active person."

ME: Is that what your background is in?

ULLIKA: I'm originally from Germany, and they have an

YOU ASKED . . .

"What do you do when you feel like you just want to give up?"
—KAYLEE, AGE 17

ULLIKA ANSWERED . . .

"I usually try to tell myself that maybe I'm just at a moment of my life where things are not quite going the way I want them to go. But I try to stay positive and focused on the future rather than the moment. I'll tell myself, 'Look, this is a difficult situation and this is hard, but there are good things to come and there is more to come. I just need to focus on that rather than what's happening right now.'"

apprenticeship program there. So I did that for three years and got a degree in visual merchandising and shop window design.

ME: When did you begin working for IKEA?

ULLIKA: I did a store opening in 1994 and stayed there for nine years. In 2002 I became a freelancer for IKEA and now I just do international work for them.

ME: So if you're working with an IKEA in another country, how does it work?

ULLIKA: When we're doing a new store, usually I'll do the planning six months ahead of the opening, and I'll go to Holland to do that. And then once it's time to get a store ready, I'll fly to whatever country it's in. If it's a store that's already built, and the interior and shell is there, then I have an assignment of creating one of the shops. The racking is usually already up, so I start looking at the plans that I have and then do the merchandising. I usually have a group of salespeople who help me put all the goods on the shelves, trying to figure out what is the perfect spot for which kinds of products. There are a lot of special IKEA ways of doing things. Then when you're done with the merchandising, you get into the visual merchandising, which is usually organizing stuff on a shelf. You figure out how you want to display a specific candleholder or a specific quilt cover . . . that kind of thing.

THE BREAKDOWN

IN MEETINGS: 30 minutes a day

SITTING: 1–2 hours a day

STANDING: 6 hours a day

WORKING SOLO: 2–3 hours a day

ME: How long will it take you if it's a new store you're opening up?

ULLIKA: Six weeks.

ME: Six weeks that you would be in that country? Wow. What is it like to travel so much for your job?

ULLIKA: The reality is that you never actually quite know where you are, and you spend a lot of your free time flying, living out of hotels, and being in places that you don't really know. So you have to be really, really flexible when you do this kind of work. It can be very lonely at times. And it's not like you get someplace and somebody is right there to explain to you where to find your groceries. You have to do a lot of that stuff by yourself. So you have to be very self-motivated. We do have pretty good working hours and we don't do a lot of overtime, because things are very organized. But when I'm in another country, we get off work and I have a hotel room to

WHY WAIT?

- Try to get a job in retail while you're still in school, and get involved in how displays at the store are put together.
- Sign up for set design for your school theater productions to get experience working with tools and your hands.

myself that IKEA pays for, and that's it. So I try to organize myself—do I want to sightsee or do I just want to hang out in the hotel? I think the hardest part is that because I'm on the road thirty-eight weeks of the year, when I'm at home, I don't have time to have a "regular life," as in Tuesday nights I go to yoga, Wednesday nights I see my girlfriends. I don't have that at all.

ME: That's really intense. So where are you off to next?

ULLIKA: Australia.

ME: Cool . . .

ULLIKA: Yeah, this is the part that sounds really fabulous. And it is fabulous. I do love my job. It's the best thing that I've done.

ME: Do you get to travel business class?

ULLIKA: No. IKEA is about low cost and low budget, and the company expects its employees to not waste money. So we never have any kind of first-class or business-class travel.

THEN TO NOW

1992: Received a certificate of shop window design and visual merchandising from Hamburg Trade School, Germany	1993–1994: Worked at Nordstrom doing visual display and holiday setup	1993–1994: Worked at the Gap doing sales and visuals	1994: Started working at IKEA	2000–2001: Participated in IKEA's Leadership and Management Training

ME: What kind of personality do you think is a good match for this type of work?

ULLIKA: You have to be open-minded and friendly, you have to like being around people, and you have to like working with your hands. It's hands-on work. You have to like taking a drill in your hands, you have to like to hammer, to paint, get dirty, get on your knees, get a ladder . . . You have to be a very active person.

ME: What are the other challenges of your job, besides the travel?

ULLIKA: It can be challenging to always be working with different kinds of people. You never know who you're going to team up with, and you never know what kind of personality they have. Sometimes it can be very tough, especially because, although we work in English, for most of us English is our second language. So it's a challenge when you have to explain things to people.

WHAT IT TAKES

- Being comfortable with getting dirty and doing physical work
- Having a good sense of color and design
- Persistence . . . It's a tough field to break into

ME: And what's the best part about your job?

ULLIKA: It's never boring. I learn so much every time I go

2000: Worked at IKEA in Budapest, Hungary, as visual merchandiser

2002: Became freelance visual specialist

2007: Became visual merchandising manager, IKEA Portland

2009: Became store planner for IKEA North America

someplace, and because IKEA brings out new products every year, there are new ideas, new concepts every year, so that keeps the job really fresh all the time. And then, of course, being in all the countries and learning so much about other cultures is just fabulous and amazing. I feel really fortunate to have that.

ME: If you're having a really great day at work, what makes it so?

ULLIKA: If I listen to people's ideas and we can come together and brainstorm as a team and by the end of the day, we've done a whole display and it looks beautiful . . . that's wonderful.

ULLIKA'S ADVICE

- *Believe in yourself and believe in what you can do with your hands and your creativity. Don't let other people tell you that you're not good at something.*

- *It's a bit tough to get into visual merchandising, but when you're in, you're in, and that's the nice part about it. The best places to try to break in are department stores, the Gap—even galleries or small shops.*

- *Take a summer job in something that you like to do or that sounds interesting to you. Do it for a few weeks or a few months and check it out before making a decision about if it's really something you want to do for life.*

In the Field

FIVE MORE CAREERS IN DESIGN

INTERIOR DESIGNER Interior designers pay attention not just to aesthetics, but also to designing spaces that are based specifically on how they will be used by the client. They must be

licensed by the state and know how different design materials
react or hold up in various situations.

HOME PRODUCT DEVELOPER   Kind of like the fashion designers of the interior decorating industry, product developers might work for home furnishing stores like Crate & Barrel or Pottery Barn, and develop new products and furniture lines to be carried there.

KITCHEN AND BATH DESIGNER   Kitchen and bath designers specialize in designing the two rooms that are used the most in any house, and they create kitchens and bathrooms that are not only attractive, but functional as well.

TEXTILE DESIGNER   Textile designers usually have a background in art and design, and they use their creativity to develop new designs for textiles to be used in the home, such as sofa covers, pillows, curtains, and bedding, while also paying attention to things like durability and how the fabric will be used.

FURNITURE MAKER   Blending their love of creativity and design with the practical aspects of construction using wood, fasteners, fabrics, and other materials, furniture makers might create furniture for designers like Ethan Allen or hand-make unique pieces of furniture for individual customers.

YOU NEED TO KNOW ABOUT

Visual Merchandising and Store Design (www.vmsd.com) is a website focused on the work of visual merchandisers in the world of retail. Visit their website to view design galleries, read articles on visual merchandising, see what kinds of jobs are out there, and more.

ELLEN GOLDSMITH-VEIN

Talent Agent

*Ellen Goldsmith-Vein,
Owner and CEO,
The Gotham Group*

The Facts

WHAT? Talent agents represent performers like actors, writers, animators, musicians, and comedians. They find work for their clients, but also negotiate their clients' deals, guide their careers, and represent their involvement in a project or gig.

WHERE? Many agents work at large firms in New York or L.A., while others work for smaller boutique agencies or, like Ellen, start their own!

HOW? Agents don't need a particular educational background, although a BA doesn't hurt. Breaking into the industry is very competitive—most people intern first and then start out in the mailroom at an agency, working their way up to a receptionist or assistant before representing clients themselves.

$$$: $30,000 a year for agents just starting out, but there's no cap on earning potential, as agents earn a percentage of their clients' income

DRESS CODE? In most agency environments, the dress is very businesslike . . . suits and other business attire

STRESS FACTOR: On a scale of 1 to 10, Ellen says it's a 40!

when i say that Ellen Goldsmith-Vein has built her own Hollywood empire, I'm not exaggerating. Ellen is the founder and CEO of The Gotham Group, a representation firm in the heart of Beverly Hills that focuses on the animation and family entertainment business. Ellen's agency reps everything from show creators to film directors to artists and writers, not to mention publishers like Scholastic, Simon & Schuster, and HarperCollins. Ellen and The Gotham Group are also actively on the producing end of the industry, producing films like *Camp X-Ray* (starring Kristen Stewart) and *Abduction* (starring Taylor Lautner), and the FOX movie *The Maze Runner*, to name a few.

I visited Ellen in her loftlike offices on Sunset Boulevard, and the energy in the air was intense—it was obvious there was lots going on and plenty of smart, attentive people working their butts off in every office and cubicle. Ellen had just gotten back from a business lunch, so I hung out on the plush couch in her office while she caught up with her assistant (who sat in Ellen's office next to her desk) and simultaneously returned a phone call, had a conversation with a colleague down the hall, and made notes on a stack of papers on her desk.

"I feel like I have a responsibility to my clients, but I still am able to have a critical eye when it comes to their work and ideas."

As an agent and manager in the animation and family entertainment biz, Ellen represents directors, artists, animators, writers, producers, animation studios . . . even publishing companies. She and her team act on behalf of the firm's clients, negotiating deals with studios and production companies, setting up pitch meetings, finding work for their clients, and being an advocate for anything related to their clients' careers. It's a big job, but somebody's got to do it. I had a chance to pick Ellen's brain and get all the details about what her daily life is really like.

ME: What were your career aspirations when you were a teen?

ELLEN: When I was a teenager, I think I had sufficient delusions of grandeur. I wanted to be the first woman justice on the Supreme Court. You know, that's the kind of "middle-of-the-road" thinker I was. Obviously that was not meant to be, because look where I am now—I'm in the cartoon business. When I went to college, I was initially pursuing a political science route in the hopes that that's what I would end up doing. And that was the dream until I took a creative writing class in college and somebody said, "You're a great writer" and I kept getting As on anything that I had to write. So then I decided I wanted to be a novelist. And so I went into banking, which is exactly what you do when you are a novelist who wanted to be a justice of the Supreme Court. *(Laughs)* After five years of doing that, I decided that I was going to come back to Los Angeles, and I went to work for the William Morris Agency. I thought that would be a way to get back into the creative process. And from there I ended up representing writers as opposed to actually being a writer.

YOU ASKED . . .

"What difficulties did you have to go through to get to where you are?" —MANDI, AGE 17

ELLEN ANSWERED . . .

"From the outside we look like a small company. But we're actually a pretty big company, both in terms of client revenue generation and material and bodies. We control an entire family entertainment industry, which is a billion-dollar business. I don't know if it's because people don't understand the economics of this business or they believe that actors and directors are the business that you need to be in, but getting that recognition has been the hardest thing."

ME: Did it all sort of click for you when you realized that this was what you wanted to do?

ELLEN: Well, I had really been an agent when I was in the banking world. It was just a different commodity—money as opposed to talent. And I was pretty good at it, so it seemed natural. I was more of a caretaker. I feel like I have a responsibility to my clients, but I still am able to have a critical eye when it comes to their work and ideas.

ME: There are all of these Hollywood takes on what an agent does—can you set us straight? What does an agent actually do?

ELLEN: Essentially, agenting, at its very core, is representation. And by that I mean it's going out into your client's world, whether it's publishing or film or television or music, and acting on their behalf. So you have to decide what projects and material make sense for your clients, and what other elements you can bring into a project that make sense for your client, and you have to make a determination about who the best people are for your clients to be in business with. It's sort of like being the angel on their shoulder if it happens the right way and if it's a good relationship.

ME: So how do you literally spend your day?

ELLEN: My day may be different from a lot of other people's days here, because a lot of the managers here do "coverage," which means they go out and talk to the studios and the production companies and figure out what's going on in

THE BREAKDOWN

IN MEETINGS: 1/3 of the day

ON THE PHONE: 1/3 of the day

E-MAILING OR IMING: 1/3 of the day

SITTING: All day

READING: Whenever I can

MULTITASKING: All day long!

the world and what's open in terms of writing and directing assignments. For me, it's not only checking in with clients, but it's talking to their other representatives and keeping everyone informed, because in the entertainment industry, information means everything. It's also finding out what the status of client activity is. We usually "go out" with one piece of material a week, whether we have a book that we're out in the marketplace with, or a comic book, or an article, or we've got a pitch. So there's managing that process—talking to movie studios and producers, assigning territories. It just goes on and on and on. That's why my job is a 40 on the stress level!

ME: What are the hours like?

ELLEN: It's pretty much 24/7.

ME: If you're working those kind of hours, how do you juggle it with being a mom?

ELLEN: I have to get up at the crack of dawn. I basically spend time with my kids in the morning and then when I get home.

THEN TO NOW

1986: Graduated UCLA with a BS in sociology	1984–1989: Mortgage banker at Merrill Lynch	1989–1990: Assistant to an agent, William Morris Agency	1990–1992: Development executive, Nelvana Entertainment

For example, tonight I have a dinner, so I'm going to leave early, go home, spend a few hours with my kids, and then I'm going to go to meet my clients for dinner.

ME: What's the first thing that you do when you get to work in the morning?

ELLEN: First I check my e-mail from home at six in the morning, because I have clients in London and all over the place, and I need to make sure that I know what they're doing. Then I read the trades* online and the newspapers and then I start making phone calls from home. Once I get in the car, I'm on the phone the entire way here. So usually it's a case of the tail wagging the dog. I may get on the phone with somebody, which precipitates needing to make another phone call, and so on.

ME: What does a great day at work look like?

ELLEN: I feel like I'm really lucky, because we are surrounded by so many incredibly talented people that every day for us is a great day. I remember I was so desperate when I first got into the animation business, all I wanted to do was represent Henry Selick, who directed Tim Burton's *The Nightmare Before Christmas*—that's all I wanted to do. I couldn't get him to return my phone calls. I just worshiped him. And about five or

---

* THE LINGO: **Trades** is another word for trade magazines or publications that relate to a specific industry. In Hollywood, the trades typically refer to the *Hollywood Reporter* and *Variety*.

| 1992–1994:
Manager/
partner at Atlas
Management | 1993: Founded The
Gotham Group | 1999–2003: Partner/
head of Animation and
Family Entertainment,
Artists Management
Group (AMG) | PRESENT: CEO,
The Gotham Group |

six years after I started this company I started having conversations with Henry and then we actually signed him, which was a big milestone because I think he's such a genius. So every day I just think to myself, *Man, I can't believe I'm lucky enough to be in business with the people we represent.* So whether it's Henry or it's an author or a publisher or Dark Horse Comics, or we just signed another Academy Award–winning director . . . How could every day not be a good day?

ME: What do you think are the most important traits of people who are successful in this business?

ELLEN: You have to realize that you're committing to making people's careers move along beyond where they are when they first come to you. So you have to take that obligation seriously. I always tell people that if you get into this business to make a lot of money, you never will. It's about having enough of a commitment to your clients that you can continue to move their projects forward. The other thing is having patience. There are times where I'm not up to the task—I don't have the patience. And when I'm not up to the task, I have to take a beat or I have to ask other people for their help. It's really important when you're in the representation business to work collaboratively. The ultimate downfall of any agency is working in little fiefdoms as opposed to as one unit.

ME: Do you think there are any misconceptions about what it's like to be an agent?

PAYING YOUR DUES

Believe it or not, many agents start out working in the mailroom (the official entry-level job at an agency), where they'll spend a year or two learning the ropes and soaking in the atmosphere before being bumped up to an assistant.

ELLEN: Yes . . . I don't think people realize how much incredibly hard work it is. I can't tell you how many people have come in here who just don't get that it's as intense as it is, and the incredible pressure that you're under when people's lives hang in the bal-

WHAT IT TAKES

- Amazing networking and schmoozing skills
- A drive to succeed
- Business savvy
- Being great with people

ance based on what you do or don't do, whose call you return or what you say or don't say. That's why I think the training programs at the agencies are important, because it gives you a great overview. It's really vital.

ME: Do you expect to stay in this career for the rest of your life?

ELLEN: I can't imagine doing anything else. At least until my kids stop liking cartoons and I'm no longer a hit at all their friends' parties.

In the Field

FIVE MORE CAREERS WORKING WITH TALENT

MAKEUP ARTIST When celebrities are performing, making a guest appearance, or attending a red carpet event, makeup artists work their magic, giving them a finished, flawless look. Makeup artists may work long or irregular hours on television or film shoots.

TALENT MANAGER There are some similarities between managers and agents, but while agents' primary role is negotiating deals for their clients, managers play more of an advisory role in terms of what projects make the most sense for their clients to work on.

PERSONAL ASSISTANT Celebrities have busy, busy lives. Personal assistants are the celebrities' right-hand people, organizing their schedules, running errands, answering phones. Many are on call 24/7 and have to drop everything to attend to their boss.

PUBLICIST Publicists shape a celebrity's image for the public. For example, if there's big news about Angelina, her publicist will figure out the best way to get the word out, including identifying the magazine or television show that might get the exclusive interview.

TALENT SCOUT We've all heard stories about a celebrity being "discovered." Talent scouts find new talent by going to concerts, comedy clubs, improv shows, local theater . . . and sometimes just by keeping their eyes open as they walk down the street.

YOU NEED TO KNOW ABOUT

The industry trade magazines *Hollywood Reporter* (www.hollywoodreporter.com) and *Variety* (www.variety.com) publish daily and weekly editions, and while subscriptions are pricey, many libraries carry the weeklies, and you can view some headlines and articles for free online.

For more on careers in Hollywood, check out the publicist profile on page 208 and the movie studio executive profile on page 65.

lunch break

THE FREELANCE LIFE

Have you ever met someone who works as a "freelancer"? Being freelance essentially means that you're self-employed, and although you may take on jobs for one or more companies, you're not actually employed by them. For example, a freelance photographer might be hired by a magazine to do occasional editorial shoots, but she isn't actually on their payroll—the magazine just hires her when they need her.

If you're considering a career as a freelancer, make sure you're a motivated self-starter, since it's a lot of hard work to build up a sustainable freelance career. Like any career, being a freelancer has its upsides and downsides. Here are some things to consider if you think you might want to go this route:

UPSIDES	DOWNSIDES
You can work on the projects you really want to work on, and say no to the projects that don't interest you.	There is little to no job stability for a freelancer, and sometimes it can be months or longer between paying gigs.

UPSIDES	DOWNSIDES
The pay for freelancers might be better for certain jobs than if you were being paid as a full-time employee.	Freelancers have to pay for their own medical insurance and don't get any other paid benefits.
You can wear anything all day long, even your pajamas.	Working from home can be isolating.
You can set your own hours and work as much or as little as you like.	You often have no control over when jobs come up, so you might have no work for months and then get slammed with three jobs all at once.

CLAUDIA POCCIA

Business Executive

The Facts

Claudia Poccia, President, Gurwitch Products

WHAT? Business executives work at high levels at a corporation, running either divisions within a company or an entire business.

WHERE? Every for-profit company in every city has business executives running it.

HOW? A BA or BS in business, marketing, or finance is a great start, but most people get an MBA to accelerate their quest to be a high-level business executive.

$$$: From $75,000 up to a million plus, depending on the level and size of the company. At very high-level positions, bonuses and other financial incentives are usually an additional benefit.

DRESS CODE? Business dress

STRESS FACTOR: On a scale of 1 to 10, a 7

i was lucky enough to find time on Claudia Poccia's overbooked calendar for a phone interview, which Claudia conducted out of her Manhattan office. She is president and CEO of Gurwitch Products, the global luxury cosmetics and skincare enterprise best known for its Laura Mercier, RéVive, and nyakio brands. Since joining in 2011, Claudia has established Gurwitch as one of the leading prestige beauty companies in the world.

Known as a leader and a mentor in the cosmetics industry, Claudia has built a career on giving back. In September 2012 she and Laura Mercier, founder of the Laura Mercier cosmetics brand, joined together to launch a lifesaving mission to shine a light on ovarian cancer, a disease that touched both of them through the experiences of loved ones. Together they established the Laura Mercier Ovarian Cancer Fund (LMOCF). The fund is dedicated to raising awareness and funding research and educational efforts that will help diagnose, treat, and support women with ovarian cancer.

"The challenge is to try to keep up without feeling overwhelmed. . . . I think it's important to be able to figure out what's 'need to know' and what's 'nice to know.'"

Claudia loves the complexity of her job, and the fact that as president of Gurwitch, she gets to work on a variety of brands. "I am fortunate to work with three beauty brands, all of which have founders with very distinct beauty philosophies. Each has an authentic story that attracts a passionate consumer following. For Laura Mercier, we have found that Laura's belief that flawless beauty has many faces translates in every market around the globe. Likewise, for RéVive, the merging of science and beauty resonates with consumers everywhere. The nyakio brand is rich with rituals and ingredients from its founder's African heritage," she explains.

"My vision is to bolster and exponentially grow each brand while staying true to its DNA and to ensure our global operating model is in place to support those businesses; this includes

ensuring the correct strategy and supporting business plan for
each of our portfolio businesses."

To accomplish this, Claudia utilizes a foundational approach
that translates to any business practice. "We must ask ourselves, how do we connect with our consumer in an authentic
and integrated way? How do we ensure our consumer-facing
message remains relevant? What is the appropriate product
proposition to support each brand's DNA? What is our global
expansion strategy? Is our operational framework capable of
supporting our growth objectives? Do we have the correct
structural economics to support our long-term business plan?"

Okay, I know what you're thinking: *big job.* Keep in mind,
though, that Claudia isn't doing all these things by herself. "It's
important to surround yourself with highly skilled, experienced
individuals, and then make certain that you bring out their best
in service to the vision of the company," she says.

"I have a responsibility to set the vision and empower the

YOU ASKED . . .

"Was it all worth it?" **—COURTNEY, AGE 15**

CLAUDIA ANSWERED . . .

*"Absolutely, and on so many levels. I've had to do some things
along the way that were anything but glamorous. Early in my
career I was working on a major fragrance launch, and we
had all of the fashion windows at Saks Fifth Avenue for the
launch. We had these wonderful tulips in the window, but it was
unseasonably cold and they wouldn't open. So there we were
at six in the morning with blow dryers trying to get the flowers
to open without fogging up the windows. At moments like that,
you say to yourself, 'Is this really what I want to do with my
life?' But it was definitely worth it, because I also have moments
where the work I do really makes a difference. And at the end
of the day, I always go back to the fact that I truly and sincerely
love the beauty business."*

THE BREAKDOWN

IN MEETINGS: At least 6 hours a day

ON THE PHONE: 30–45 minutes a day

ONLINE: 1–2 hours a day (usually during my commute)

PUBLIC SPEAKING: Occasionally for conferences

READING: Usually during commute

COACHING AND MENTORING YOUNG TALENT: All day long

team to deliver against it and to ensure that we are aligned on our shared objectives. I coach. I mentor. But I also believe at the end of the day, you can't lead by consensus. Someone has to make the call and someone has to be accountable, and that's the job of the leader."

So, we know what kind of big-picture things Claudia is doing, but how does she actually spend her day? Two words: meeting central. I asked her to give us the rundown.

CLAUDIA'S (UN)USUAL DAY

Today is actually a great example of a typical day.

I start every day at four thirty a.m., and spend a half hour doing what some may refer to as "meditating," but to me, it's "quiet time." I focus and calibrate for the day ahead, writing my intentions in my journal. I encourage everyone to take a few moments out of their day for themselves to get centered and balanced.

After quiet time, I spend an hour getting ready for the day; I walk my dog, get ready, and try out the latest beauty innovations from our brands.

During my commute into the office, I check e-mails and often take conference calls with my international colleagues, who are in different time zones and ending their days as I'm beginning mine.

Today I was the first person in the office, so I was able

to organize my thoughts and get a to-do list ready for my assistant.

At seven forty-five a.m. I met with our SVP of operations. Each day he brings me up to speed on our brands' manufacturing and shipping schedules, ensuring we're on track to meet our retailers' sales orders.

At eight thirty a.m. I attended a meeting with the head of our public relations department to review a speech I'm making at a major retailer partner's event next week.

At nine a.m. I had a status meeting with my assistant. We reviewed my schedule—meetings for the day and weeks ahead, any new deliverables required of my team.

The next meeting on my calendar was with the head of our human resources department. We are in the midst of our annual performance reviews, and she and I discussed our talent calibration sessions as well as merit-based salary increases.

At ten thirty a.m. I met with the company's CFO, who updated me on our outlook for the first quarter's results. Immediately following that meeting, I met with the heads of our sales and marketing departments to review upcoming programs and commitments to our key retail accounts.

I then attended a twelve thirty p.m. lunch with a strategic manufacturing partner and the SVP of product innovation to review our future pipeline and discuss proprietary formulas and launches.

After that, I had a meeting with a film industry leader to discuss how we could strategically collaborate on initiatives that would generate awareness for our brands.

At four p.m. I met with the company's chief

WHY WAIT?

- Get a job working retail in beauty, fashion, or cosmetics.

- Join (or start) a chapter of Future Business Leaders of America (FBLA) at your high school.

creative officer for a "creative review." We reviewed several items to ensure they were on-brand, including a corporate social responsibility video, educational video segments, a new store design concept for a retailer in France, and the packaging concept for a major launch.

My final meeting of the day was with my assistant to discuss priorities for the evening and next day. After that, I spent an hour returning calls and following up on items requiring immediate attention. I also use the time between meetings for calls and e-mails.

At six thirty p.m. I either begin my commute home or attend an industry function. During my commute home, I visit the brands' social media channels to see what consumers are saying about our products and brand experience.

WHAT IT TAKES

- Passion about what you do
- The confidence to take the lead
- The ability to inspire and motivate others
- Strong business skills

Claudia works long hours Monday through Friday, including commuting time, where she's reading, texting and e-mailing via her iPhone, and doing phone work, as well as a

THEN TO NOW

1980–1981:	1980–1984:	1984–1986:	1987–1992:	1992–1994:
Worked as a flight attendant	Director of in-flight training, Air Florida, Inc.	Account executive, designer fragrance, Cosmair, Inc.	Various positions at Giorgio Beverly Hills, Inc.	Director of field marketing, Avon

few hours over the weekend so she can get a head start on the week.

"The challenge is to stay on top of your game in a balanced way. I believe in being 'present in the moment,' whether at home or at work. I also work at keeping it all in perspective in order to focus on what really matters at that particular moment in time. I think it's important to ascertain what is 'mission critical,' 'need to know,' and 'nice to know,'" she says.

I asked Claudia what she loves best about her job, and I could tell by her answer that she loves just about everything, which is probably why she's so good at what she does. Claudia has two qualities that business leaders need in order to be successful: vision and passion.

"Every day I am given the opportunity to do something I love. When I was in college, I worked behind a cosmetic counter and fell in love with the beauty industry when I saw, firsthand, the confidence-boosting power of a makeover. Empowering someone to recognize her beauty—that just never gets old."

CLAUDIA'S CAREER ADVICE

There are going to be parts of your job that you love and that you don't. But if when you wake up in the morning you can feel great about going to work, you have a spring in your step and you know that in some small way you'll make a difference, then you're in a good place.

| 1994: Began working with Estée Lauder USA | 2000: Became VP sales & education, Stila | 2003: Promoted to SVP, general manager, Stila | 2005: Named president of *mark*, Avon's teen brand | 2011: Became president of Gurwitch Products |

FIVE MORE CAREERS YOU CAN HAVE WITH A BACKGROUND IN BUSINESS

TRADER "Online trading" gets a lot of press, but many traders work for international banks where they trade, or manage the buying and selling of, different assets such as bonds, stocks, futures, or options, worth millions of dollars. Traders try to predict the financial markets and figure out when to buy or sell to make the most profit.

FINANCIAL ANALYST Financial analysts typically work in-house for corporations, analyzing financial transactions involving their business. Financial analysts might do things like work up budgets to determine if a project is worth taking on, develop financial plans for programs within the company, or analyze the finances of a competitor.

MUTUAL FUND ANALYST Mutual fund analysts are like researchers. Their job is to research and analyze different potential investment opportunities for mutual funds or pension funds, and make recommendations on which funds are good investments and which are risky.

MERGERS AND ACQUISITIONS MANAGER People who work in mergers and acquisitions, or M&A, typically structure deals for two companies who are merging or when one is acquiring the other. People in M&A might provide advice, figure out the finances, or set up deals for their client.

VENTURE CAPITALIST Venture capital firms are companies that invest in what are usually considered to be high-risk opportunities, like start-up companies or young, struggling businesses. Though these investments are typically much riskier than more traditional types of investing, the financial payoff can be high.

YOU NEED TO KNOW ABOUT

Future Business Leaders of America (www.fbla-pbl.org), otherwise known as Phi Beta Lambda, is a national nonprofit organization whose aim is to help middle school, high school, and college students prepare for business careers. You'll find a ton of resources at this website, including an online kit to help you start a chapter at your own school.

For more careers as an executive, check out the nonprofit director profile on page 184.

TAMARA HAYMAN

Engineer

Tamara Hayman,
Systems Engineer,
Lockheed Martin

The Facts

WHAT? Engineers use math and science to design and develop anything from small machines and computers to space shuttles. Systems engineers, like Tamara, develop the requirements for a system, like a computer program, and make sure it gets built the way it needs to, from start to finish.

WHERE? Depending on their field, engineers might work for private corporations, local governments, pharmaceutical companies, or big government contractors.

HOW? A bachelor's degree is all an engineer needs to work in this industry, but getting a graduate degree will open up doors to more advanced opportunities and promotions.

$$$: An average of $85,000 a year, while top engineers can make $150,000 and beyond

DRESS CODE? Business casual to casual

STRESS FACTOR: On a scale of 1 to 10, between a 7 and an 8

tamara is a young star in her field. At the age of twenty-four, she juggles a demanding job as a systems engineer at Lockheed Martin in Bethesda, Maryland, a company that develops everything from space stations to defense systems for the military; graduate school; and taking part in a supercompetitive three-year program for young engineers called the Engineering Leadership Development Program. Only five engineers get into this program at Tamara's site each year, and in addition to training in all the different engineering disciplines, she participates in national conferences and mentors younger engineers as they pursue their own graduate degrees.

"I'm a nosy person, so this job is perfect for me because it allows me to know what everyone is doing."

I recently had the chance to talk with Tamara about her job and her life.

ME: How did you get started in engineering?

TAMARA: I've always been involved in internship programs or leadership development programs. If someone told me about an opportunity, I'd apply. I kind of fell into engineering because everyone said that this is where the money is. Now that I'm here I can say, "Okay, I can do this." I remember one mentor who said to me, "Stop trying to figure out exactly what you

YOU ASKED . . .

"How have you stayed motivated?" **—BRIE, AGE 14**

TAMARA ANSWERED . . .

"I'm one of those people who wants to be the best at whatever I do. I love it when people know my name and know who I am, and I have a drive to keep learning more so I can be the best in my job and my field. And in a place where you have six hundred employees, in order to stay on top you have to work really hard. So that's my motivation. I know that if I work hard now, I'll get recognition later."

want to do and just take advantage of every opportunity that comes your way, because one day someone will pull you into a position that you never thought you wanted to do or even knew existed, and that's when you'll realize that's the place you want to be."

ME: What does a systems engineer do?

TAMARA: A systems engineer writes the requirements for a system. So, say a computer needs to have an on and off power button. It must have a keyboard and the keyboard must interface with the CPU system. The user should be able to press T and T shows up on the monitor. Those are all the kinds of things we tell the designer of the hardware so that the final system can do all of those things. The designer can make it look any way that they want to, but it must still meet the system requirements that I set up.

Part of what I love about this job is that I get to be involved in every stage of the process. So, while my job is to write the requirements, when we go into design, I'm making sure that the person designing the system is designing it according to the way that I wrote the requirements. Then when we move into development, I'm making sure that the person is developing the system in the way that I wrote the requirements. The same thing goes for the testing phase—I'm making sure that they're testing it to meet my specifications. I'm a nosy person, so this job is perfect for me because it allows me to know what

THE BREAKDOWN

IN MEETINGS: Sometimes all day, some days not at all

ON THE PHONE: 4 hours a week

ONLINE: On and off throughout the day

SITTING: Most of the day

PUBLIC SPEAKING: Occasionally for presentations

READING: On and off throughout the day

WHY WAIT?

- Take math and science courses in high school—they'll be a prerequisite to most engineering programs in college.
- Look for apprenticeship and mentoring programs specifically designed for girls interested in engineering.
- Join an "Advocates for Women in Science, Engineering, and Mathematics" (AWSEM) club in your school or start one! Find out more at www.saturdayacademy.org.

everyone is doing throughout the whole life cycle of the system we're developing.

TAMARA'S (UN)USUAL DAY

7:30 A.M.: I get up, get ready for work, and head out. It takes me about thirty-five minutes to get to work. When I get here, I get something to drink and get settled in. The first thing I'll do as soon as I get to work is look at e-mails to see what meetings I have and see what my day looks like. I'll go through e-mails and respond to those I can. I write myself a "to do" list for all the things that I plan to accomplish that day. I don't necessarily accomplish everything, but at least I have a plan.

10:00 A.M.: A lot of mornings I have meetings at ten or eleven, so I'll grab my little engineering notebook and scribe all the information I get from each meeting, any important discoveries that came out of that meeting, or things I want to follow up on. If I don't have a meeting, it will pretty much be me starting to accomplish some of my tasks for the day.

12:30–1:30 P.M.: I take an hour for lunch, and my other engineering friends and I will sit in the cafeteria and just talk about how our day's going so far or what was on TV the night before or the difference between men and women in relationships . . . that kind of thing.

1:30–6:00 P.M.: In the afternoon I tackle more of the tasks on my "to do" list. Sometimes the things I'm working on are related to the Engineering Leadership Development Program (ELDP) that I participate in at work. The ELDP is a competitive program for young engineers that gives them the chance to work

WHAT IT TAKES

- Paying attention to detail
- Having good math and analytical skills
- A desire to want to figure out how things work
- Being able to work in a team

in different engineering disciplines at the company. I'm the deputy manager of that program here, so I handle all the day-to-day operations of the program at this branch of Lockheed Martin. So the rest of my day will be juggling the work of an engineer—attending design reviews or writing requirements for new systems—and the work of managing the Leadership Development Program and being a mentor to entry-level engineers.

6:00 OR 7:00 P.M.: Leave work.

ME: What's your work space like?

TAMARA: Most engineers sit in cubicles. I sit in a three-person cubicle, but there are only two of us, so the other person and I share the third desk. My desk is always cluttered because of

THEN TO NOW

| 1997: Interned at law firm through Law Links | 1998: Interned at University of Maryland through Youthworks | 1999: Graduated high school in Baltimore | 2001–2003: Worked as part-time cashier at university bookstore | 2003: Graduated University of Maryland, BS in computer science |

PAYING YOUR DUES

Wannabe engineers usually start out as associate engineers, a position they have for about two years. Associate engineers have an engineer mentor and learn the ropes by doing the job with supervision.

the two different jobs I'm juggling, so I try to stay organized and keep the paperwork for each job separate, but it never works out that way. Because I work on government systems and we have a whole bunch of requirements, each system has its own requirements documents. I have all of these thick notebooks laying on my desk. I also keep notes from any training course I've had since I started—I've been here for three years, so you can just imagine how many notebooks I have. I like to say that I'm organized, but my desk is just a cluttered mess. I can find everything, though, even though somebody else might not be able to.

ME: What's the toughest part of your job?

TAMARA: Because we're developing systems that are used on actual navy ships, you really have to pay a lot of attention to detail and keep the end goal in mind all the time, because whatever you do in your job today is going to affect someone's life later. So just because I'm tired or I really don't want to go through all the details or research a system like I should, I have

2001–2003: Interned at Lockheed Martin through INROADS	2003: Hired at Lockheed Martin as software engineer	2005: Began working as a systems engineer at Lockheed Martin	2006: Graduated Johns Hopkins University, MS in technical management	2011: Promoted to open innovation deputy program manager at Lockheed Martin

to remember that my taking the easy way out now could affect the way the system runs later. It could ultimately backfire and even affect someone's life. So you really have to pay a lot of attention to detail.

ME: How do you deal with that pressure?

TAMARA: Lunch is my refresher every day. My friends and I go to lunch and we don't talk about work. . . . We just talk about "stuff." I'm also a serious soap opera junkie, so even though I can't watch them, I'll go to CBS.com and read what happened yesterday on *The Young and the Restless* if I feel like I need a quick break or distraction.

ME: What's the best part of your job?

TAMARA: With everything that I work on, we have meetings and peer reviews, which means my coworkers from the different engineering areas come in and review the requirements that I wrote. I'm writing from a systems perspective, but an electrical engineer might approach the project in a different way, and the same goes for a mechanical engineer and a software engineer. So having the other engineers come into a meeting to review my work and find no defects in my requirements is the best thing ever, because it means that I really am doing my job well.

INTERESTED IN A CAREER IN ENGINEERING? HERE'S TAMARA'S ADVICE

- *Pay attention to detail, be nosy, and want to know how things work.*

- *Be a people person. We're not all geeks or bookworms—we have to be able to interact with people.*

- *Remember that engineering is not just about math and science—it's about making your ideas a reality.*

FIVE MORE ENGINEERING CAREERS

MECHANICAL ENGINEER There is an engineer behind every machine—dishwashers to jet engines. Mechanical engineers know all about how machines work, and they might have jobs developing and testing new products for companies or maintaining equipment for major manufacturing plants.

CIVIL ENGINEER Civil engineers design and maintain the infrastructures that we encounter in our everyday lives—things like highways, bridges, airports . . . even skyscrapers. They consider how these infrastructures will be used, what their impact will be on the environment, how much energy they'll use, and how safe they will be.

AGRICULTURAL ENGINEER There are actually engineers who spend their workday figuring out the most efficient ways to handle, process, and distribute the food that ends up in our kitchen. Agricultural engineers develop new and better ways for preserving or packaging food or even create new and improved technologies for cooking food.

AEROSPACE ENGINEER Flip through the employee directory at NASA and you'll find it's full of aerospace engineers. They're the ones who design and test new space shuttles, military jets, missiles, and commercial airplanes. They usually work for organizations like the Federal Aviation Administration (FAA), NASA, or private companies.

INDUSTRIAL ENGINEER Industrial engineers figure out the best way to keep everything moving smoothly in the production and distribution of a product or service. They may work on anything from a radio station broadcast to a bank service—and integrate people power, budgets, schedules, and the mechanics of how to actually get the process done.

YOU NEED TO KNOW ABOUT

The website Engineer Girl (www.engineergirl.org) is part of the National Academy of Engineering. Its goals are to expose women and girls to engineering careers, and this awesome website includes tons of info on how to get ready for college, inspirational books to read, fun facts about engineering, quizzes, and essay contests.

BECCA WERTHEIM

Teacher

The Facts

WHAT? Teachers educate students, from pre-schoolers through high school.

WHERE? There are teachers everywhere there are schools and students. They might work in private or public schools, or teach preschool, elementary, middle school, or high school.

HOW? At the very least, teachers need a bachelor's degree in education or the subject they want to teach, although teachers with a graduate degree will be more competitive and earn more money. To teach in a public school, teachers need to pass a licensing test in their state.

Becca Wertheim, Second-Grade Teacher

$$$: An average salary of $56,000, depending on school, geographic location, and level of experience

DRESS CODE? Casual

STRESS FACTOR: On a scale of 1 to 10, a 7

i've known becca since she wrote and published her book *Live High on Life for Teens: 12 Simple Ways to Make the Most of Your Teenage Years* as a teenager, and I've loved watching her work hard to reach her goal of becoming a teacher in the years since. She's finally realized her dream, and at the time I was writing this book, she was just finishing up her first year as a second-grade teacher at a magnet elementary school in Asheville, North Carolina. In our interview, she describes what it's really like to be doing what she's wanted to do since she was a little girl.

"The biggest challenge for me as a beginning teacher was finding a healthy balance between work and my personal life. It was tempting to work all the time, even on weekends, but I had to remind myself to take time to rejuvenate."

ME: When did you first know you wanted to be a teacher?

BECCA: I've wanted to be a teacher for as long as I can remember. My parents have photos of me "playing school" with my stuffed animals when I was just four years old, before I was even in kindergarten. I've always loved school and the classroom atmosphere. When I'm in a classroom, I'm in my element.

ME: Did you change majors at all during college, or was it a straight and steady path?

BECCA: I received my undergraduate degree in psychology and earned my elementary education teaching license. Because of my love for the outdoors, at one point I wanted to be an environmental studies major in addition to elementary education, but I realized it just wasn't the right fit for my career path. Psychology was a perfect match because I learned about developmental psychology, including important skills and strategies that I now apply to my current career as a teacher.

ME: So, I know you're kind of a newbie at this. Where are you in your career journey?

YOU ASKED . . .

"How do you manage to keep yourself motivated when there are students who just don't want to learn?" —ASHLEY, AGE 16

BECCA ANSWERED . . .

"Although there are times when students don't have the motivation to learn, I don't let it discourage me. I've learned that if I show excitement and enthusiasm for what I'm teaching, my students are more likely to be excited about it too. I bring art, music, and movement into a lot of my lessons, which keeps my kids engaged. I also remind them of the purpose behind what they're learning and relate my lessons to the real world. When they see the value in what I'm teaching them, they're better able to focus and retain the information I'm teaching. You have to find what interests your students and be relatable!"

BECCA: This is my first year teaching, but it feels like my second year, because I currently teach in the same classroom where I did my student teaching, which is a dream come true! Since I completed my student teaching at the school where I now work, I had a better understanding of what to expect going into my first year. I already knew my coworkers, the routine of the school, and the overall environment. This preparation was invaluable in helping me transition from college to the huge responsibility of being a teacher. Although I had an idea of what to expect, teaching is much more challenging than I thought it would be when I was in school. Teachers have a lot of "behind-the-scenes" responsibilities such as paperwork, conferences, meetings, training, professional development, assessment/testing, and data analysis in addition to teaching children. Although it's more challenging than I anticipated, it is also far more rewarding than I could've ever imagined!

ME: Can you tell us about what grade you teach and what your students are like?

BECCA: I teach second grade, and I absolutely love it! My students are seven and eight years old, which is such a fun age. They are funny, creative, energetic, compassionate, caring, and optimistic. They're old enough to be able to participate in challenging activities and do things independently, yet young enough to still think I'm the coolest person in the world just for being their teacher.

ME: Wow . . . I can imagine that teaching a bunch of second graders could be absolutely exhausting. Is it, and if so, how do you recharge?

BECCA: I honestly had no idea how exhausting this job would be. By the time two thirty p.m. rolls around and the students are dismissed, I am ready for a nap! But my day doesn't end there; I have endless responsibilities even after the school day ends. The first semester was really tough, because I was getting to work extra early and staying up super late. I struggled to find time for myself and was often tired. After winter break (an opportunity for rejuvenation), I realized that in order to be the best teacher I can be, I have to make my personal life a priority outside of work. I started eating healthier, exercising nearly every day, making time for my hobbies, getting more sleep, and making sure to keep a positive attitude. Now I feel like I finally have the hang of things and have much more energy each day. And believe me, when you're surrounded by twenty seven-year-olds all day, you need *all* the energy you can get! Thank goodness for coffee, yoga, and bubble baths!

THE BREAKDOWN

IIN MEETINGS: 30 minutes a day

E-MAILING OR IMING: 1 hour

SITTING: 1 hour

STANDING: 6 hours

PUBLIC SPEAKING: 6 hours

READING: 30 minutes

WORKING SOLO: 30 minutes

ME: Yes, I've heard the first few years are the most difficult, so I'm glad you've found ways to practice self-care! But it sounds like it's also super rewarding. . . . What do you find the most fulfilling part of your job?

BECCA: It's extremely fulfilling to go to work each day knowing I'm making a difference by sharing my knowledge with the

WHY WAIT?

- Look into being an assistant or aide to a teacher at your school.
- Volunteer at a preschool or summer school as an assistant teacher.
- Be a volunteer tutor in a subject you're an expert in.

younger generation. I love teaching a lesson and then watching light bulbs go off as students discover new information. In social studies we've been learning about global citizenship, and we're fund-raising all year to sponsor a year of education for a child in rural Nepal. One of the ways we raised money was by making bracelets, scarves, and magnets to sell at a craft fair. It was rewarding to see all my students engaged in the project and proud of themselves for using their talents to make a difference in the life of a child on the other side of the world. They asked tons of questions because they were interested in the topic and wanted to know more. You know you've impacted your students when they're eager to learn more about a topic you've introduced them to.

ME: What has been more difficult than you expected?

BECCA: The biggest challenge for me as a beginning teacher was finding a healthy balance between work and my personal life. It was tempting to work all the time, even on weekends, but I had to remind myself to take time to rejuvenate. It's also challenging to teach so many different types of students who all have different personalities. I deal with that challenge by implementing a strong classroom management system,

WHAT IT TAKES

- Being enthusiastic, patient, and positive
- Staying calm even when frustrated
- Being an expert in the subject(s) you want to teach
- Being adaptable and flexible, because the world of education is constantly evolving

creating a positive classroom environment, and bringing creativity into my lessons. I use a variety of teaching strategies so that I keep students interested and engaged, no matter what type of learner they are.

BECCA'S (UN)USUAL DAY

6:00 A.M.: *Wake up.*

7:00 A.M.: *Arrive at work to ensure I'm ready for the school day.*

7:40 A.M.–8:00 A.M.: *The students arrive, and we begin our day. The students take care of their morning duties and I lead our morning meeting. Then students go to specialists (art, music, computer lab, Spanish, or PE), and while they're there, I have a "planning period," which means I run errands around the school, make copies, prepare materials, or attend meetings.*

9:00 A.M.–11:45 A.M.: *Phonics, spelling, reading workshop, and writing workshop integrated with science and social studies.*

THEN TO NOW

2010: Becca published her book *Live High on Life* when she was eighteen years old

2013: Named She's the First Chapter President of the Year

11:45 A.M.: *Recess and lunch.*

12:30 P.M.: *Math and an intervention block where students get extra practice in areas they may be struggling with.*

2:30 P.M.: *The students are dismissed! I have meetings or parent-teacher conferences and stay to clean and organize my classroom and prepare for the following day.*

5:30 P.M.: *I leave work and go to the gym for a quick workout or yoga class.*

7:00 P.M.: *Get home, make dinner, prepare my lunch for the following day, check e-mail, and try to relax a bit before going to bed.*

ME: If young women reading this book have an interest in teaching, would you encourage them to go for it?

BECCA: If you love to learn, love to teach, and love being around kids, then I highly recommend a career as an elementary school teacher. If you're considering a career in teaching, take time to reflect on the best teachers you've had throughout your years in school. Ask yourself what made them have a positive impact on your life. If you want to have that same impact on young people, then a career in teaching may be the perfect fit for you!

2013: Graduated from University of North Carolina–Asheville with a degree in education and psychology

2013: Began teaching second grade at Claxton Elementary School of Arts and Humanities

---

BECCA'S ADVICE FOR FUTURE TEACHERS

- *Come to work each day with a positive attitude and a purpose*

- *Never forget why you're there—for the kids. They need you. You have one of the most important jobs in the world!*

- *Be a lifelong learner, a hard worker, and a great example for your students*

In the Field

FIVE MORE CAREERS IN EDUCATION

PRINCIPAL   Principals are the heads of schools, and they oversee teachers and staff, make decisions about the school rules, and enforce the rules. Since they're usually appointed by the school board, principals also deal with administrative duties like managing the school budget and making policies.

COLLEGE PROFESSOR   There are some similarities between college professors and middle school or high school teachers, but in addition to preparing lectures and educating students, professors spend a good deal of time doing research and writing papers to help them become experts in their academic field.

UNIVERSITY DEAN   If professors are like teachers, then deans are like principals. They are generally former college professors who have moved from being immersed in their research area of expertise to overseeing a larger unit within the university, such as a group of departments or an aspect of student life.

SPECIAL EDUCATION TEACHER   Special education teachers might work with students with physical disabilities, emotional or mental disabilities, or gifted and talented students. They provide specialized instruction to students who have special needs outside the general student population.

SCHOOL NURSE School nurses manage the overall health of the student body, from scheduling health-related educational programs to figuring out the best way to manage an outbreak of chicken pox. They might administer hearing tests one day, and make sure that a child with special needs is being taken care of on another day.

YOU NEED TO KNOW ABOUT

The website TeachersCount (www.teacherscount.org) has resources for teachers and people interested in the teaching profession. Here you'll find a whole section dedicated to people who want to teach, including info on why it's such a great career, how to go about doing it, and info on scholarship opportunities.

For more careers working with children, check out the educational psychologist profile on page 140 and the child therapist profile on page 55.

KAY LAKEY

Physical Therapist

Kay Lakey, Physical Therapist, Private Practice Owner

The Facts

WHAT? Physical therapists work with people's physical structures, whether to help them recover from an injury or because they're experiencing chronic pain. They use a blend of exercises, stretches, massage, electrotherapy, and other tools to help rehabilitate their clients.

WHERE? You'll find physical therapists in hospitals, clinics, schools, or, like Kay, in their own private practice.

HOW? Physical therapists need undergraduate work heavy in biology, anatomy, and other sciences, and they must attend an accredited graduate program for physical therapy and become licensed to practice.

$$$: An average salary of $84,000

DRESS CODE? Depends on the work venue . . . business casual for private practice or maybe scrubs if at a hospital

STRESS FACTOR: On a scale of 1 to 10, between a 5 and a 6

physical therapy is a very popular field among women—in 2009 more than 68 percent of physical therapists were female. I interviewed Kay Lakey, who runs her own physical therapy clinic, to find out what a physical therapist's work involves.

"Basically what we do is work with people's structure—their muscles, their bones, their tendons, their ligaments—and help them improve function. So if you were to get hurt doing a sport, a physical therapist would be the one who would help you transition back into your sport with no pain, or if you have a spinal cord injury or a head injury, they would help you get back into society without any assistance or with minimal assistance. So we're helping people get back to being functional in their life, and hopefully, pain free," she explained.

"That is the piece that is so cool about physical therapy and working with people—as soon as you're the teacher, the students actually teach you."

As the owner of her own clinic and the only person on staff, Kay wears many different hats. To give us a better picture of what her day looks like, I asked Kay to break it down.

KAY'S (UN)USUAL DAY

I start my day by opening the office. I don't have an assistant or anything—I'm a sole practitioner. So just like anybody, I come in and turn the coffeepot on, open everything up, unload laundry because I need to keep clean sheets on my massage table, those kinds of things. Throughout the day I'm answering phones and taking appointments, canceling appointments, dealing with faxes and e-mails from doctors, insurance companies, and patients.

I schedule my appointments from nine to six, usually seven a day. But that's just me. I've worked in hospitals

YOU ASKED . . .

"How did you know what you wanted to do with your life?"

—JESSIE, AGE 15

KAY ANSWERED . . .

"When I was a kid, I always wanted to be a doctor or an astronaut, so there was a part of me that always knew that I was going to do something that was not just getting married and having kids. I had no idea that I'd become a physical therapist, but when I took a college course for it and saw everything that was involved in the field, I thought, 'Oh, this is really cool.'"

before where I've had twenty-four patients scheduled a day, for fifteen-minute appointments. But I can't schedule as many now because I handle all of the administrative parts of running my business too.

When my clients come in, I do an evaluation of them. I'll watch them walk, watch them move, test their range of motion and joint function and strength. I'll have them fill out a form with specific questions about what their pain is and what their function is, what their goals are or what they want to accomplish. Then I'll do some work with them, like joint mobilization or ultrasound or craniosacral. We decide together what their program is going to be, and each time I see them, I reassess them. Based on what I see, the program might shift slightly. These appointments typically

THEN TO NOW

Graduated from University of Montana with BS in health education and recreation

Received certificate from the Mayo Clinic School of Health Related Sciences, Rochester, MN

1977–1981: Worked as physical therapist at Elks Rehabilitation Hospital in Boise, ID last fifty-five minutes or so. When we're done, I come into my office and make notes on their chart about what we did, what I observed, and so on.

THE BREAKDOWN

IN MEETINGS: Not often

ON THE PHONE: 1–2 hours a day

ONLINE: Maximum of 1 hour

SITTING: 2–3 hours a day

STANDING: 7–8 hours a day

READING: 1 hour a day

At lunch I'll run errands. I'll go to the bank, I'll go to Kinko's to make copies, I'll go to the post office. So the tasks of running a business get slipped in since I don't have anybody who's working for me. In between all of the appointments, I'm doing other work, like calling insurance companies, calling doctors' offices, or dictating my notes.

As a physical therapist, Kay puts together a plan of action to help her patients reach their goal, whether it's to free themselves of pain or to run a marathon someday. I wanted to get a better sense of what a physical therapist does in working one-on-one with patients. These are the kinds of things that Kay might do with a patient who's come to see her for an appointment, using some of the techniques she used while studying physical therapy at the Mayo Clinic:

1985–1987: Worked at the Sports Physical Therapy and Back Clinic, Davis, CA

1988–1994: Worked at the Puget Sound Physical Therapy Registry, Redmond, WA

1993: Started own physical therapy practice

- Have the patient walk around the room and see what part of the patient's body her eye is drawn to

- Gather information about what's happening in a patient's body through her hands

- Check range of motion in an area that they're working on

- If she picks up that there's a misalignment, then she'll use an osteopathic muscle energy technique.

- If it's the first time she's seen the patient, Kay will teach him or her how to do the energy technique for themselves at home.

While Kay's work clearly has a positive impact on her clients, it's not without its challenges, the biggest of which, according to Kay, is dealing with insurance companies and all the paperwork that goes along with it. On top of that, she finds herself challenged by working with clients who have been treated poorly by the medical system, mainly because no one has been able to diagnose what's wrong with them.

"Those people who have been severely curbed and not supported are the hardest. They get cut off by insurance companies, but they're still disabled and are struggling to figure out how to function with a level of pain that most of us couldn't handle. And there's a lot of anger and emotion around that. So it's harder to figure out what to do to help those people. I feel really bad for them because I'm a pretty compassionate and empathetic person," Kay explains.

Despite these challenges, Kay finds her work as a physical therapist extremely fulfilling. "One of the true gifts of what I do is watching and witnessing the journey of us as

WHAT IT TAKES

- An abundance of patience
- Being able to tune in and connect with people
- Physical stamina—you're on your feet a lot

human beings and supporting a person's struggles. I'm learning all the time, and that is the piece that is so cool about physical therapy and working with people—as soon as you're the teacher, the students actually teach you. When I started my own business, my life began to get healed in ways you would not believe," she says.

KAY'S CAREER ADVICE

- *Have the courage to do what excites you and what fulfills you, even if it's not going to make you a lot of money.*

- *If you're going to take a profession for status, money, or power, you're not going to be happy in it. Keep asking yourself, "What makes me happy and what do I enjoy doing?"*

In the Field

FIVE MORE CAREERS WORKING AS A THERAPIST

OCCUPATIONAL THERAPIST These therapists work with people who have permanent disabilities or have been injured, to give them tools to become as self-reliant as possible. They teach their patients how to do everyday things, such as grocery shopping and using public transportation.

SPEECH LANGUAGE PATHOLOGIST Also known as speech therapists, they work with people who have difficulties speaking. Patients can include children who are slow in developing their verbal skills and victims of head injuries who have lost language skills.

RECREATIONAL THERAPIST Activities like playing music, making art, even cooking and hiking can relieve stress. Recreational therapists work with physical therapy patients and find ways to incorporate these sorts of activities into their work to speed up recovery and strengthen their clients' overall mental, physical, and emotional health.

MASSAGE THERAPIST   Massage therapists are trained in massage and anatomy, and they provide massages to relieve stress, promote recovery from an injury, reduce pain, and improve the overall well-being of their clients. They often work in spas or gyms.

KINESIOLOGIST   Kinesiology is a science focused on healing pain and illness in people by tuning in to the body and figuring out what is at the root of the imbalance that is causing the pain. Kinesiologists look at the whole body as opposed to just the symptom, and they perform muscle testing on their patients as part of their therapy.

YOU NEED TO KNOW ABOUT

The American Physical Therapy Association (www.apta.org) is the national organization for physical therapy professionals. The website features a whole resource section for students interested in becoming physical therapists.

SUSAN HYATT

Life Coach

The Facts

Susan Hyatt,
Life Coach and Author

WHAT? Life coaches help people create more of what they want in their life (fulfillment, peace, a better job, a better relationship), using a variety of self-awareness, motivational, and accountability tools.

WHERE? While some coaches work in person, many connect virtually, working with their clients via phone or Skype.

HOW? The coaching industry isn't regulated, but most coaches are professionally trained and certified by a coaching school.

$$$: An annual salary of $45,000, but can be much lower or much higher depending on coach's niche, experience, and number of clients

DRESS CODE? Casual

STRESS FACTOR: On a scale of 1 to 10, a 2

when I decided to feature a life coach in *In Their Shoes*, I knew I wanted to interview Evansville, Indiana–based Susan Hyatt. That's because Susan has found a way to build a dynamic, exciting brand to support her coaching career, including helping to train and support other coaches, authoring books, and hosting an online show, *Life Is Delicious TV*. Here's a peek at Susan's fascinating job!

ME: Before we jump into the nitty-gritty details, can you just set us straight about what a coach does that is different from what a therapist might do?

"It was one of those moments where the skies parted and a lightning bolt hit me on the head, and I just remember thinking, 'Oh my gosh, I think this is what I'm supposed to do.' So what ultimately led me to coaching was being in the darkest spot of my life that I was ever in."

SUSAN: Sure. A life coach is someone who can help you figure out what you want and how to get it. So just like sports teams and athletes have a coach who helps them to perform to their highest potential and ability, a life coach can help you do that with different areas of your life. By and large, therapists will help you heal a wound, often around something that has happened in the past. A life coach is much more focused on what's happening in your life right now and where you want to go in the future.

SUSAN'S TYPICAL DAY*

4:30 A.M.: *Wake up and have coffee.*

5:30 A.M.: *Work out at the gym.*

6:30 A.M.: *Have breakfast with my kids (thirteen and fifteen) and husband and get everyone off to school and work. If it's a smooth morning getting everyone out the door, I'll shower and change into jeans and a sweater or T-shirt. Otherwise I'm wearing running tights, a sports bra, some kind of sports shirt, and a zip-up hoodie.*

8:00 A.M.: *Everyone else is gone, and I walk into my home* office to get started with work, usually answering e-mails, doing administrative work, writing, or working on special projects like my TV show. My office is a really bright, sunny, comfortable space, although my office is really mobile—all I need is my cell phone and my laptop.

9:00 A.M.–11:30 A.M.: I might have one one-on-one coaching session in the morning, and then I spend quite a bit of time checking in and out of social media to promote projects that I'm working on and connect with clients, readers, and viewers.

11:30 A.M.–12:00 P.M.: I usually eat lunch before my noon class. I make myself something high protein in the kitchen, like a salad with grilled chicken and avocado, or a breakfast burrito with eggs, black beans, avocado, and hot sauce.

12:00 P.M.–1:30 P.M.: Teach a virtual class like a telecourse over the phone or an online webinar.

1:30 P.M.–2:30 P.M.: I go back to answering client e-mails, coaching a lot via e-mail. Other times I might be creating a newsletter or answering questions from my virtual assistants, who are also working on sending out special e-mails to my clients and potential clients, marketing pieces, and those kinds of things.

2:30 P.M.: I finish my work and switch gears to move into "mom mode." Then I'm taking my kids to music lessons and

YOU ASKED . . .

"Can you change your career after you've already started?"
—TEAGAN, AGE 16

SUSAN ANSWERED . . .

"Yes, you absolutely can. I've reinvented myself. This is my third reinvention. So many people get stuck and think they cannot. But if you find you want to create something new—whether it's for your level of interest, or passion, or income—you can absolutely make a change."

sports practices. If I'm waiting around for my kids or sitting in the car, I will also take that opportunity to answer client e-mail or check in on Facebook. It's great to have a mobile office.

5:00 P.M.: *I come home and do all sorts of glamorous things like cook dinner, fold laundry, and clean up. We usually eat dinner around six, and that's my day.*

* This schedule goes for Monday through Thursday. Friday's are "fun Fridays," and are all about doing whatever the hell I want. So I'm resting, and reading, and getting massaged, and stuff like that.

ME: I know that coaches can wear many hats and have to focus on different pieces of their business. Is that a requirement for being a successful coach?

SUSAN: I think so. I think most coaches are solopreneurs. So until they reach a point where they're hiring an assistant, they are typically doing many different kinds of things. I think most coaches are doing one-on-one coaching, or facilitating seminars and workshops. But there's also a whole business side to being a life coach. So coaches find themselves in the role of being a marketing director. So unless they belong to a firm or have reached a point where they have hired a lot of help, coaches are juggling a variety of activities.

THE BREAKDOWN

IN MEETINGS: 30 minutes a day

ON THE PHONE: 3 hours

SOCIAL MEDIA: 1 hour

SURFING THE WEB: 1 hour

E-MAILING: 1 hour

SITTING: 5 hours

PUBLIC SPEAKING: 1 hour

READING: 1 hour

WORKING SOLO: 6 hours

WHY WAIT?

- Scour the self-help aisles and read books about personal growth and life coaching.
- Focus on doing your own personal growth work—coaches have to be able to "live it to give it."

ME: What would you consider to be the highlights of doing this work?

SUSAN: My favorite part of being a coach is being able to witness clients admit what they want and then create it. I used to be in real estate, and I can remember just dreading checking my cell phone and my e-mail, because there was a lot of highly charged emotional negotiation going on. I'm not knocking real estate. It's a great industry, but it wasn't pleasant for me. But now when I check my e-mail, I get so excited because it's full of either e-mails about the potential for a client, or the excitement about what they're creating. My favorite part is being able to witness that. I also think it's really cool to be in an industry where all your time is spent around the possibility for the human race. It's not a bad gig thinking up ways to help people get what they want.

ME: That does sound super satisfying. Can you explain to us exactly what you do to help your clients get what they want? What does the actual "work" entail?

SUSAN: Before I have a session with a client, I have them fill out a pre-work workbook. It helps answer a lot of questions about why they want coaching, what kind of change they want to experience, and what's going on in their past and in their life right now that has led them to this point. Then, when I get on the phone with them, I ask questions to get access to what they're thinking and what their deepest hopes, dreams, and fears are so that we can get to work on those. So I use a variety of coaching tools to gain access to that information, which may or may not be conscious to them. Once I get access to what they're thinking, then I can help them create a plan. A lot of times what needs to happen before they do anything is that we help them create a positive mind-set that what they want is possible for them—without that, they can't really do anything. Then I typically assign them some fun and challenging homework.

ME: Can you give us an example of how that works?

SUSAN: Sure! I had a client who was all about fun. She was going to gallery openings, dinner parties, and concerts. I mean, it was unbelievable the amount of fun this woman packed into every single day. And she was exhausted and enjoying none of it. So my homework to her was to cancel just about everything for two weeks and lay on her butt. So it just really depends on what's going on with the client. But I like to assign real-life practical homework, so we're not just talking about the change that they want to make, but they're actually taking baby steps toward implementing it.

WHAT IT TAKES

- The ability to see possibility and vision
- Empathy
- Open-mindedness

ME: It sounds like such good, positive stuff! Are there downsides or challenges to being a life coach?

SUSAN: One challenge can be if you're working from your home

THEN TO NOW

1994: Interned at Lisboa Associates Public Relations

1995: Graduated from Hood College

1996: Became account executive, Ed Lewi Associates Public Relations

1997: Marketing and promotions director, Dame Media Communications and you're not used to that. For some people the distraction of working from home can reduce their productivity, so they'll find themselves eating, folding laundry, playing with the pets. None of which are bad, but if you have deadlines and need to be working, it's not good. So I think working by yourself in isolation and not in an office full of people can be a challenge, particularly for extroverts. I also think many coaches aren't used to the business side of being a life coach. So they enjoy the actual work of coaching but are surprised at all the other hats they have to wear to market their business. Lastly, because coaches want their clients to get what they want, I think it can be challenging to just allow the client to have their process and journey without being attached to the results.

ME: Yes, I can see how it might be easy to get emotionally involved or be overly empathetic to what a client is going through. Is that a problem?

SUSAN: My first year it was a big issue, and I had to learn energetically how to buffer myself and have boundaries around my own energy. But yes, many times clients are coming to you in a negative space and are dealing with deep issues. That can be taxing energetically and emotionally.

ME: Wow. You must come across such a wide range of people from all different walks of life. Does that feed your own life?

SUSAN: Yeah, I mean, I get so jacked up! I'm always hanging

| 1998–2002: Stay-at-home mom | 2002–2007: Residential Realtor, Prudential Prime Locations Real Estate | 2007: Trained to be a life coach with Martha Beck | 2007: Launched Susan Hyatt, Inc. |

up the phone or getting off Skype going, "Oh my gosh." I get to witness such a variety of amazing things. My clients inspire my life.

ME: You mentioned that you used to work in real estate. How did you get turned on to this career of life coaching and make the decision to change?

SUSAN: I was always someone who felt super envious of people who knew what their thing was, like my husband. I was never someone who felt super talented at anything. You know, I couldn't play the piano. I was an okay singer. I would look at people who really excelled at something and think, "Dang, what's my thing?" So when I was in college, I changed my major four times.

ME: What happened after college?

SUSAN: I worked in marketing and public relations until I had children. Then I stayed at home for a little while with the kids and re-emerged as a residential Realtor with the sole goal of making enough money so we wouldn't starve if my husband, also a Realtor, didn't sell a thing. At first I really liked it. I was excelling in that industry and making quite a bit of money, but I started to realize that while I liked helping people, a lot of the job sucked my soul. I found myself in this place of feeling trapped and stuck, so I started reading everything I could get my hands on. I read Martha Beck's book *Finding Your Own North Star* and began applying things from the book in my life. I started to watch how quickly my life, especially internally, was changing. I didn't realize that what Martha did was called life coaching. It was one of those moments where the skies parted and a lightning bolt hit me on the head, and I just remember thinking, "Oh my gosh, I think this is what I'm supposed to do." So what ultimately led me to coaching was being in the ~kest spot of my life that I was ever in.

ME: One last question! Can you tell us a little bit about the other juicy projects you're working on that tie into your life coaching?

SUSAN: Sure! I've written two books—*Create Your Own Luck: Steps to Get Your Luck On*, and an ebook on green smoothies called *Jacked Up on Greens*. Right now what I'm most excited about is a reality show I'm doing called *Life Is Delicious TV* where I work with real-life clients who want to make change in their life, as well as a dinner series called *Girlfriends Gone Wild*, where I bring twenty women together at a time to have an amazing dinner party and we talk about personal transformation.

SUSAN'S CAREER ADVICE

- *Listen to your gut. You have all the answers you really need inside you.*
- *Be yourself and fly your freak flag. All that stuff that makes you different will actually be the things that make you the most money and bring you the most joy.*
- *It's okay to not have all the answers right now. Allow things to unfold for you.*

In the Field

FIVE MORE CAREERS AS A COACH

CORPORATE COACH Corporate coaches either work in or consult for corporations to help employees reach their goals. They tend to focus on supporting individual employees, with an overall goal of helping a business or organization thrive.

PARENTING COACH When parents are facing challenges with their children, they may work with a parenting coach. These specialized coaches offer parents tools and strategies to problem-solve around issues such as sleeping, education, and emotional, behavioral, and neurological challenges.

FINANCIAL COACH Financial coaches support their clients in not only making sound, smart financial decisions when it comes to things like debt, savings, budgets, and retirement, but they also help them deal with their emotional baggage as it relates to financial issues. They're not the same as financial planners, but there can be some crossover in the work they do with clients.

WEIGHT LOSS COACH When people are trying to lose weight in a healthy way, they might hire a weight loss coach. These coaches help people understand the root causes of their over-eating and develop new, healthier relationships with food and their bodies.

CAREER COACH Career coaches help people navigate their careers, whether that means figuring out how to thrive in the career path they've already chosen, or uncovering a new, more fulfilling career that reflects a client's passions and taps into their talents. People work with a career coach when they feel dissatisfied with some aspect of their career and they want help determining their next steps.

YOU NEED TO KNOW ABOUT

The International Coach Federation (ICF) is the largest organization and support network for professional coaches. Their extensive network offers a slew of information about coaching, including links to training and accreditation programs, hiring tips, information about coaching conferences, and more. Visit them online at www.coachfederation.org.

MAURA TIERNEY

Actor

The Facts

Maura Tierney, Actor

WHAT? Major movie stars . . . The gal in a Wendy's commercial . . . The extras in the background of the new Bond film. They're all actors—getting paid to play a role in order to entertain or inform.

WHERE? Actors perform in television shows, movies, regional theater, Broadway, commercials, cartoons . . . even marketing gigs for corporations. The main hubs for this profession are New York City and L.A.

HOW? Most actors hone their craft by studying dramatic arts in college or even grad school. For access to most auditions, actors need an agent, and to get an agent, they need some experience, a prepared monologue, and a head shot.

$$$: While big-time actors can earn more than a million dollars a year, the average salary for an actor is around (gulp) $5,000 a year. Many actors supplement their income with full-time or part-time jobs.

DRESS CODE? Actors wear whatever their role or audition calls for, whether it be a suit, jeans, or a chicken costume.

STRESS FACTOR: On a scale of 1 to 10, a 7

maura tierney has, by any definition, enjoyed a very successful career as an actor. For the past twenty-six years Maura has been seen on big and small screens everywhere, from starring with Jim Carrey in the movie *Liar, Liar* (1997) and with Ben Affleck in *Forces of Nature* (1999) to playing leads in NBC hits—sitcom *NewsRadio* and medical drama *ER.* More recently, Maura has been featured in CBS's *The Good Wife* and stars in Showtime's dramatic series *The Affair.*

I had a chance to catch up with Maura at her home in New York City to find out what life as a successful actor really looks like.

"Acting really is a collaborative art . . . no matter how prepared you are, you have to be ready to throw everything out the window once you start working."

ME: It seems like starring in a weekly TV series must be pretty demanding. What kind of hours do you work?

MAURA: It varies. A standard workday for us is twelve hours, and if you have a lot to do, you can have a week where you work a twelve- or thirteen-hour day every day. And then some episodes, I'm a little bit lighter. So it really varies according to the script.

ME: Could you walk us through a typical day on a busy week?

MAURA: Every day is different, but I seem to be on the set a lot. On a busy week, my call time is six a.m., which is an hour before the crew gets there. I have to get up around five fifteen, which is a drag if you're not a morning person. I've been doing it for eighteen years, and still my body has not switched around to enjoying the mornings, but that's okay. So I get up really early and get there about six, go through hair and makeup, and then the crew and the director and everybody else arrives and we go to work at seven. We shoot for six hours and then we break for lunch. Then we shoot four or five more ꞏꞏrs in the afternoon.

ME: Do you have work to do once you're home?

MAURA: I do have work to do. I live close to the studio, so I get home probably around seven fifteen. Luckily, I don't have too much trouble remembering and learning lines. In the beginning it was a lot more arduous learning my lines, but fortunately for me, it's not something I have to work so hard at. Unless it's more of an emotional scene, a personal scene for the character . . . that stuff I have to prepare for.

ME: Many people forget about that part of the job—memorizing lines. Are there any other behind-the-scenes challenges that people might not be aware of?

MAURA: Well, you never know what can happen on the set when you show up. You can sit at home and work on a scene and think, "This is the way I think it's going to go, and this is what I think my character is thinking and feeling," and then you get to the set and the director or the actor you're acting with has a completely different idea, and the whole thing is sort of turned on its ear. Acting really is a collaborative art, whether it's theater or TV or the movies or whatever. No matter how prepared you are, you have to be ready to throw everything out the window once you start working.

YOU ASKED . . .

"How have you stayed grounded?" —ALEXANDRA, 16

MAURA ANSWERED . . .

"Well, I do love acting. I think that's part of it—I love the work. And I still have all my same friends that I met in college twenty-five years ago who I'm very close to, and I think that that's helpful because in this business you can sort of get turned around easily. Having remained friends with this group of people who I love so much has been very helpful."

WHY WAIT?

- Join the drama club at your school, or if there isn't one, start one yourself!
- Audition for school productions or local community theater and see how you like being on stage.
- Take acting classes, or if you're interested in musical theater, try dancing or singing lessons.

ME: You also mentioned that it's a lot of work to prepare emotionally . . . is that challenging?

MAURA: Again, that depends. Sometimes it is, sometimes it isn't. Sometimes the writing and the material is very moving to me and I respond to it almost immediately when I read it. I sort of know, "Okay, so that's in my body . . . I know that." Other times, the muse is not with you, and you have to work a little harder to try to find an authentic emotional place. I guess the gist of what I'm saying is that there's a fluidity. You can't be rigid about anything.

ME: And what are the best parts of your job?

MAURA: My favorite part of this job? Well, I don't know. . . . It's a wonderful job. If you get lucky like I did, it's a great job. I mean, it's difficult in terms of the fact that everybody's a critic of your work, but if you're okay with that inside yourself, then it's great. I love how many different people I meet. And because

THEN TO NOW

| Attended New York University | Studied drama at Circle in the Square Theatre School, New York City | 1995–1999: Starred in NBC sitcom *NewsRadio* | 1997: Starred opposite Jim Carrey in *Liar, Liar* | 1997: Profiled in *InStyle* magazine |

they're actors or actresses or writers, you know, sometimes they're kind of weird and usually very interesting. (*Laughs*) It's kind of like being in a circus.

ME: I haven't heard that one before.

MAURA: I love that aspect of it.

ME: And what about the recognition factor? Would you consider that a pro or a con? Or is it just part of the job?

MAURA: It is a pro. I mean, sometimes people are so sweet about it, and it's really nice when they come up and say, "I watch your show with my daughter every week." It's a great thing to hear. Sally Field and I did a big story line together on *ER* where Sally's character has a mental illness, and people have come up to me and talked about how real that was and how much it meant to them to see it portrayed realistically on TV. So that kind of stuff is really rewarding.

ME: Yeah, I can see that. . . . Just to know that you're really having an impact on people.

PAYING YOUR DUES

Breaking into the industry can be tough, but many actors gain valuable experience, make connections, and find an entryway by doing small theater work, student films, and extra work.

1999: Began her tenure on the drama *ER* as Abby Lockhart

2001: Nominated for an Emmy Award for her role on *ER*

2006: Starred with Eric McCormack in the off-Broadway play *Some Girls*

2014: Cast as lead in the Showtime series *The Affair*

MAURA: Yeah. And today, someone said to me, "You know, from across the street you looked like that chick from *ER*!" And then I was ordering coffee and he said, "Jeez, you even sound like her." *(Laughs)*

> ## WHAT IT TAKES
> - Patience . . . Your dream gig may take a while to land
> - Persistence and passion
> - A high tolerance for stress and pressure

ME: That's funny.

MAURA: It was really funny.

ME: Acting is one of those careers that a lot of girls are interested in pursuing. Is there any one thing you could pinpoint that they might be surprised to find out about the job?

MAURA: I'm always very encouraging to people who want to do this, but they should realize that it's hard work. You need to have a lot of stamina in terms of putting yourself out there. For many people it does involve a lot of rejection in the beginning. And you need to find a way not to take that personally, because it's not personal. I've been on both sides of casting—I've auditioned for a million things that I didn't get, and I've also been in the room auditioning other actors. A lot of times three great actors will come into the room and then a fourth one comes in and that's just the person who's going to play the role. And it has nothing to do with how talented or not talented anybody is. So it's important that you go into it knowing that if you don't get a job, it's not necessarily personal. I don't want to be negative about it, but sometimes you don't get a job you want and it's really, really hard, but you know, you have to keep going.

> ## INTERESTED IN ACTING? HERE'S MAURA'S ADVICE
>
> *You have to love acting. I think a lot of people perceive it as glamorous, which it can be—you get to go to parties, dress up, be on TV, and have people recognize you. But those trappings should not be the reason why someone wants to get into this field, because again, it's hard work. If you're in it just for the celebrity, I think there's less of a chance of enjoying a long or satisfying career.*

In the Field

FIVE MORE CAREERS WORKING AS A PERFORMER

STAND-UP COMEDIENNE Being a stand-up comic has got to be one of the toughest jobs out there, but women who do it say they love performing in front of a crowd and getting laughs. And while most never land on *The Tonight Show*, there are plenty of opportunities for gigs in small comedy clubs or open mic nights.

STUNT DOUBLE Some actors do their own stunts while filming, but most of the time the more challenging stunts, like jumping off the roof of a tall building onto an air mattress, are performed by stunt doubles. Though doubles are highly trained in safety techniques, the work is not without risk, and it definitely never gets boring.

DANCER Whatever your dance style—ballet, hip-hop, tap, ballroom—there are opportunities to dance and get paid for it. Some dancers are part of touring companies, while others might become teachers, open their own studios, become choreographers, or perform on variety shows and TV specials.

TV SHOW HOST With the boom in reality shows, job ops for TV show hosts keep growing and growing. Think about it. . . .

Where would we be without Ryan Seacrest guiding our journey on *American Idol*? TV hosts have to be comfortable in front of the camera, charismatic, and quick on their feet.

VOICE-OVER ACTOR   Turn down the volume the next time you watch *Family Guy*. Without the distinctive voices of Stewie or Peter, something will definitely be missing. Some voice-over actors bring animated characters to life, while others find work narrating documentaries or performing voice-overs in commercials.

YOU NEED TO KNOW ABOUT

Back Stage (www.backstage.com) is the main online resource for actors. Here you'll find career resources, advice for dealing with agents and casting directors, interviews with and articles about important people in the biz, and notices for auditions.

For more careers working in Hollywood, check out the movie studio executive profile on page 65 and the TV show creator profile on page 1.

ROXANNE COADY

Independent Bookstore Owner

The Facts

Roxanne Coady,
Owner, R.J. Julia

WHAT? Independent bookstore owners typically run the day-to-day business operations of local bookstores, as well as interact with customers, organize community and author events, and keep the shelves stocked with books.

WHERE? Wherever there are people who love to buy books!

HOW? There are no formal educational requirements for this career, although a love of books, business savvy, and perseverance are essential.

$$$: An annual salary of $35,000 to $45,000 on up, depending on the size and success of the store

DRESS CODE: Casual

STRESS FACTOR: On a scale of 1 to 10, an 8

independent bookstores have often been romanticized by Hollywood. Rent the oldies but goodies *You've Got Mail* with Tom Hanks and Meg Ryan (1998) or *Notting Hill* with Julia Roberts and Hugh Grant (1999) and you'll see what I mean. There is something very appealing about the idea of spending long days in a warm, cozy bookstore, sipping hot tea, surrounded by books.

The reality may look different, but for Roxanne Coady, owner of the well-known indie bookstore R.J. Julia in Madison, Connecticut, setting up her own cheerful reading nook was a way of creating a comfortable space that would have a positive impact in the community. She opened her store in 1990, when after nearly twenty successful years working in accounting, Roxanne realized it was time to make a major career shift.

"I thought, I'm forty years old and I have enough money and enough time to have a career that feels like it makes a difference in society. So I made the decision to leave my firm. I always knew my new career would have something to do with reading, so I thought about starting a publishing company or a bookstore. But I realized that I really didn't know anything about publishing—I wasn't an editor, I wasn't a writer. But what I always loved doing was picking out the right book for somebody. So I thought about opening a bookstore, and that's what I did," she explains.

"I may have challenges and sleepless nights worrying about cash flow and hiring and firing people, but still, my life is about books."

Owning an independent bookstore is, in many ways, like running any small business. There are general operations tasks to do, such as renting and maintaining retail space, handling the financial side of things (such as payroll and accounts with vendors), and managing a staff of employees. And like other jobs in retail, bookstore owners might spend a fair amount of time behind the cash register or on the floor arranging displays or helping customers. More specific to the world of books, independent bookstore owners also have to

YOU ASKED . . .

"Once you've achieved a certain level of success, does running your own business ever get easier?" —CHLOE, 17

ROXANNE ANSWERED . . .

"I worry every day. I've had to put another ton of money into the store this year. No . . . it's never out of the woods in a kind of sustainable way, but I just keep on doing it. And part of it is that I'm also on the board of a publicly held bank, which both keeps the other part of my brain occupied and helps me earn additional money. I do a bit of consulting for publishing companies, and I'm very active in the nonprofit world. It's a very full and satisfying life."

figure out ways to raise the store's profile in the community, as well as find creative ways to keep the store thriving even as competition increases every year.

Books are now sold just about everywhere—from online sites such as Amazon.com to the big chains such as Barnes & Noble and specialty stores such as Urban Outfitters. A career as an independent bookstore owner can be a precarious one, since the competition is fierce and the financial risks are high. Yet there are more than 1,900 such bookstores across the country facing these challenges every day, and keeping their community hub afloat. According to Roxanne, one of the biggest challenges of running an independent bookstore revolves around money.

"When you run something like a bookstore, there's not a clear line of whether it's for-profit or not-for-profit. You know, there's a kind of expectation that running an independent bookstore is about being a good member of the community. So we're stuck in the middle—there are people who expect it to be like the library, yet we need to make money in order to pay staff, pay rent, and run a business in a smart way.

WHY WAIT?

- Read books from different genres to expand your literary knowledge.
- Attend author events at bookstores near you to see how they are organized and promoted.

"What has intensified that challenge is that we sell a commodity—books. And this commodity has a fixed price, and we have formidable, well-capitalized competitors. It's harder to find a tougher business environment than that. So the real challenge is, how can we add value to what is basically a commodity? You know, a copy of *State of Denial* by Bob Woodward is still a copy of *State of Denial* by Bob Woodward, whether the buyer gets it at a discount online or pays full price at a bookstore. And so we have to find ways to add value—by the experience of coming into the store, or by the experience of talking to us on the phone, or by being sold a good book," Roxanne says.

But like many independent bookstore owners, Roxanne couldn't imagine doing anything else, despite the challenges. When I asked her what she loves about her career, Roxanne emphasized that it has enabled her to create her ideal work environment.

"It's worthwhile to run an organization where the employees are treated in a way that's respectful, and to create an

THEN TO NOW

Graduated from University of New Haven, Connecticut, with a BS in accounting and economics	Became partner and national tax director at BDO Seidman, New York, New York	1989: After a twenty-year career in accounting, quit job and moved to Connecticut	1990: Son, Edward, was born	1990: Opened R.J. Julia bookstore in Madison, Connecticut

environment where there's mutual goodwill. It's pretty satisfying to go to work every day when people are collaborative and kind to each other. Having a place that matters to the commu-nity and the customers— that's pretty satisfying too. And I like that my world is

WHAT IT TAKES

- A willingness to devote time and energy to your vision
- Love for books of all kinds
- A desire to be a visible community member

books. I may have challenges and sleepless nights worrying about cash flow and hiring and firing people, but still my life is about books. On really bad days, I might wish for a job pump-ing gas. But most days I feel like I'm doing exactly what I want to do. I just wish it were a little easier financially," she says.

As owner of her own business, Roxanne has also managed to create a flexible schedule that allows her to be where she needs to be, when she needs to be there. That's an import-ant factor since she's involved in a number of other business and volunteer activities, from participating on a bank board to consulting for publishing companies. She also created Just the Right Book in 2010, an online service that taps into her business's knowledge as booksellers to create a human algo-rithm that allows readers to have books handpicked by a lit-erary expert based on their personal tastes and preferences.

She explains, "My workday totally varies. There are some

1995: *Publishers Weekly* named R.J. Julia its Bookseller of the Year

1996: Founded the *Read to Grow* literacy initiative

2006: Roxanne's book, *The Book That Changed My Life*, is published

2010: Launched her complementary business, Just the Right Book weeks where I'm in the bookstore every day early to late, although sometimes even when I'm there every day, some of what I'm doing is not about the bookstore. But if I work sixty hours a week, probably thirty-five or forty of those hours are devoted to the bookstore, on average. When you're talking about the pros of owning your own business, you do have a lot of autonomy. Not freedom. You don't have freedom because you have employees and you have responsibilities. But you have a lot of autonomy. So I can decide how my day is going to go. That's a big deal to me.

Is it possible to have any downtime when running a business that needs so much hands-on involvement?

"If I'm exhausted, and I want to take a day off, I'm a little bit torn, because there's always something to do. And that's the tough part. There really aren't good boundaries, but I make it work."

ROXANNE'S CAREER ADVICE

It's important for teenage girls not to react to the noise around them, and instead really think about what it is they want to do in their heart. Girls shouldn't let society dictate whether they should or shouldn't have kids, or whether they should or shouldn't get married, or whether they should or shouldn't make money. Talk to women who are happy and content in their lives and try very hard to think independently about what it is you want to do.

In the Field

FIVE MORE CAREERS WORKING WITH BOOKS

EDITORIAL DIRECTOR Editorial directors work for publishing companies and oversee the authors writing books for their imprint (publishing brand), as well as coordinating the different stages involved in successfully publishing and promoting books. They play a key strategic role in the editorial direction for an imprint.

BOOK COVER DESIGNER You can't judge a book by its cover, but the design of a book cover will most likely have an impact on sales. Book cover designers create covers that will be noticeable, will appeal to the book's target demographic, and will hopefully lead a potential reader to pick up and purchase the book.

LITERARY AGENT Like a talent agent, literary agents are in the business of representation. They present their authors' work to editors at publishing houses in the hope of getting publishing deals for their clients. Literary agents work on commission and earn a percentage of their clients' publishing income.

SALES ACCOUNT MANAGER Sales account managers work for publishing companies, and their job is to ensure that their books make it from the publisher's warehouse to the shelves of independent bookstores, bookstore chains, and other retail outlets. They also help develop marketing and promotional plans for book launches.

ACQUISITIONS EDITOR These editors have one primary responsibility, and that is acquiring new titles for their publishing company's imprint. Acquisitions editors nurture relationships with literary agents so they can be apprised of up-and-coming talent, as well as actively solicit new authors and projects to fill out their publishing slate.

For more careers working with books, check out the librarian profile on page 84.

YOU NEED TO KNOW ABOUT

The American Booksellers Association is the national organization devoted to supporting independent booksellers. On their website (www.bookweb.org), you'll find interesting articles and research, resources, and a directory of independent bookstores nationwide.

lunch break

WOMEN IN THE WORKFORCE

While a lot of progress has been made in the past century when it comes to women in the workplace, things are not equal—not yet, anyway.

Some careers have been traditionally female-dominated, like nursing, and others have been traditionally male-dominated, like engineering. That remains the case even today. Here are recent statistics about where women are working, courtesy of the U.S. Department of Labor, Bureau of Labor Statistics. As of 2011, women made up:

- 96 percent of speech language pathologists
- 82 percent of elementary and middle school teachers
- 71 percent of psychologists
- 34 percent of computer systems analysts
- 34 percent of physicians and surgeons
- 32 percent of lawyers
- 14 percent of architects and engineers
- 4 percent of all aircraft pilots and flight engineers

Any shockers there? If not, this next statistic ought to do it. Are you ready? On average, a woman still earns 19 percent less than a man who's doing the *exact same job*. That's right . . . the *exact same job*. However, recent research shows that "millennial" women (young women born between 1980 and the early 1990s) are closing the earnings gap, which is the difference between what men and women earn. In 2013 they earned 93 cents for every dollar earned by a man.

Here are examples from the Bureau of Labor Statistics for 2011:

- Female chief executives earn 31 percent less than their male counterparts.

- Female college and university professors earn 19 percent less than their male counterparts.

- Female computer programmers and systems analysts earn 19 percent less than their male counterparts.

Disturbing numbers, to be sure, but it's not all bad news. Women have made serious headway in the past century, especially when you consider that in the year 1900, women made up only 18 percent of the labor force, while today we make up nearly 50 percent. And women are surpassing men when it comes to education—more women than men today go on to get bachelor's and master's degrees.

Karen Lederer, a professor at the University of Massachusetts, teaches a class called Career and Life Choices for Women, and she shared her thoughts on how these statistics actually trickle down to working women.

Karen suggested that at some point in their careers, most women are going to encounter a situation where their gender impacts their career in a negative way, like being given different responsibilities from a male counterpart or being passed over for a promotion.

As I talked with Karen about this reality for women in the workplace, she said something that really resonated with me. Karen said that it's important for young women to remember that if and when this sort of gender discrimination happens, don't take it personally. There is a tendency for women to wonder what we did wrong, or even worse, what's wrong with us.

My hope is that some of you reading this book are going to be the first women not to experience any gender discrimination in your career journeys. To get off to a solid start, join up with professional women's organizations—most industries have them—and connect with experienced women who've successfully navigated their own careers despite these inequalities and ask them how they did it.

CAREER CHOOSER

*Check out this checklist of job traits to
help you choose your ideal career!*

get to attend hip work parties

Actor

Advertising Executive

Architect

Business Executive

Design Creative Director

Independent Bookstore Owner

Life Coach

Magazine Editor

Movie Studio Executive

Museum Curator

Photographer

Professional Athlete

PR Specialist

Publicist

Screenwriter

Senator

Stylist

Talent Agent

TV Show Creator

Urban Planner

Video Game Programmer

have own office

Advertising Executive

Animator

Business Executive

Child Therapist

Coast Guard Lieutenant

District Attorney

Educational Psychologist

Life Coach

Magazine Editor

Marine Biologist

Movie Studio Executive

Museum Curator

Nonprofit Director

Publicist

Real Estate Agent

Senator

Sheriff

Talent Agent

TV Show Creator

get lots of free stuff

Actor

Advertising Executive
Business Executive
Magazine Editor
Movie Studio Executive
Professional Athlete
Publicist
Screenwriter
Stylist
Talent Agent
TV Show Creator

have stocked kitchen at work

Actor
Chef
Movie Studio Executive
TV Show Creator
Video Game Programmer

never off duty

Business Executive
Coast Guard Lieutenant
District Attorney
Educational Psychologist
Entrepreneur
Environmentalist
Forensic Scientist
Independent Bookstore Owner
Journalist
Magazine Editor
Movie Studio Executive
Nonprofit Director
Photographer
PR Specialist

Publicist
Real Estate Agent
Relief Worker
Senator
Sheriff
Talent Agent
TV Show Creator
Veterinarian

up against inflexible deadlines

Actor
Animator
Business Executive
Journalist
Magazine Editor
Movie Studio Executive
Photographer
Screenwriter
Stylist
TV Show Creator
Video Game Programmer
Visual Merchandiser

can create flexible work schedule

Accountant
Actor
Chef
Commercial Airline Pilot
Dental Hygienist
Design Creative Director
Entrepreneur
Environmentalist

Independent Bookstore Owner
Life Coach
Museum Curator
Nurse
Nurse-Midwife
Photographer
Physical Therapist
Professional Athlete
Real Estate Agent
Screenwriter
Social Messaging Strategist
Stylist
Talent Agent
Urban Planner
Video Game Programmer
Yoga Instructor

can work from home

Child Therapist
Design Creative Director
Entrepreneur
Environmentalist
Life Coach
Photographer
PR Specialist
Professional Athlete
Real Estate Agent
Screenwriter
Social Messaging Strategist
Stylist
Talent Agent

involves travel to interesting places

Actor
Advertising Executive
Business Executive
Coast Guard Lieutenant
Commercial Airline Pilot
Design Creative Director
Environmentalist
Journalist
Life Coach
Magazine Editor
Marine Biologist
Museum Curator
Photographer
PR Specialist
Professional Athlete
Publicist
Relief Worker
Screenwriter
Senator
Stylist
Talent Agent

frequent business lunches

Actor
Advertising Executive
Business Executive
District Attorney
Magazine Editor
Movie Studio Executive
Nonprofit Director

Publicist
Screenwriter
Senator
Stylist
Talent Agent
TV Show Creator
Urban Planner

can be your own boss

Architect
Business Executive
Chef
Child Therapist
Educational Psychologist
Entrepreneur
Independent Bookstore Owner
Life Coach
Nonprofit Director
Nurse-Midwife
Photographer
Physical Therapist
Publicist
Real Estate Agent
Screenwriter
Social Messaging Strategist
Stylist
Talent Agent
Veterinarian
Visual Merchandiser
Yoga Instructor

job might entail significant busywork

Accountant
Engineer
Independent Bookstore Owner
Librarian
Nurse-Midwife
Physical Therapist
Real Estate Agent
Teacher

might receive public recognition through work

Actor
Advertising Executive
Animator
Architect
Business Executive
Chef
District Attorney
Educational Psychologist
Environmentalist
Independent Bookstore Owner
Journalist
Magazine Editor
Marine Biologist
Movie Studio Executive
Museum Curator
Nonprofit Director
Photographer
Professional Athlete
Publicist

IN THEIR SHOES

Screenwriter
Senator
Sheriff
Talent Agent
Teacher
TV Show Creator
Urban Planner

Engineer
Forensic Scientist
Life Coach
Photographer
Screenwriter
Video Game Programmer

collaborate with others as part of job

Actor
Advertising Executive
Agent
Architect
Business Executive
Chef
Design Creative Director
Engineer
Magazine Editor
Marine Biologist
Movie Studio Executive
Nonprofit Director
Relief Worker
Senator
Sheriff
Social Messaging Strategist
TV Show Creator
Urban Planner
Visual Merchandiser

job involves interaction with the public

Actor
Chef
Commercial Airline Pilot
Dental Hygienist
District Attorney
Independent Bookstore Owner
Journalist
Librarian
Life Coach
Museum Curator
Photographer
Real Estate Agent
Relief Worker
Senator
Sheriff
Social Messaging Strategist
Urban Planner

work alone much of the time

Animator
Child Therapist

CAREER INDEX